What people are saying about ...

Running to the Fire

"This book is as fun and adventurous as the author himself. I would travel anywhere with Ken Isaacs because he's like a cross between MacGyver and Ethan Hunt in the *Mission Impossible* series—he's a troubleshooter, a fixer, a strategic analyst, and highly adaptable to any situation. *Running to the Fire* takes you on his harrowing journeys across the globe into some of modern history's worst catastrophes—both natural and man-made—to show you how Christ's love can transform people and nations. This book will challenge you to put your own faith on the line to see the same transformation in the lives around you."

Skip Heitzig, senior pastor at Calvary Church, Albuquerque; board member of Samaritan's Purse

"A searingly intimate memoir that reads like a thriller. And a moving testimony not only to the power of faith but also to faithfulness—a necessary antidote for our fickle age. The instinct to help another in distress is innate in humanity. But how many heed the call to serve by turning wishful words into practical deeds? Many more than we may think. Ken Isaacs delves into his decades of experience at the front lines of global suffering to show that Good Samaritans of all shapes and sizes—and blessed with the right skills—pop up on cue when most needed. In his passionate call for us to join them lies Ken's message of stubborn hope for our dark times."

Mukesh Kapila, CBE, professor, former director at the United Nations, author of *Against a Tide of Evil*

"Kenney is the most fascinating person I have ever met and has helped thousands and thousands of people. I have traveled with him and have seen the work firsthand. This book powerfully tells much of the story. Fabulous, so beautifully written."

Greta Van Susteren, 30-year award-winning news anchor, decades-long world traveler with Samaritan's Purse

"A powerful reminder that hope in Jesus shines brightest in the world's darkest places. This book is not just a story; it is a call to action."

J. Frank Harrison III, chairman and CEO, Coca-Cola Bottling Co.

"*Running to the Fire* is exciting to read and deeply biblically instructed. This book takes it to another dimension with its globe-trotting narrative of faith and action. Isaacs tells how commitment of faith changes his life and helps millions. Read this book."

Mike Pompeo, former Secretary of State

"*Running to the Fire* offers a powerful and compelling account of Ken Isaacs' leadership during some of the most demanding humanitarian crises of our time. Through vivid, real-life experiences, Isaacs demonstrates unwavering dedication, courage, and humility. Drawing from his firsthand involvement in the evolution of modern humanitarian aid, he has tirelessly worked to protect the lives and dignity of the world's most vulnerable. This book is an inspiring call to action for anyone driven to serve humanity."

Michael VanRooyen, MD, MPH, professor at Harvard Medical School, director of the Harvard Humanitarian Initiative, author of *The World's Emergency Room*

"*Running to the Fire* is more than just a story; it is a call to action, a call to risk, a call to go! When we give God the little we have, it multiplies, and men like Ken generate extraordinary results. Ken captivates us with his adventures and challenges us with his questions. Now it's up to us to find the answers—not for Ken, but for ourselves."

Lucio Malan, Senate Majority Leader
in Rome, Italian Parliament

"Ken and I have traveled and collaborated across many nations together. Few have gone to the places Ken has gone, and fewer have deeply helped so many. *Running to the Fire* is a fearless firsthand account capturing the power of faith and healing in action."

Bill Frist, MD, former US Senate Majority Leader

"*Running to the Fire* is a powerful story of letting God use you as you are. Ken Isaacs, a leader in global humanitarian response, is a pioneer, problem solver, humanitarian, diplomat, well driller, and all around make-it-happen man of God. From responding to natural disasters to combating famine and assisting those impacted by war, Ken Isaacs and Samaritans Purse have been in the forefront of helping people in Jesus' name."

David Eubank, director, Free Burma
Rangers, Free the Oppressed

"A powerful testimony of radical compassion and unshakable faith in action in some of the world's most dangerous and destitute places—ranging from war, famine, and epidemics in Africa to Bosnia's Sniper Alleys, from violence in Afghanistan and Iraq to Haiti's earthquake and Japan's tsunami. Isaacs embodies the heart of the Good Samaritan, vividly illustrating the Gospel by showing that the cross stands at the center of the cosmic battle between light and darkness, displaying God's love in Christ as humanity's only true hope. Sustained by the prayers and sacrificial love of his late wife, Carolyn, Isaacs' courageous commitment brings Christ's hope to the broken and forsaken."

Girma Bekele, PhD, adjunct professor of mission studies,
Tyndale Seminary, Toronto; former colleague in Ethiopia

"I appreciate the work Ken Isaacs has done with Samaritan's Purse over his many years of traveling to difficult, often dangerous, places to help those in desperate need and to bring them the hope of Jesus Christ. Ken has made a lasting impact following the call of Jesus to 'go.' Ken doesn't just talk about it; he does it."

Frank R. Wolf, former member of Congress

"I've had the privilege of serving with other Christ followers at Samaritan's Purse and have been humbled by the experience. *Ordinary* people willing to do *extraordinary* things for God. I usually come away asking, 'Where does this ministry find such amazingly committed and sacrificial servants?' Ken Isaacs provides an answer and an example in *Running to the Fire*. He embodies the way God uses common, surrendered believers to do uncommon acts of service. Ken's global journey of devotion and dedication will ignite a desire to serve God and people, no matter who you are and no matter where you live."

J. Warner Wallace, *Dateline*-featured cold-case detective, senior
fellow at the Colson Center for Christian Worldview, adjunct
professor of apologetics, author of *Cold-Case Christianity*

KEN ISAACS

WITH ROBERT NOLAND

HELPING
IN JESUS'
NAME

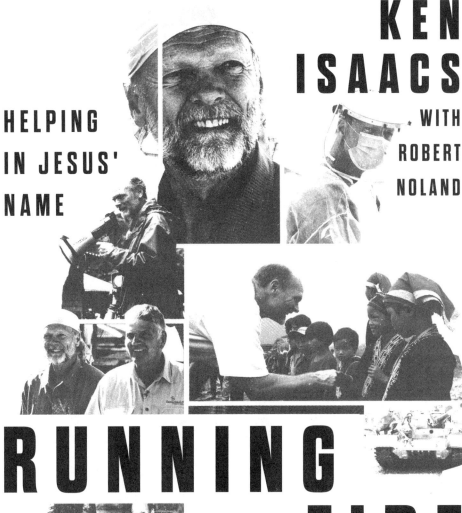

RUNNING

TO THE FIRE

150 YEARS STRONG

DAVID C COOK

Samaritan's Purse

RUNNING TO THE FIRE
Published by David C Cook
4050 Lee Vance Drive
Colorado Springs, CO 80918 U.S.A.

Integrity Music Limited, a Division of David C Cook
Brighton, East Sussex BN1 2RE, England

DAVID C COOK®, the graphic circle C logo and related marks are
registered trademarks of David C Cook.

Library of Congress Control Number 2025931579
ISBN 978-0-8307-8845-3
eISBN 978-0-8307-8846-0

The Team: Michael Covington, Luke McKinnon, Stephanie Bennett,
Caroline Cilento, Judy Gillispie, Karissa Silvers, Susan Murdock
Cover Design: Brian Mellema
Cover and Interior Photos: Samaritan's Purse

Printed in the United States of America
First Edition 2025

1 2 3 4 5 6 7 8 9 10

053025

> **We don't run away from the fire—we run _to_ it.**
> Franklin Graham

CONTENTS

Foreword

Let your good deeds shine out for all to see, so that
everyone will praise your heavenly Father.

Matthew 5:16 NLT

You are about to peer into the great big heart of Ken Isaacs—rugged, reflective, and resilient. I have known him forty years and haven't changed my mind about him. If need be, this guy could jump from a plane or helicopter above the jungle, land on his feet, and find his way to civilization while helping people along the way.

A big challenge invigorates Kenney regardless of the obstacles (sometimes they're land mines). In earlier days, though, when faced with a perplexing problem that seemed insurmountable, he would say, "Franklin, remember, I'm just a well driller!" But when God drilled deep into his soul, he submitted to Christ and said, "Yes, Lord, I'll follow and obey You." Never did he imagine that God would use a well driller from America's southland in the ways He has.

You hold in your hands the chronicles of Kenney Isaacs. He changed direction and migrated to doing life God's way. Before I really knew him, he drilled a well on my mountain property not too far from where our Samaritan's Purse International Headquarters stands today. When he finished, he said to me, "Franklin, if I can ever help you in your work, let me know." I dismissed it. Then came the death-gripping famine and drought of the 1980s in Ethiopia. News headlines wailed like sirens. Video footage rendered horrific images not easily ignored. The world watched the masses dying of starvation, thirst, and disease.

We were a small Christian organization at the time, but God had plans for our ministry that led us in the footsteps of the Good Samaritan, a man featured in a parable Jesus told. His message pricked the ears of those listening, as recorded in Luke 10:33, where a wounded man had been left along the road to die: "But a Samaritan on his journey ... had compassion" (HCSB).

I was compelled to respond to the crisis in the Horn of Africa, and the Lord brought back the words of the well driller's offer, but his name slipped my mind. After quite a search, Kenney and I reconnected. As God's hand moved, particularly in the heart of Ken's wife, Carolyn, this couple in the prime of life left their home in the Blue Ridge Mountains of North Carolina and took up residence in a mountainous region of Ethiopia. They couldn't speak the language, and the culture was filled with ancient folklore.

And have I mentioned that Kenney is a "can do" kind of guy? With enthusiasm and practicality, Ken not only established and directed the monumental work of drilling wells to provide lifesaving water, but together with Carolyn (now in Heaven), they brought to hopeless and helpless people God's message of mercy and love by letting their lights shine in the darkness and offering a cup of cold water in Jesus' name. "The water I will give [them] will become a well of water springing up within [them] for eternal life" (John 4:14 HCSB).

We can follow Christ and reach out to others, or we can turn aside from those in need and miss the enriching purposes of God. Aren't we grateful that Jesus did not pass us by? We can praise God that His Son traveled from Heaven to earth to meet us just as we are—sinners in need of a Savior. His name is Jesus, "for He will save His people from their sins" (Matt. 1:21 NASB). It is Jesus who comes to our rescue, pulling us from the flame of despair, saving us by the truth of His Gospel, and giving us the assurance of Heaven.

Since 1988, Kenney has traveled the world with me. He has led many others to hot spots where God had work for us to do. There is no greater purpose than telling people from every nation, "Come and see the works of God" (Ps.

66:5 NASB). And while God does not need us, He grants us the privilege to serve Him. This is the ministry at Samaritan's Purse. We do not run away from the fire; we run *to* the fire. Why? In the brief but power-packed book of Jude, a half-brother of our Lord, we read Jude's words: "Show mercy.... Rescue others by snatching them from the flames" (vv. 22–23 NLT).

I know Kenney well enough to tell you that his desire is that, through his story, your heart will be moved to consider how God might use you to carry His message to those who need a saving touch from the Savior.

Kenney's accomplishments don't include the college degree he longed to earn. His possessions are void of a dusty and framed university diploma hanging on a wall. Rather, he is an effective diplomat with foreign governments as Samaritan's Purse seeks entrance to build field hospitals in war zones for the sick and wounded and temporary shelters for refugees driven from their homelands.

Kenney is a ready soldier commissioned by God to run to the front lines of world catastrophes, putting God's love and mercy on display. Human credentials would never have prepared him for what God had in store. I am thankful the Lord called Kenney to step out of the ordinary to do the extraordinary. It is God who enables us as we walk in His way. It is Jesus who commissions His people and credentials us with everything we need to obey Him, helping others in Jesus' name. Ken Isaacs is more than a colleague; he's my friend. And, by the way, he's still running to the fire, to the glory of God.

Franklin Graham
President and CEO, Samaritan's Purse
Billy Graham Evangelistic Association
Boone, North Carolina
April 2025

What If?

I bet I know what you're thinking.

When you picked up my book and read the back cover or scanned the table of contents and saw the many years I have served with Franklin Graham on the Samaritan's Purse team, along with the countless destinations I've been to and the disasters I've responded to, you may have gotten a certain image in your mind. You might have made some assumptions about me. So right out of the gate, I want to make something clear.

I hold no degrees and had no special training to equip me to live the life I have experienced. Yet when I read my Bible, I realize that puts me in some good company. When the angel of the Lord called Gideon a "mighty warrior" and told him he would save Israel, he responded, "Pardon me ... but ... my clan is the weakest in Manasseh, and I am the least in my family" (Judg. 6:12, 15). After Moses was called by God, he asked, "Who am I that I should go to Pharaoh and bring the Israelites out of Egypt?" (Ex. 3:11). When Saul invited David to marry into the family and fight battles for the king, the young man questioned, "Who am I, and what is my family or my clan in Israel, that I should become the king's son-in-law?" (1 Sam. 18:18).

As Jesus was teaching by a lake, He stepped into the boat of a struggling, exhausted fisherman named Peter. When Jesus miraculously produced a net full of fish, Peter begged, "Go away from me, Lord; I am a sinful man!" (Luke 5:8). Jesus' response? "Don't be afraid; from now on you will fish for people" (v. 10).

Gideon said, "But I'm just a farmer." Moses, as well as David, said, "But I'm just a shepherd." And Peter said, "But I'm just a fisherman." When God called me, my response was much like theirs: "But I'm just a well driller." For the first two decades of my working life, I drilled water wells. That was the worldview through which I learned how to solve problems and fix things that were broken.

So the real difference maker, the game changer, the common denominator is I serve the same God as those men in the Bible did. From the pages of Scripture, we find that it's not about what any of us *can't* do; it's about what He *can do*.

Whatever your "But I'm just a _____" may be, as you read my story, please keep this in mind: If God can choose to work in and through Ken Isaacs, a blue-collar common man from Boone, North Carolina, then why in the world would He not work in your life too? So here are my questions:

What if you fully surrendered your life to Jesus?
What if He wants to speak to you?
What if He asks you to follow Him?
What if He asks you to go?
To run *to* the fire?

If You'll Open the Door

Boone, North Carolina

When I was just two years old, my biological father abandoned my mother and me. For the next four years, she raised me as a single mom. When I was six, she married a man named Coy Isaacs. At ten years old, Coy adopted me, and my last name was legally changed from Warren to Isaacs. That Father's Day in 1962, as a gift to him, I began calling Coy "Daddy." From that year on, I considered him my father.

I soon came to the conclusion that my parents liked to move. In my twelve years of education, I went to thirteen schools in seven cities in four states throughout the Southeast. So I was always "the new kid." One day, when I was in third grade, I looked outside to see our 1956 Chevrolet loaded with my bed strapped on top. We drove all day into the night to the new town my parents had chosen. Around the time I might be able to start settling in, we'd leave for the next stop. The longest time I spent in one place was my last two years in high school in Boone, North Carolina, where I graduated.

Sadly, my daddy, Coy, died in 1979 of a massive heart attack when I was twenty-seven. In 2002, after deciding to try to find my biological father, I was able to locate him. After just one visit, I was grateful that he left Mom and me all those years ago. We were clearly better off and so blessed that Coy had come into our lives.

I can look back and see how God used that nomadic lifestyle to prepare me to be able to adapt and go to work in different places all over the world—to always stay flexible, get along with new people, and quickly adjust to unique and unfamiliar circumstances. I learned so many lessons from living the life my parents chose for our family. Over the years, I've found the folks who can best relate to my childhood are those who had a parent in the military, those for whom the idea of home was always somewhat of a moving target.

Those last two years of high school when I finally had the opportunity to be in one place for a while, I met a girl named Carolyn Wright. We fell in love, and right after graduation we got married, and I went to work for her father in their family business—the Dewey Wright Well and Pump Company. Based out of Boone, we drilled water wells and installed pumps. As far as I could see, that would be my life's work.

A Blue-Collar Calling

In November of 1984, I walked into a store where the owner, Harris Campbell, began telling me about a man named Don Norrington, who had spoken at his church. Don had recently returned after spending a month volunteering in Togo, Africa. In his testimony, he talked about a specific need there for well drillers. Harris told me, "Kenney, I thought about you, and if you ever want to go, I'd like to help." Obviously, the thought of going to Africa—something that had never even crossed my mind—was a lot to take in, so I just responded with, "Um ... okay, thanks."

A few minutes later, another man walked in that Harris knew. Making the connection to what he had just told me about the need for wells in Africa, he brought the man over to introduce us.

"Hey, Kenney, I want you to meet someone. This is Franklin Graham."

"Good to meet you, Franklin. I'm Kenney Isaacs."

As we shook hands, Harris told Franklin I was a well driller and talked about our previous conversation. Franklin smiled, responding with, "Yeah, that would be good. You should go to Africa."

God worked through Harris to make the initial introduction between Franklin and me. The conversation about mission work in Africa was enough to prompt him to feel like we should meet. Moments like that are proof that on any given day you just never know what God might bring into your life. Some of the constant mysteries of living by faith are those ordained, sometimes mystical, appointments that change your destiny.

A couple of weeks later, curious about the opportunity in Africa, I called Harris to get Don's phone number. Turned out Don was the campus minister with the Southern Baptists at Appalachian State University. When I met him at his office, I was quickly struck by his strong enthusiasm. He was clearly passionate about their mission in West Africa, working in partnership with the North Carolina Baptist Men's Association. From that moment, something new and fresh began to take hold in me. God used this introduction to His work in the world to bring Carolyn and me, now in our early thirties, to a crossroads of faith that led us both to recommit our lives to Christ.

In March of 1985, I made my first trip to Togo, Africa, to work as a volunteer drilling water wells. When we arrived and got off the plane, I met the other dozen or so folks in the mission group. I could quickly sense they were frustrated with the hassles of getting through customs. But I have always enjoyed a good challenge. For me, this was new. It was fun and exciting—an adventure. I was energized by it *all*. Soon after we arrived at the mission base, I was out with two local well drillers applying my everyday, familiar skills, yet in a totally different environment on the other side of the world.

During the month I spent in Africa, I began to sense that God was calling me to the world, to take Jesus' Great Commission in Matthew 28 seriously and allow His words to become personal to *me*: "Therefore go into all nations in My name." These words were no longer just part of a familiar story that happened to the disciples thousands of years ago. I felt the command was now directed at me. It's funny how we talk about "a personal relationship with God" but somehow don't personalize the words of Scripture as if He is talking to us today. My first experience in Africa led me to a new place in my faith from which I knew it would be very difficult to turn back.

Not long after I returned home from Africa, Carolyn asked, "Why are you so quiet?" Still processing my thoughts, I answered the best way I knew how: "I don't know, honey, but I feel like God's calling me to the world. I'm going to pray about it." I could tell she was a bit surprised by my answer. But I did just that. I began praying, "Lord, if You will open the door, I'll go through it."

June 1988

I sensed I had heard Him "calling me to the world." I felt God had placed this very powerful phrase in my heart, but I had no basis of experience to know what to do with the feelings associated with the call.

At that time, I had never heard of any "humanitarian organizations" or the term NGO (nongovernmental organization). The only connection I could make was to being a missionary. But all the missionaries I had met in Africa had graduate or postgraduate degrees. They were doctors or nurses or pastors, white-collar folks from the States. Let's just say—then and now—I am *not* a sophisticated guy. I'm blue-collar. Street-smart and straightforward. I had developed my career from a mix of common sense and trial-and-error—not by going to school but by being thrown into the deep end.

Based on my brief experience thus far with navigating a calling, I was feeling a bit "less than" in the missionary department. I had met some amazing, talented people, but not anyone like me. Yet here was the other side of the coin: what I *had* acquired through my work was a strong commitment to serving my customers, getting along with people, constructively correcting those who worked for me, and effectively managing a business.

As a thirty-four-year-old well driller with a wife, two sons, and a big God, I prayed faithfully, conscientiously, and intentionally. I would get up in the morning around four thirty, read the Scriptures, and talk to God. I could empathize with Abram when God said, "Go from your country, your people and your father's household to the land I will show you" (Gen. 12:1). While I was trying to stay faithful to seek Him, life just seemed to be on a normal track. Nothing else happened. But then the next year, a drought in our county in North Carolina created an on-site meeting with a new customer.

The Dream Job

In June of 1986, our crew was out at a drilling site when they called in on the radio, "Hey, we're about to finish up with this job. What's next?" I answered, "All right, hang on. I'll be there soon, and we'll head to the next location."

The address belonged to Franklin Graham, the man I had briefly met at Harris's store.

When we got there, like most folks, Franklin came out, wanting to know if we thought we could hit a well and get enough water. I assured him from what I saw, he was good on all counts. At that point, all I really knew about Franklin was that he was Billy Graham's son and had a ministry in Boone called Samaritan's Purse that worked with global missions. I had no idea that he could potentially be an answer to my prayer. After we finished talking and I was about to leave, I felt compelled to give him my business card. As I did, I said, "Hey, if something ever comes up regarding water in Africa, let me know if you need some help." He took the card and thanked me. That was it.

During this new season in my faith, every time I brought up going back to Africa to Carolyn, she would look at me with wide eyes, responding with something between an accusation and a legitimate question: "Have you lost your mind?!"

After praying for a year and a half with nothing happening, I finally resigned to God's apparent silence on the matter, thinking, *Well, He obviously doesn't want me in the world, or He would have answered by now.* While I kept my head down and worked hard to make a living, I began to question my future in the family business. As we all gathered for Thanksgiving in 1986, a talk I had with my father-in-law, who was also my boss, allowed me to see I had no real future in his company. That was the day I decided the time was drawing near for me to leave.

In the spring of 1987, I had the opportunity to go back and volunteer again in Togo on a two-month trip. In my mind, this was going to be my goodbye to the dream of going to the world. I figured I would take this final adventure and then come back to find a new job in the drilling world. While there, I contracted malaria, which took me awhile to fully recover from when I returned home.

In June, I gave my father-in-law my notice and took a job with Graves Well Drilling in Sylacauga, Alabama, which had been bought out by the Alabama Gas Company. Because of my experience, they made me a regional director with a salary, full benefits, and the keys to a company truck. With that package, I felt like a Fortune 500 executive. Pay and perks aside, this new career path was really exciting with plenty of learning opportunities doing different kinds of horizontal and diagonal drilling. Everything was on a much larger scale. I was assigned to the regional office in Jackson, South Carolina, where the majority of our work was at the Savannah River nuclear plant. Every Monday I would head there for the week, then come home on Friday night to spend the weekend with my family.

One Saturday that summer, while at home, I got a call from Preston Parrish, who worked for Franklin.

"Are you Kenney Isaacs?"

"Yessir. That's me."

"Kenney Isaacs, the well driller?"

"Yessir."

"Are you Dewey Wright's son-in-law?"

"Yessir."

Franklin had given him my card and all the information he could recall about me. Finally assured he had the right man, Preston continued, "Great. Well, would you be willing to come and talk to Franklin? He needs some advice about drilling equipment in Ethiopia."

Of course, I agreed.

Over the next several months I met with Franklin to advise him on a proposal they were working on to partner with a church in Ethiopia for a clean water program. Beginning in 1983, there was a historic drought and famine there that lasted for years. You may recall the response from famous music artists who put on the Band Aid concert and released the legendary "We Are the World" song. Those efforts brought a lot of global attention to the humanitarian crisis there. Franklin's vision for Samaritan's Purse has always been to meet needs anywhere in the world, all while sharing the love of Christ.

By late 1987, the answers that kept coming back to Franklin from Ethiopia were not actually addressing our questions. Out of desperation, I told him, "Listen, this doesn't have to be hard. I think you just need to get someone to go there with the questions to make sure you get the right answers. Someone needs to go on-site to get eyes on the situation."

Franklin responded, "Kenney, would you be willing to do that? To go and get those answers?"

I told him I was on board, but my boss would have the final say (the boss at my job that I really loved). He would make or break the deal. That next week I went to the company's headquarters. When I explained the situation, his answer took me by surprise. Not only did he say I could go, but they would also pay me. There was just one stipulation. They would write a story about my trip and put it in their monthly newsletter. As a smart boss, he saw this as a great PR move.

In January of 1988, I went to Ethiopia for a month. On the long flight back home, I wrote a full report detailing all the information—an itemized list of necessary equipment, contact information for the best vendors, and estimated costs that included a spare parts package. I also gave Franklin an operational plan for how to install the pumps, as well as how to educate people in every community or village on pump repairs. To me, this seemed like common sense stuff.

A Change of Heart

After I returned home in February, the day I met with Franklin in his office, I walked in and handed him the report. I sat quietly in the chair across from his desk as he began to look over the first page. Just as he flipped to the second, his eyes cut up toward me. Very matter-of-factly, he stated, "I don't believe it's an accident that you and I have been brought together."

Now, a sidebar about that moment: Over these many years as I have faced so many difficult trials and insurmountable challenges, even at times numbing grief, Franklin has reminded me of that day, stopping to ask, "Do you remember when I told you that I didn't think we were brought together by accident?" Many times I have drawn encouragement from that ordained moment.

At the time Franklin made his veiled prophecy about the future, I had not yet shared with him my burden of feeling like God had "called me to the world." Because of my great job, the company truck and all, I had moved on, assuming the answer was no. After all, isn't a year and a half long enough to wait for

Ken, Carolyn, Jamey, and Coy at departure from Boone, August 1988.

something to happen? And wasn't it God who blessed me with the dream job? Why would He give it to me and then ask me to leave? But a crucial lesson we all have to learn is that God's timing is not our timing. Remember what He said through the prophet Isaiah,

> "For my thoughts are not your thoughts,
>   neither are your ways my ways,"
>   declares the LORD.
> "As the heavens are higher than the earth,
>   so are my ways higher than your ways
>   and my thoughts than your thoughts." (55:8–9)

To say that Franklin Graham is persistent or tenacious is an understatement. Deciding that I was the man to go back to Africa and run the project, he began to call me one or two times a week for the next two months. Every time, he would ask, "Are you praying about going to Ethiopia? Are you putting this before the Lord?" To be honest, at first, I wasn't serious in my prayerful exploration of his request. But as he kept pressing me, I started talking to Carolyn. Her answer? "There's no way. I am *not* going to Africa!" At that time, our son Jamey was a junior in high school and our son Coy was in third grade. (Yes, we named our youngest son after my adopted father.)

Seeking the Lord, I landed on two places in Scripture. One was when God called Moses to go to Pharaoh. Moses argued with God, explaining why he wasn't the right guy for the job and how he wasn't equipped:

> "Who am I that I should go to Pharaoh and bring the Israelites out of Egypt?" (Ex. 3:11)

> Moses said to God, "Suppose I go ... and say to them, 'The God of your fathers has sent me to you,' and they ask me, 'What is his name?' Then what shall I tell them?" (Ex. 3:13)

> Moses answered, "What if they do not believe me or listen to me and say, 'The LORD did not appear to you'?" (Ex. 4:1)

> Moses said to the LORD, "Pardon your servant, Lord. I have never been eloquent, neither in the past nor since you have spoken to your servant. I am slow of speech and tongue." (Ex. 4:10)

And finally, when God had offered an answer for every question, Moses went with what is so often our go-to response to tough assignments:

> But Moses said, "Pardon your servant, Lord. Please send someone else." (Ex. 4:13)

As I meditated on those divine conversations, I prayed, "God, if You're asking me or guiding me, I don't want to be out of Your will." The second place I camped out was the book of Jonah when God sent him to Nineveh. The familiar but strange story is that Jonah didn't want to go, got swallowed up by the whale, and spit out. After all that, he ended up going anyway! (Ironically, I worked in Nineveh several times over the years, but that's for a later chapter.) I could clearly see how fighting God created a lot of needless hardships in Jonah's life. In that season of seeking, God's Word was a strong influence and constant encouragement for me.

Weeks into Franklin's phone calls, our company moved into a brand-new building. And I got a corner office. Anyone in corporate America will tell you that the corner office is the end goal, right? Now, I had it all. Heaven on earth. Or was it? These were blessings from God, weren't they?

But, before long, I actually began to feel like God was indeed calling me. I mean, I could *feel* it. My original sense of His calling was now coming back full circle. Even stronger this time. Yet there was still one very major roadblock to me saying yes. My wife, my soulmate, my better half, was not on board. That made me question if I was actually hearing God. Was I really understanding His will for my life? Why was there confusion with the two of us not being on the same page?

From Cussing to Quiet

One Friday afternoon, Franklin called. As I sat in my new office, looking out the corner windows, he asked his now familiar question, "Are you praying about this?"

"Yes, I am. And I feel like God is calling me ... but my wife's not on board with it."

"But what I asked you was, 'Do *you* feel like God is calling *you* to go to Ethiopia?'"

Again, I said, "Yes, I feel that He is."

"Then your real decision is what are you going to do about it? ... Can I pray for you now?"

As Franklin began to intercede over the phone, that "peace that passes understanding" the apostle Paul talked about came over me. As I sat there, my eyes closed, taking in the words for Carolyn and me, I felt like the Holy Spirit was confirming the decision in my heart.

Right after Franklin's "amen," I told him, "I'll be there in two weeks."

Hanging up the phone, I stepped out the door to speak to my boss. (The same guy who agreed to let me go to Africa for a month with full pay.) His name was Don Harvard. Don smoked cigars, cussed like a sailor, and had a good heart. I said, "Hey, Don, I need to talk to you." He motioned for me to step outside. Never being one to waste words, I got straight to the point, "I'm giving you my two-week's notice. I'm going to work in Ethiopia."

With that, Don lit into me with a string of profanities mixed with a few rhetorical questions, like "What do you think you're doing?!" Finally, he yelled, "Get your butt in the truck!" As he started driving who knows where, he just kept unloading on me until he finally got it all out and appeared to calm down. Pausing to catch his breath, he said, "All right, I know I'm gruff. I know I'm being grumpy about this. But I do understand what you're doing. If you feel like this is what God is calling you to do, I'll support your decision."

I was grateful I hadn't interrupted his rant or gotten defensive, because he made a 180 after being able to vent. I understood Don's anger because, one, I took him by surprise with no warning and, two, I knew he valued me and didn't want me to leave the company.

His next question was obvious, "What did your wife say?" When I answered, "I haven't told her yet," well, that set Don off again. Then came round two of another string of profanities mixed with more rhetorical questions. When he calmed down a second time, he gave me my marching orders, "I think you need to fly home. Not drive the six hours. Fly. You need to get home right away and talk to your wife."

Abiding by my boss's advice, I caught the next flight out. Carolyn picked me up in our tiny orange Honda sedan at the Hickory, North Carolina, regional airport. Just as I had with Don, I wasted no time in telling Carolyn. I knew she was wondering what in the world was going on, and I had to put us both out of our misery of waiting. Pulling out of the airport, I blurted out, "I gave Don my notice. I'm going to work for Samaritan's Purse, and I'm going to Africa."

In our two and a half years of dating and, ultimately, in our forty-six-year marriage before she passed in October 2017, that was the only time that Carolyn's response was to not speak to me. I think she was both shocked and infuriated that I had made this decision on my own. In fact, for the next three days, she didn't say a word to me. Three *very ... long ...* days. That's an excruciating length of time to have the person you love the most ignore you. She said nothing. No words. To say you could cut the tension with a knife isn't strong enough. *Chain saw* would be more appropriate.

Even though I had no idea how to deal with her silence, I knew full well that I had absolutely shaken her world.

Buckle Up

On April 11, 1988, I went to work for Samaritan's Purse. At home, my marriage was strained. I was open with Franklin about it, and he said, "We're going to start praying for your wife." Now, I am not sure *who* he asked to pray, but I do know this: with Franklin, it's not some little group or intimate prayer circle. On major issues, he asks a *lot* of people to pray.

In May, Franklin talked to me about going back to Ethiopia and also to London and Kenya. Then he added, "Why don't you take your wife with you? Yeah, take Carolyn on this trip. Let her see another part of the world." Surprised, I responded, "What?! No, she's made it clear to me she has no desire to go to Africa." Seeing I was reluctant to ask her, Franklin offered, "Bring Carolyn up here. I want to talk to her myself."

That night at home, I delivered the request. "Carolyn, Franklin would like to talk to you."

"What does he want to talk about?"

"I don't know," I said, clearly faking ignorance. "Why don't you come up and talk to him?"

Begrudgingly, Carolyn agreed.

The very next day, she walked into his office, sat down on the couch, folded her arms across her chest, let out a big sigh, and stated, "I understand you want to talk to me."

Franklin is not taken aback very often, but in that moment with my wife, he certainly was. Yet he pressed on with his pitch. "Carolyn, Kenney needs to go back over to Ethiopia. I'd like you to go with him and see what it's like. You can go to London first. There's an organization there partnering with us in Africa. Then on to Kenya where there's a great missionary couple that I would love for you to meet. From there, you can go to Ethiopia."

Franklin felt like it might be easier if Carolyn got to see London first and then Kenya before getting the full exposure to the poverty, drought, and famine in Ethiopia. That sounded logical, I know, but my wife had lived her entire life up to that point in Watauga County, North Carolina. Europe and Africa were only places she had seen on TV and in magazines.

When Franklin finished his presentation to my wife, after a long pregnant pause, with her arms still crossed and expression stoic, Carolyn asked, "Is that all?"

When he answered yes, she closed with, "Okay, thank you." She then stood up and walked out.

(During the final months of Carolyn's life, she came up to our staff devotions one morning, and, in a very endearing manner, Franklin told that story to everyone and shared how he didn't know how to react to her. It was a comical and nostalgic moment.)

After just two days, Carolyn announced to me that she would go to Africa. Taking in her words, I was somewhere between shocked and elated.

Our trip went exactly as planned. After a stop in London, then a week in Kenya, we went to Ethiopia for the next nine days. We drove south into areas in dire need of water. The harshness of life in Ethiopia was tough to witness; the people were desperately poor under a communist regime during wartime. Yet their genuine and deeply respectful manner touched us both. I could clearly see the things we witnessed were very difficult for Carolyn, as they are for most anyone seeing those conditions for the first time.

For our flight out of Addis Ababa, Ethiopia, we boarded a Lufthansa flight for Frankfurt, Germany, which would be our last leg back to the States. As the plane began to go down the runway and pick up speed for takeoff, at the point where you feel the front wheels lift off the ground and you get pushed back into your seat from the force, I leaned over to Carolyn. In a quiet, intimate tone, I asked her, "So what do you think about Ethiopia?"

She turned her face toward me, our noses about an inch apart, her eyes locked in on mine, and stated, "Well, I think there is a lot of need there. I believe you can help. And I can see that God is calling you." Pausing, she brought up her hand and pointed her finger in my face. "But I'm *never* coming back."

That was the moment I knew my wife was giving me her blessing to pursue this new calling from God that would be a part of our life and marriage for the next twenty-nine years.

Coy and Ken at Samaritan's Purse

Chapter 2

Go, Even Though There Is No Road

Ethiopia
1989–1991
Drought/Famine

Working from our last communication that my wife would not be going back to Africa, I continued to pray for the Lord's will to bring His resolve to us. Meanwhile, Franklin and I were figuring out how I could go on two- to three-month rotations, traveling back and forth. Yes, in effect, commuting between North Carolina and Ethiopia. But, of course, there was no getting around the reality that the distance was going to create a strain on our marriage and family in every possible way. The time difference and lack of communication options in Africa would definitely be a constant challenge. This was back before cell phones, and international long-distance calls on landlines cost ten dollars a minute. (For perspective, in today's economy, that would be about twenty-five dollars a minute.) While the initial upset over my decision to leave my dream job appeared to be behind us, we had to try to find the best way forward.

At home in the early summer of 1988, with our sons out of school, we would often go to my mom's house after work to visit. (By this point, she had remarried.) We would snack on cucumbers or watermelon or her legendary coleslaw.

Sitting around the table, we'd catch up on life, then go home for the evening. On this particular day, I had arrived first and was enjoying a plate of slaw.

When Carolyn came in the door from her job as an accountant, my mom asked, "Hey, honey, how are you?"

"Oh, I'm doing good."

"Well, come on and sit down. Have some coleslaw."

Needing no further convincing, my wife sat down and joined me, indulging in Mom's slaw.

Making her usual conversation, Mom asked Carolyn, "So, what did you do today, honey?"

"Well, I gave my two-week's notice."

When I heard her news, my eyes widened, and my jaw dropped, revealing a mouthful of coleslaw. I was shocked. Speechless. Confused. Questioning if I had somehow misheard her, I froze, feeling like the room was suddenly made of extremely fragile glass and any abrupt movement or word spoken would shatter it into a million pieces.

My mother, God bless her, never missed a beat. She didn't show any emotion or change the inflection in her voice at all as she asked, "Oh, really? And what are you going to do?"

"I think God is telling me to go to Africa with Kenney."

Yes, my wife had quit her job exactly as I had mine with no discussion and no explanation. She believed she had heard from God and was being obedient. Like me, Carolyn knew what she had to do and just did it. That was indicative of the way we were both wired and the way each of us responded to the movement of the Holy Spirit in our hearts. Regardless, if back when we were flying home from Africa, you would have told me about this moment in my mom's kitchen, I would have said you were crazy. But, like I said before, the life of faith is always an adventure.

God had answered my prayer in a way that was beyond my wildest imagination. He had also confirmed the calling He had placed in my heart of going to the world. I was a guy with no preparation and no training wanting to take on the challenge of meeting the overwhelming needs in Africa. And now my family would be with me on this new journey. True to her word, Carolyn followed through, and, in late August of 1988, we moved to Ethiopia. That decision totally altered the course of our lives forever.

Changes and Challenges

I hit the ground running on a new well-drilling project owned by the Ethiopian Kale Heywet Church. Founded in 1927, the church is now its own denomination of 10 million members with headquarters in Addis Ababa. The immediate dilemma was working within the church's structure to establish the program while having to liaison with a communist government that was oppressive to Christians. Quite the challenge. On the logistics side, I had to locate and acquire equipment, organize the entire project, and hire workers.

For our family, a huge part of the move was adapting as quickly as possible to different social norms, a different culture, a different language, different weather, different smells, different foods, and a totally different government. For example, a curfew forced everyone off the streets by 7:00 p.m. The authorities were very strict, navigating two wars that were going on at the same time. One was essentially a civil war with the Tigray People's Liberation Front (TPLF). The other was with the Eritrean People's Liberation Front (EPLF). At the time, there was a lot of

Drilling a water well in Addis Ababa

military activity, with approximately 5,000 Russian and 25,000 Cuban military advisers stationed around the country supporting the Ethiopian government's war efforts.

Living under communism created serious constraints regarding goods, with most Western commodities not allowed. For the first month, our family lived in a missionary guest house. The government did not allow Ethiopians to rent their houses. But we were finally able to work out an arrangement to get into our own place. After moving in, like most kids, the boys adapted quickly and took well to life in Africa. Jamey, our oldest son, sixteen at the time and in his senior year of high school, went to International Community School in Addis Ababa. Coy, who was eight years old and in third grade, went to Bingham Academy, a missionary school.

One advantage of moving to a foreign country was discovering that Jamey had a natural gift and affinity for learning languages. He graduated from high school at seventeen, and to our surprise, he told us he didn't want to attend university. Instead, he asked to take a gap year and go to Argentina on an exchange program. After two years of Spanish in high school and six months in Argentina, he became fluent and began his PhD studies, having not even done his undergrad work. Later, he moved to Leipzig, Germany, for a year after he won an essay competition sponsored by the Rotary Club network. Jamey wrote his entry in German after going through a course on tape. After living in Germany for six months, he also became fluent in their language. From there, Jamey enlisted in the Marine Corps and eventually graduated from naval postgraduate school with the Commandant's Award in Thai, his third fluent language, aside from English.

Coy, starting in fourth grade, went to Rift Valley Academy, a missionary boarding school in Kijabe, Kenya. Carolyn and I had to travel all over Ethiopia for the drilling program, so keeping him in one safe spot was best for us all. But this meant we would see him only every three months. Being separated from him at such a young age was very hard on Carolyn and me emotionally. Such a choice made for a very difficult dynamic for us all.

We received letters from Coy written on paper that served double duty. After he wrote the letter on the thin blue parchment, the paper would be folded to create an envelope that could be sealed, stamped, and mailed. The postal system typically took three or four weeks to deliver one of his letters to us. I recall a few times seeing what was clearly his dried teardrops on that paper, evidence he was crying as he wrote us. Needless to say, as parents, reading his words while seeing those stains was tough.

The separation made our opportunities to go visit Coy such wonderful times. We always loved those days, as all three of us enjoyed going to the restaurants there, as well as the other first world comforts that we didn't have in Ethiopia. One time when Coy was only nine years old, we flew him to visit us. Not many kids that age can say they have gone through customs with a passport and boarded an airplane to fly internationally to another country completely on their own. After Coy got his degree in business from North Carolina State University, he went to work for Samaritan's Purse and served in Darfur for two years. Today, he works for another NGO doing humanitarian work.

Even with the separation and inherent difficulties, we grew very close as a family. Simultaneously, we also grew close to the Lord because we had to rely on Him every single day for everything. I believe that is part of the testimony that God had planned for our family all along. Just like Jesus said in John 17:22–23, "I have given them the glory that you gave me, that they may be one as we are one—I in them and you in me—so that they may be brought to complete unity."

While the world saw Ethiopia at the time as a drought-stricken and famine-ridden nation, what we witnessed daily from the inside was the callous brutality and oppression of the communist government toward its own people. Because of this, thanking God for our food before a meal was not just some religious exercise for us. We were very sincere and filled with gratitude. For so many people around us, there was no food. They weren't just hungry; many were dying of starvation and related illnesses. So when we gave thanks, we were specific, "Lord, thank You for the clean water, for the tea, for the rice," and so on. Grateful for whatever we had the privilege to be able to eat that day, we recognized God's hand and His daily

Solomon and Ken at a well pump, southern Ethiopia, 1990

provision, which was so much clearer when we lived there than it was when we had lived in a land of abundance.

One of our staples, considered the national food of Ethiopia, was called injera, a fermented sponge bread rolled out about a foot and a half in diameter, set on a cooker, and then cut. You tear off a piece and pick your food up with it. Throughout Africa, people commonly have some sort of bread they use to scoop up meat, vegetables, or gravy.

We once had a major treat when we got a call from some friends we had made at the American embassy. They invited us to come on a Wednesday night for a hamburger meal with the Marines stationed there. In those days, we could drive right up to the gate and the guard would smile and say, "Hey, Mr. Isaacs, come on in." After that, anytime we got to go there and eat actual American food with our servicemen and servicewomen was a true privilege.

During those years in Africa, the separation of our family affected all our lives and changed us radically. Yet we had so many amazing adventures together. We each learned how to live differently, how to be adaptable, and, like I said, how to be grateful and rely on God for everything. In the US and the rest of the first world, we refer to our life filled with material possessions as our "comfort zone." In Ethiopia, our family discovered our true comfort zone as we pursued God's will. Psalm 119:76 tells us the Source: "May your unfailing love be my comfort, according to your promise to your servant."

You Get What You Pay For

To give you an example of the kind of day-to-day issues we had to solve to keep the work of Samaritan's Purse going in Ethiopia, in February of 1989 on one particular project, I needed to pick up an air compressor in Djibouti. My only viable transportation option was a plane. I went to the Ethiopian Airlines office to inquire how to go about flying cargo. Even though they were under a communist government, for some reason, they allowed the airline to operate in a free market system, outside the regime. They informed me that I could schedule a charter for $10,000. Thinking that was a fairly good deal under the circumstances, I asked if they would take American Express. Not a gold or platinum or black card, just the regular working man's green card. After I contacted Franklin back home at Samaritan's Purse, we both agreed the value of the compressor was worth the cost to our project. When Ethiopian Airlines said they would accept American Express, I laid down the plastic and charged the airplane. (If you're not rich, then you must be in some sort of mission work to do something like that.)

A week later, I was in a C-130 cargo plane, a massive four-engine aircraft that can carry up to twenty tons, flying from Ethiopia to the capital of Djibouti, a city of about 200,000 people. On the way, I began to feel the plane descending. I knew we couldn't possibly be near our destination yet, so I was immediately concerned there might be a problem. I asked what was going on, and the pilot informed me that all was well; he just had to make a brief stop in Dire Dawa. As the plane rolled in and the massive rear door came down, a crew began to load some unidentified cargo. When I asked what we were taking on "my plane," they told me they were transporting khat to Djibouti.

Khat, or qat, is an indigenous flowering plant. The leaves are harvested and sold as a recreational drug to produce a stimulant effect. They can be chewed (much like dipping tobacco), brewed in tea, sprinkled on food, or smoked. Khat is considered an addictive and dangerous substance due to its chemical compounds, which are similar to amphetamine. The effects create an immediate increase in blood pressure and heart rate with potential long-term effects such as paranoia, nightmares, hallucinations, and violence. While illegal in the US, it wasn't in that part of Africa and much of the Middle East.[1]

Once I understood the nature of the cargo, I told the pilot, "Now, wait a minute, I didn't charter this airplane for you to fly a drug into Djibouti!" The pilot calmly responded, "That's right. You chartered the plane to get freight back to Ethiopia *from* Djibouti. This is *our* freight on the way *in*. We'll unload it there, get your compressor, and fly you back, just like you paid for." Because this guy was clearly in charge of the plane, there wasn't much I could say at that point. While I had no idea another stop would be made on my flight, I also hadn't asked if there would be. Yet another important lesson to learn when you're in other parts of the world. (For a brief moment, headlines flashed in my mind that read, "American Arrested as International Drug Runner.")

Let Your Yes Be Yes

In May of 1989, with the air compressor now in our possession, we needed two trucks to complete the project. In those days, there weren't many logistic lines in and out of Ethiopia. The two largest thriving ports in this region at that time were in Assab and Djibouti. (In 1994, Assab became the sovereign territory of the newly formed state of Eritrea.) We had to get permission to retrieve both trucks. While there were some bureaucratic hoops to jump through, Assab was fairly straightforward. Carolyn, Coy, Desta Demessie (a close friend of mine), and I went there to get the service truck, which was outfitted with a water tank and fuel tank. We got the vehicle out of customs to drive back to Addis Ababa. The other truck with the drilling machine was in Djibouti. I found out that was going to be an entirely different matter. They informed me that no one had driven from Djibouti to Ethiopia in the past eleven years! That was going to make getting everyone to sign off on that transaction very challenging.

A major lesson I learned in those early days stayed with me, and I have utilized it all over the world—namely, you must be extremely careful when you need an answer and, in particular, permission. You need to go to the right person first because if you talk to someone and get a no, it's almost impossible to get that decision reversed. Nobody wants to change course and admit they were wrong, and any superiors involved are always going to support the guy who originally gave the no. Because what I needed had apparently not been done in an incredibly long time, if ever, I knew my chances of getting a yes were right up there with winning the lottery.

To get permission to bring the truck into Ethiopia from Djibouti, I had to go to the Ministry of Foreign Affairs, the Office of Customs, the Office of National Security, and the Relief and Rehabilitation Commission. I had decided my best chance would be to *not* ask anyone a direct question, so what I came up with was, "If I can get permission from the other government offices to drive a truck from Djibouti into Ethiopia, would you object to it?" Each office's answer? "No, we would not object *if* you can get permission from the other Ethiopian and Djibouti government offices." At each place, I asked for an official letter stating their answer, to which each agreed. Essentially, the message was, "We have no objection if no one else objects."

When we got to Djibouti, I went to all the offices there that had anything to do with taxes, national security, or exports, even the Ethiopian embassy—essentially anyone I could think of that might lend credence to the case I was building. As I began to gather these letters, I placed them in a protective folder that went everywhere with me. I was prepared to show anyone my documentation, declaring, "Look, these are the offices that do not have an objection." Before long, my folder was several inches thick, filled with letters from the various entities.

Dead Reckoning

After we were able to secure the truck with the drilling machine, it was time for Desta and me to make the trip from Djibouti to Ethiopia on the road that hadn't been traveled in over a decade. I was told to use a compass to drive through the desert until we came to an asphalt road. Finding that road would be the only way I could know I was back in Ethiopia. We drove through a place called the Plain of Galafi where the weather was extraordinarily hot.

At that time, there were concerns about attacks from the two rebel groups. In Djibouti, I met a Frenchman named Gino Pecol who had contacts that advised him on the best times for me to travel. He assured me there would be no fighting in the areas I would be driving through. So, armed with my folder of paperwork and local intelligence from Gino, Desta and I got in the truck and started our drive.

When we finally arrived at the gate on the border between Djibouti and Ethiopia, a guard walked up to the truck. Once again, working my principle to keep the communication to a minimum, I simply told him, "We're taking this truck to Ethiopia." No questions. No pushback. He quietly went over and opened the gate. It was that easy. Now, here's the very ironic and comical thing (now, not so much then): in all my preparation, when I did get to the border, they just waved me on through. They didn't look at *anything*! Talk about "measure twice, cut once." I had measured five or six times. But in my line of work, you can't overprepare.

After we drove through and he closed the gate behind us, we were staring at nothing but sand as far as we could see. You couldn't even see a road. Why? Because there was no road! Was it once there and now it was covered up with sand, or had there never been a road past the border? We had no idea. All we knew was we had to start driving.

Now, think about that border guard for a minute. Imagine being stationed at a gate where no one ever tries to get through. For a fleeting moment, I wondered if he just complied because he was thinking, *I'm going to be the last person to see these guys. They're either desperate or crazy.* I could clearly see why no one had been on that "road" in more than ten years. But any questions I had simply didn't matter now. We checked the compass and started driving, exactly as I was told to do.

I remember stopping along the way to get out to stretch our legs and being amazed at how incredibly hot it was. Breaking down would have been a death sentence. Knowing no one had been out there for so long, I understood that help was not going to be coming along—ever! I've been in extreme heat many,

many times, but never in a place like this where I questioned if my skin was actually going to start melting.

Finally, by the grace and mercy of God, we came upon that stretch of asphalt I was told was there. Even with a road to drive on, I stuck to my plan of dead reckoning. Checking the compass, I turned south onto the blacktop. Within about five miles, we came upon a military checkpoint that was manned by the Ethiopian army. Immediately, I could see this was going to be a much

different situation than the lone guard back at the other border who said nothing and just politely opened the gate.

As I stopped, way too many armed men for my comfort surrounded the front of the truck. Looking stern and carrying weapons, they began speaking very loudly in Amharic, the Ethiopian Semitic language. My friend Desta spoke it, but our concern was that me being an obvious for-

Rick Auten, Mitchell Minges, Solomon Gebre Yohannes, and Ken, western Ethiopia, October 1991

eigner might create a problem with them. While, at that point, I had learned a few words and key phrases in their language, I certainly wasn't anywhere close to fluent.

In Amharic, a guard asked, "Are you Russian?"

Much like a witness in a court of law, I simply answered his question, "No."

"Are you Cuban?"

"No."

Having no idea how they were going to take it, I decided to cut to the chase. With the most nonaggressive tone I could manage, in their own language, just above a whisper, I said, "I'm an American." That's one of those moments where your brain tells you to shut your eyes so you don't see them raise their rifles to fire, but you know you really need to maintain eye contact. After all, these were soldiers serving a communist government.

To my surprise and relief, they understood me enough to begin to call out to one another, "American!" Big smiles replaced the stern scowls as at least a dozen of them ran up to the truck to shake my hand. With one word, I went from potential threat to beloved celebrity. They were clearly happy to see an American, making that moment incredibly uplifting.

After I shook the hands of all the Ethiopian soldiers, with me smiling and waving, they gladly let us drive through their checkpoint. We spent the night in a little town called Mile, where, even after dark, the heat was sweltering. Several days later, we finally made our way back to Addis Ababa.

Surviving Our First Coup

Late in 1989, one Monday morning, I was at a place called Nazreth, forty miles south of our home. I noticed there were a lot of jets flying overhead. Even with our proximity to an air force base, hearing the constant whooshing sounds of the jet engines coming in and out, I knew there was an unusual amount of traffic. When I finished work, I drove back to our little office at the church compound. A friend called me and asked, "Hey, how's your family?" A bit confused, I answered, "They're fine." Realizing how I sounded, he offered, "You haven't heard, have you? There's been a coup. You need to get to your family right away. You have to make sure they're okay."

Thanking him, I immediately called Carolyn. I was grateful and relieved when she answered and told me they were safe. At that time, she was going a couple of days a week to use the exercise equipment in the Marines' gym at the embassy. Earlier that day, she had gone there to work out. On the drive, she noticed tanks in the road. She also saw large piles of dirt with mounted machine guns fixed on top to create protective barriers. Yet Carolyn drove on, right through the middle of it all, with no idea there was actual fighting.

She told me when she arrived at the gate, the guards opened it quickly, telling her, "Mrs. Isaacs! Get in here now!" Once she was safely inside, Carolyn asked, "What is going on?" When they informed her there was a coup, she responded, "Oh my goodness! Then I have to get back home. I have to get to my children," to which the guard answered, "No, no, you can't go out. It's not safe for you to go back." Now, the same woman who had told me in no uncertain terms that she would not be going to Africa informed those guards, "Well, I'm leaving, so you had better open that gate." Since she was not affiliated with the US government in any way, they complied and let her go. Carolyn drove back through the coup, except this time she heard gunfire along the way.

The next day, Tuesday, the town was locked down, and an impromptu national holiday was declared. In total, the whole country was shut down for three days. We learned that around twenty Ethiopian officers had been shot. There were secret security forces everywhere with everybody watching everyone. The president, Mengistu Haile Mariam, had been in East Germany, and, upon hearing what was happening at home, he quickly returned late on Tuesday night. Once he was back in the country, he was able to restore his communication and shut down the coup. While some of those who had carried out the plan were killed right away, a trial would follow for the men who had been captured in the failed takeover.

The final day of the trial happened to coincide with the World Cup soccer championship game. Our family was down in Shoshamani in a hotel restaurant that had a TV. The place was packed with folks enjoying the game. Suddenly, a breaking news bulletin interrupted the action announcing that the verdict had been given, everyone charged in the coup had been declared guilty, and the sentence had already been carried out by the time the station reported the event.

Immediately following the news, everyone got up and solemnly walked out without talking. The manager switched off the TV. The men who had attempted the coup were actually beloved by the people. They were officers who saw a window of opportunity to try to change things when the president left the country—more evidence that the people were both suppressed and oppressed under the communist regime.

Babies in a Battle Zone

In March of 1991, we received word that the US ambassador at that time, Robert Houdek, was summoning us all to the embassy (Robert is still a friend to this day). At the gathering, I saw that most of the people I recognized from Canada were not wearing the Canadian flag pins they typically wore to distinguish themselves from us Americans.

Ken and Solomon on a Russian tank, Simien Mountains, 1991

Ambassador Houdek told us that the TPLF was at Dessie and headed toward Addis. With the Ethiopian army seemingly unable to stop them, the paramilitary group would be in the capital city in a matter of days. He advised us all to get a flight out as soon as possible. The ambassador warned that if the US government had to order an extraction, the charge could be as much as twenty thousand dollars, an outrageous number at the time.

Right away, I heeded the ambassador's advice. Our third year in Ethiopia, we had brought Coy back to Addis with us. Of course, I didn't want my family exposed to open conflict, placing their lives in danger, so we got the next flight out on March 22, 1991. Ambassador Houdek's wife was also on our plane.

After being back in Boone for several days and getting my family settled, I returned to Ethiopia. This would be the first time I would work with people who were fleeing a combat zone. The word *refugee* is actually a technical term for people who have been forced to flee conflict or persecution and have crossed an international boundary to seek safety. Internally displaced people (IDPs) are those who have fled their homes but are still within their own country's borders.

By the time I returned, everyone was fearful of the TPLF's takeover. Hoping for safety in numbers, tens of thousands of IDPs had congregated in a football stadium, attempting to live there. Many were soldiers who had thrown down their weapons and taken off their uniforms. They had brought their family members with them and were now living in squalid conditions. A good number of the women there were pregnant, with some getting close to giving birth.

Seeing that need at the top of the list, I knew I had to come up with some way to help those women and their babies. I had an idea: We had built a greenhouse nearby with tables covered with plants. We had plant beds made out of plywood mounted on steel poles. The greenhouse had a staff of about twenty men, so, mobilizing that team, we cleared away the plants, covered the beds with plastic, and brought all the pregnant women there to get ready to deliver their babies. With the help of a local doctor and several nurses, we quickly turned a plant nursery into a human nursery.

Being in that stadium and seeing the horrific, filthy conditions these people were living in offered me the opportunity to better understand how to assess and meet needs in a crisis situation. Setting up a birthing center on the fly and using only what we had at hand was a unique experience that helped me develop skills I would use my entire career. My time in Ethiopia taught me so many amazing lessons as I learned to discern what people needed, pay attention to how they reacted, and figure out how I could best meet their needs.

I received an amazing education living the one-day-at-a-time lifestyle of someone called to leave their comfort zone and go where people were fighting for survival every day. From navigating bureaucracy in a communist government to meeting the needs of impoverished and oppressed people to having to rig solutions, like converting a greenhouse into a birthing center, Africa gave me a crash course in how God can work in and through humanitarian assistance.

First well in Selam Children's Village. Addis Ababa. 1989

The story I told you of driving through endless sand, navigating by dead reckoning, is actually such a powerful metaphor for the life to which God calls each of us as His followers. To go, even though there is no road.

> See, I am doing a new thing!
>> Now it springs up; do you not perceive it?
> I am making a way in the wilderness
>> and streams in the wasteland. (Isa. 43:19)

Carloyn and Kenney at Debre Zeit, 1990

Addis Ababa market, 1990

Chapter 3

Now's the Time

Afghanistan
1991/2001
War

Following the takeover in Ethiopia by the Tigray People's Liberation Front, I was concerned about the safety of the drilling equipment we had invested in and worked hard to secure. To protect the rig, we moved everything south, as far away from the line of fire as possible. Needless to say, these events immediately impacted the future of my work in Africa.

I know this sounds funny with all our amazing technology today, but a game changer arrived with the introduction of the fax machine, allowing me to handwrite a letter to Franklin on paper, feed it into the machine, dial, hit Send, and watch the page transmit to our office back in Boone in seconds. Typically, within a few hours, I would get a written answer back, all at a fraction of the cost of an international landline call. The ability to communicate across the world in writing seemed miraculous to us.

I faxed Franklin a letter explaining that, due to the escalation of violence, we had to transport the drilling rig to a safe location and close the program down for now. I also let him know that I still felt called to the work and would like to stay on with Samaritan's Purse. His response came back that I should return home and we would discuss that possibility. As I left Ethiopia, little did I know that this frequency of international travel would soon become an ongoing and distinct rhythm in my life.

A Black Hawk and a Blanket

After returning home to Boone in May of 1991, I went to meet with Franklin. The first Gulf War had started in August of 1990 and was still in its first year. Franklin asked me if I would travel to Turkey to assist a group of missionaries who were helping displaced Kurdish people near the border of Iraq, fleeing Saddam Hussein's military forces. While I didn't assume this new assignment meant I was officially hired, the reality was that from Ethiopia on, my involvement in the work continued.

A colleague at Samaritan's Purse had contacted the US ambassador to Turkey, Morton Abramowitz. Appreciative of our help, he agreed to make arrangements for the two of us to have access to a Black Hawk military helicopter and pilot for three days to explore the region and assess the needs of the people. During the Gulf War, Black Hawks "participated in the largest air assault mission in Army history with over 300 helicopters involved."[1]

We were to stay on the military base located outside of Diyarbakir in southeastern Turkey and were assigned to a tent where a Special Forces unit was stationed. (If you're unfamiliar with this branch, the Army's website describes them as "expert[s] in guerrilla warfare [who] use unconventional tactics to take on missions abroad."[2]) Because of their unique training and skills, Special Forces have the reputation of being a very tight-knit and private group. As we invaded their domain, these guys didn't know what to do with us.

On the first day, we met our pilot, who was with the First Air

Dr. Ed Carns showing Nurse Mary Lou Fisher the secrets to a PalmPilot, Kholm, 2002

Cavalry, a combat aviation brigade of the US Army. He was all business, carrying a .38-caliber revolver in a chest-mounted holster, positioned underneath his armpit. After takeoff, I asked him, "Captain, what will our altitude be today?" The glaring look on his face said, *I can't believe I have to tolerate this guy*. But instead, he answered like a seasoned soldier, "Our altitude today will be about seventy-five feet above ground level, son." With that, I decided to keep quiet and not attempt any more small talk.

Flying in a Black Hawk is an adventure every time, and my first trip was one wild ride. The pilot kept us seventy-five feet above ground level because we were flying in a combat zone. He was constantly maneuvering up and down, following the topography of the landscape. We flew over Duhok, located in the northwestern region of Iraq, a city with historical ruins dating as far back as 700 BC, with forty-two known archaeological sites.[3] From there, we flew over Zakho, as well as a multitude of small villages and areas where displaced people had gathered. With hundreds of thousands of people fleeing the invasion of the Iraqi army, Turkey had closed its border, not allowing anyone to cross. At the time, the weather was very cold and rainy with snow in the higher elevations. On my first day in this region of the world, I was getting a fast-track look at the devastation to humanity that was occurring.

Back at the base, I slept on a cot in a tent, and the nights got extremely cold and damp from frequent rains. I soon realized I had not come equipped for the weather. If I was not going to freeze to death, I had to look around the camp for supplies. Finding an area where there was a large number of crates and boxes, I thought to myself, *Surely there has to be a blanket in here somewhere!*

After I had randomly rummaged through boxes for a while, a colonel walked up and asked if he could help me. He likely knew I could be combing through those for hours and still not locate whatever I was searching for. Grateful, I answered, "I just need a blanket, sir." Without a word, he went straight over to a box, opened it, reached in, and pulled out a 100 percent wool blanket. Army green, of course. Thanking him, I took the newfound treasure back to my bunk, feeling like I might now survive the nights.

Over the years, as I have recalled that officer's hospitality to me, I've always felt gratitude for his kindness to a total stranger and civilian. To this day, I still have that blanket, and it has been with me on trips all over the world. With all the material possessions those of us in the West believe are "necessities," in my work overseas, something as simple and basic as a warm blanket becomes such a welcome blessing.

I spent about a month in Turkey, working to assess the needs of the people and helping the missionaries in the area arrange for much-needed supplies and humanitarian aid. Back home in Boone, I wanted to figure out how I could support the masses of people I had witnessed trying to escape Saddam Hussein's invasion. One of the qualities that I believe endeared me to Franklin was my entrepreneurial spirit. I've never been one to wait for someone to tell me what to do next. So I went to work searching for possible connections so that Samaritan's Purse could help the Kurdish people.

Hospitality or Hatred

By July of 1991, I had made contact with a man I had originally met in London who worked with a missionary organization. (I am intentionally withholding his name and NGO to protect their identities and missions, which is necessary for those who are living and working inside closed countries. *Closed* means a nation forbids or restricts official Christian missionary activity.) He connected me to Mark Morris, who was living in Pakistan and directing all the assistance he could into Afghanistan, as well as building relationships there. Franklin and I agreed that I would travel to meet Mark. I flew into Islamabad, the capital of Pakistan, where he lived.

I had heard stories about the rigid rules and restrictions the government fiercely imposed on Christians. Yet, at that time, I didn't fully understand the deeply entrenched animosity toward Christianity in the Islamic world. As the old saying goes, "You can't know what you don't know until you know it." We visited a home in the city where a group of about ten Christians had gathered for a secret church meeting. As they read from the Bible and prayed, everyone stayed very subdued and quiet.

After a while, a couple of other folks came in and began to share their stories. I could hear the anxiety in their voices that they would be exposed as Christians. Listening intently, I started to realize from the atmosphere in the room that they were not referring to just some passing concern. Even though they fluently spoke the local language and knew how to get around the city after having been there for years, they still lived with a daily threat regarding their faith in Christ. Letting their guard down and getting comfortable, just once, could prove to be a fatal mistake.

Next, Mark and I flew to Peshawar, Pakistan. There were an estimated four million Afghan refugees in designated areas there. Driving toward Afghanistan, we went through the Hindu Kush mountain range. I looked up to see the tall line of peaks with one single narrow gap. I knew right away this was the legendary landmark known as the Khyber Pass. The stories I had read as a boy by Rudyard Kipling came to mind, as he described it as

Ken with local friend Greg, Khyber Pass region

"a sword cut through the mountains." His poem "Arithmetic on the Frontier" opens, "The flying bullet down the Pass, that whistles clear: 'All flesh is grass.'"

The last phrase is a quote from Isaiah 40:6.[4] I also knew the history of the British losing in Afghanistan, eventually being driven out, along with the Russians. While surveying the majesty of the Khyber, I realized how easy it would be for a relatively small band of fighters to shut the pass down. The extremely harsh landscape around those mountains was foreboding.

To offer some context, five main warlords were fighting each other over the right to rule different parts of Afghanistan, primarily Kabul, the capital. Before that, in 1978, Russia had invaded Afghanistan, and their army had stayed there until February 1989. Ultimately, the Russians lost 15,000 troops with countless more injured.[5] At that time, Gorbachev was president of the Soviet Union, with Russia being one of the republics. While it may be hard to believe today in light of, for example, the war in Ukraine, the mothers of the fallen Russian soldiers rose up in such a public protest that their cries became the catalyst for Russia's withdrawal from Afghanistan.[6] Much like when the US pulled out of Afghanistan in August of 2021, the Russians left behind a graveyard of military equipment for the warlords to scavenge and use to ramp up their fighting against each other.

From this visit in 1991 to late 2001, following 9/11, to my last visit in 2007, I met three of those five warlords and actually developed a good rapport with them. The first time, I was traveling with a man named Shahzada Gailani and his wife. He was an Afghan who had migrated to San Francisco but returned to his home country with us because he cared deeply about his people. He wanted to help us help them. I recall he chain-smoked Pall Mall cigarettes, and you could hear the rattle in his chest

Kholm, 2002

when he spoke. A colleague of mine, Tom, was also with us. Shahzada had arranged for a number of bodyguards to accompany our group.

Arriving in Jalalabad, Afghanistan, we drove to a house belonging to one of the warlords—a man named Pir Gailani, who was Shahzada's uncle. Pir was one of the more moderate fighters and an advocate of a national alliance, wanting to see the return of the king after the communist takeover and the departure of Soviet troops. The goal of our meeting was to discuss how we could help their people and hopefully work out a way forward. The first thing I saw was a military tank parked in his yard. Needless to say, that sight makes quite a statement of power. We walked through the door and were introduced to the fighters gathered there. All of them were Mujahideen (a plural term for Afghan rebels, specifically members of a guerrilla group that opposed the invasion of Russia and eventually overthrew the Afghan communist government).[7] Because the Mujahideen had fought against the Soviet Union, they were supported by the US government and provided with weapons.

Every one of the men wore turbans, had beards down to their waists, and carried a weapon. On the floor was a carpet, like a large runner, with a huge feast set out, ready for us. They were well-prepared in hospitality for our meeting. (Not necessarily what you expect after seeing a tank in the front yard.) As they invited us to sit down on the floor to begin the meal, Tom realized what the men were asking us to do. That's when he stated, "I'm not going to sit on the floor to eat." Surprised at his attitude, I immediately thought to myself, *You know, I think I would be a little more accepting of their hospitality, what with the assault rifles and all.*

Somebody in the room heard what Tom said and must have understood English, because they were surprisingly gracious to him. Someone brought out a plastic chair; they didn't place it by the rug with us but rather in the corner. To go the extra mile to accommodate him, they also gave him a plate and fork.

Afghans certainly know how to put out a spread and their food is delicious—meat from their own raised animals and vegetables grown and prepared by hand. For that meal, we ate goat, mutton, whole brown rice, beans, lentils, and carrots, along with a drink that looks like milk made from fermented cucumbers. In my first visit there, I began to learn there was an essential code of conduct in Afghanistan, summarized in three words: *honor, hospitality*, and *revenge*. If you never cross the first one—honor—then you won't taste the last one—revenge. That day, I could literally feel the spirit of that code with the warlord and his fighters. While Tom sat over in the corner, I was perfectly content and comfortable eating traditionally with my hands, sitting cross-legged along the edge of the rug on the floor with the heavily armed Mujahideen.

What struck me that day was I never felt like my life was in danger. I had a peace that I was in the total protection of these Afghan men. While they had a very honorific social structure, I saw the only thing that might change my status was the knowledge that I was worth more dead than alive. Books like Marcus Luttrell's *Lone Survivor* and the movie of the same name, along with other films such as *The Covenant*, have told stories about the sacrificial honor and loyalty between American soldiers and Afghan interpreters. Their code demands they protect you with their lives. But, on the other side of that coin, I have known people who have been shot and killed, even folks who worked for the United Nations, on those very same roads I traveled. Hearing news like that was always a stark reminder of the constant dangers in that volatile region of the world.

On that trip, I wanted to visit a place in Pakistan called Darra Adam Khel, also known as "Gun Valley," a town with a population of 80,000 people and two thousand weapons shops.[8] While Shahzada was not eager for me to go there, he arranged for his men to escort me. Because my chief bodyguard didn't speak English and I didn't speak his language, we could only nod yes or no to interact. He had two bandoliers (pocketed belts or straps for holding ammo) crisscrossed on his chest, one loaded with shotgun shells and the other with hand grenades. He also carried a Colt .45-caliber pistol.

The village reminded me of the old western movies that depict Dodge City with small shops lining the dirt street. Every single store was full of swords, knives, guns, and various weapons. While there, I heard someone call out loudly, "Hey, mister!" I turned around to see this guy holding a rocket-propelled grenade launcher (RPG). As I made eye contact, he held it up for me to see the live grenade on the end and called out, "Five dollah!" The bodyguard looked at me and shook his head

Aziz Aslami and Ken watching a Northern Alliance fighter explain his tools

vigorously from side to side with a strong negative. Taking his cue, I turned and walked away, praying I hadn't offended the "salesman."

When we got back to Shahzada's house, at some point I made a comment about the beautiful large rug in the room. When I asked where it came from, he told me it was handmade in Afghanistan. I ended with, "Well, that is a *very* nice rug." About six weeks later, after I had returned home, a large package arrived via international shipping. I opened it to find the rug from Shahzada's home as a demonstration of Afghan hospitality and honor. Because I complimented his rug, he gave it to me, shipped all the way from Jalalabad.

On the way home from that trip, while waiting in London, I called Franklin and said, "I definitely think we need to do something in Afghanistan." While I didn't have a specific plan, he knew I meant an ongoing, large-scale commitment to help the people there. I just felt like it was somewhere we should be, a place of great need, a place that impressed me deeply. The starkness of the geography and the harshness of the people had a beauty all their own. The country intrigued me, invited me, and reminded me of the kind of adventure I had experienced in Ethiopia.

But, in Franklin's uncanny way, he responded, "Now's not the time, Kenney. Now's not the time." There have been situations like that when I have been a bit, shall we say, *persistent*. But Franklin has always been able to match me with being *insistent*. His answer was clear. No, for now.

Confirmation in Times Square

Fast-forward to 2001, just after 9/11, Franklin dispatched me and a group of pastors to go to Ground Zero to help the First Responders. We loaded up two Suburbans to drive from Boone to New York City. Besides a few of my coworkers, there were Pastors Sam McGinn, Wendell Capps, and Scott Andrews. (After spending time with Scott on the trip, I later began attending his church, Alliance Bible Fellowship, and had the honor of serving on the board of elders.) Pastors Skip Heitzig, Mike Macintosh, and Mike Finizio from the Calvary Chapel group also joined us.

At the time, we were in the process of starting what would later become known as the Rapid Response Team for the Billy Graham Evangelistic Association. The goal was to establish a program of rotating chaplains and pastors to minister to the people of New York, predominantly police officers, firefighters, and construction workers at Ground Zero. The Red Cross had created an opportunity to offer spiritual care to First Responders working on the site of the Twin Towers, led by Mike Macintosh, the head of spiritual care. Including our group, there were about forty pastors who would become accredited for participation in

Shahzada and his wife with Ken, Peshwar, Pakistan, 1991

the program. Once we had our Red Cross identification, we could go to Ground Zero to serve. The process took place at the wharf, just blocks away.

As I filled out the application form, there was a question: "Where were you ordained?" Not "*Were* you ordained?" but "*Where* were you ordained?" While I had obviously already taken part in a great deal of ministry around the world and had studied the Bible thoroughly for years, I had not been ordained. Honestly, the lack of those credentials had never kept me from any opportunity before. Hearing my dilemma, Mike and Skip decided they would take care of my answer to the question right then and there. As both ministers placed their hands on my shoulders, they stated, "Kenney, we're going to ordain you right now."

While a lot of churches and denominations take candidates through a rigorous process of making sure the person is fit, prepared, and truly called, these two men knew me, my background, my work, and my heart to serve both the Lord and people. I have never used titles like *pastor*, *minister*, or *missionary* to describe myself in my years of working with Samaritan's Purse, but I knew, beyond a shadow of a doubt, that God had called me. Mike and Skip believed they knew everything they needed to know to make me official in the eyes of the church and the state. Today, hanging on the wall in my office is my ordination certificate from Calvary Chapel, which they arranged for me to receive after that trip was over.

In the days following 9/11, New York was paralyzed. Everyone was in shock. Unusual things were going on, like taxi drivers taking fares for free just to help people and some restaurants providing free meals. Everyone near Ground Zero was working sacrificially.

By this point, cell phones were prevalent, and, while on that trip, Franklin called mine. He said, "Kenney, do you remember in 1991 when you said you wanted to do something in Afghanistan?"

"Yes, I do."

"Well, *now's* the time."

"Are you serious?"

"Yeah, now's the time. Let's do it."

We spent the remainder of that call envisioning next steps for my return to Afghanistan.

Franklin has stated publicly many times that wherever things are going on in the world, he wants to get his nose in the middle of it for the Gospel. At first, I was a bit hesitant to go into an area of the world where I knew the United States was getting ready to drop the hammer. But, like always, I quickly got past the initial anxiety and was ready to go.

Now, what some say is coincidence, those who follow Christ believe to be God's timing. That very same evening, not long after Franklin's call, our group was walking to Sardi's, a famous restaurant off Times Square where they have more than a thousand caricature drawings on the walls of celebrities who have performed on Broadway over decades. As I was crossing a crowded intersection, I caught a glimpse of a Samaritan's Purse T-shirt in the crowd. Looking closer, I saw that the man had it on underneath a sport coat. That's when I recognized him—Dr. Ed Carns. I had met Ed in South Sudan when he worked with us there in 1997 into 1998.

I walked up to him out of the crowd and said, "Ed! ... Kenney." He looked surprised, then launched into his trademark infectious laughter. He told me that he and his sister had planned a trip to New York City and, in spite of the 9/11 events, had decided to come anyway. So right there, on a street corner in the Big Apple, I asked him, "Would you like to go to Afghanistan?" He responded, "Are you kidding?!" Ed had suffered a severe leg injury while serving in Vietnam. Rather than amputate his leg, the doctors had somehow rebuilt it. Following his recovery, the Army put Ed through medical school to become a doctor, and he eventually retired as a colonel.

I hadn't seen Ed since Sudan, and I just randomly walked right into him in New York. And he "just so happened" to wear his Samaritan's Purse T-shirt that day. (You can't make this stuff up.) I realized that seeing him on one of the busiest blocks in the world right after Franklin had called me to go to Afghanistan was God giving me a personalized confirmation and affirmation that He was indeed telling me to go there, regardless of the risks.

Between a Rock and a Hard Place

Dr. Paul Chiles and I flew into Tashkent, the capital of Uzbekistan, then to Dushanbe, the capital city of Tajikistan.

After we had arrived and were settled, Paul had an opportunity to go with a group to the border near Afghanistan, a five-hour drive. They would then fly via helicopter into the Punjab Valley. I stayed back at the hotel and was planning to make my way into Afghanistan from Uzbekistan.

After boarding the helicopter, something in Paul's spirit told him not to take the flight. There were two reporters outside wanting to go, so he stepped out and offered his seat to one of them. At some point in the journey, the helicopter crashed and everyone on board was killed.

When I was told about the incident, as far as I knew, Paul was on that helicopter. When he walked into the lobby of the hotel

Ken in a traditional hat, 2002

soon after, I experienced one of the greatest moments of relief and shock in my life. Obviously, a special hand of protection was on Paul's life.

To be able to get safe access to the people who needed help, you had to go through the warlords. I was able to arrange a meeting with Atta Muhammad Noor, known as General Atta. Once it was confirmed, I knew God had opened that door and orchestrated the circumstances. But, just like we read about with

Paul and Peter in the book of Acts, when you go before a political or military leader who doesn't see eye to eye with your faith, you never know what you're going to get.

For some backstory here, the United States supported the Northern Alliance led by Ahmad Shah Massoud against the Taliban, who were, of course, involved with Osama bin Laden. General Atta was the Northern Alliance's second-in-command. On September 9, 2001, two al-Qaeda operatives carried out the assassination of Massoud, known as the Lion of Panjshir. The two men impersonated a reporter and cameraman to gain access through a supposed media interview where they detonated explosives disguised as camera batteries in a suicide mission.[9] My meeting was with Atta, the leader who had become the number-one man following this incident.

Besides Ed Carns, Paul, and myself, I brought Aziz Aslami, our translator. One of the details God had worked out was to be able to bring an Afghan man on this trip. He was a Christian from Saddleback Church in California whom I had connected with only a couple of weeks before the trip. Aziz was born in Afghanistan, but his parents left when he was seventeen and moved to Alabama where he had come to faith in Christ. He told me he loved his people and would do anything to help them. He actually told me, "I will go and carry your luggage." Seeing his servant's heart and passion for his people, I invited him to come and meet with me in Boone. And now, on this day, here we were in Afghanistan about to speak with a warlord, where the stakes were indeed high.

Friend Greg and a local Mujahideen with Ken, Jalabad, 1991

As we arrived at the meeting location, I immediately noticed there were military tanks in his yard, just as there had been with the first warlord I met. But this time, there was more than a houseful of fighters. Several hundred men were stationed outside with heavy weaponry. This was a very serious situation. Anticipating the moment of our introduction, I prayed under my breath, "Lord, what am I going to tell him? Tell me what I need to do."

I learned two principles from working in this region of the world. First, you always want to be transparent and let them know exactly who you are. Just be yourself and be the same to everyone. Second, if you're around people with guns, it's a good idea to try to make them your friends. Do *not* be contentious (which is why I had no hesitation to sit cross-legged on the floor to eat with the Mujahideen).

Once inside, we were escorted to a small area that had been set up like a waiting room. As we sat down, I saw there were two men already there, clearly both Americans in some sort of uniform but with no identifiable markings. They never looked at us, didn't speak to us, didn't even say hello. Each of them held a large aluminum suitcase. Putting details together later, I'm fairly confident that the men with the cases, and the two other guys I would meet later at the airport, were part of the *12 Strong* group. They were the dozen Special Forces soldiers who led the first mission into Afghanistan to try to destroy the Taliban. I have no doubt those large metal suitcases contained millions of dollars in cash.[10]

At the time, as a new government was forming, General Atta was in the process of becoming Governor Atta. Soon, we were summoned into the room, leaving the men with the suitcases to wait even longer.

After introducing myself, I simply said, "We've come to help your people."

With Aziz translating, Atta responded, "That's good because our people need help."

Following his lead, I offered, "We can build a small hospital. We can build schools. We can drill water wells. We can create women's education programs."

Listening intently, he stated, "*All* these things are good."

Deciding the time had come for full transparency, I said, "General, I'm a Christian. I follow Christ. I work with a Christian organization. If that's going to be a problem for you, please tell me now and I'll just leave."

Right away, Atta answered, "No, no, that's not going to be a problem."

"Great. Thank you, sir."

"You are welcome," the general declared.

I later learned that Atta's acceptance had a deeper meaning. We would now be under his protection. That brief, direct exchange revealed to them who we were and that our motive was only to help. Once Atta extended his hand to us that day, he faithfully maintained his hospitality. (Further evidence of the code I spoke of earlier.) From that moment on, his door was always open to me. I could even go to him if I needed access to meet other people in the region.

The first place Atta sent us was a town called Kholm where two opposing warlords, Abdul Kabir and Qari Tahir, were embedded with their fighters. One was up on top of the hill, and the other was down in the valley. They gave us a house that was located right between the two forces. With a home base established, our first efforts were to build schools.

In February of 2002, I had come back to the States to attend an AIDS conference in Washington, DC, that Samaritan's Purse had organized called Prescription for Hope. We had brought in about a thousand people from around the world, including international political leaders and media. Some of those in attendance were Helene Gayle, the head of the Bill and Melinda Gates Foundation (today, the Gates Foundation); Senator Jesse Helms, the chairman of the Senate Foreign Relations Committee; Senator William Frist, MD, Senate majority leader; and Andrew Natsios, the administrator of the United States Agency for International Development (USAID). Out of this effort would come PEPFAR—President's Emergency Plan for AIDS Relief—which went on to invest more than $100 billion in the global response to HIV/AIDS.[11]

While I was at this conference, my cell rang. It was Dr. Ed calling from Afghanistan. As I answered, he called out, "Kenney! I need to tell you something. These guys are shooting, man! There's stuff flying over our head!"

I could hear loud explosions in the background. Abdul Kabir and Qari Tahir were exchanging fire, and our house was right in the middle of the battle. Between Ed's bursts of signature laughter—a combined reaction of humor and stress—he told me, "I'm going to get everybody in the truck, and we're headed to Mazar-i-Sharif." (Mazar-i-Sharif was the fourth-largest city in Afghanistan.) "Kenney, we're going to get out of here!"

Concerned and surprised, I quickly agreed, "Yes, Ed! Go! That's fine with me. Get everyone to safety."

Ken with Team Lead Dony Sawchuk, Kholm, 2002

But the realization of our team's escape triggered something amazing. Just a few days later, the Shura, the council of elders in that community, got in their vehicles, drove to Mazar-i-Sharif, found our team, and pleaded with them to return to keep helping their people. After hearing the elders out, Ed told them, "We will only come back if both sides disarm." And they agreed. They disarmed. The story of that historic ceasefire was carried worldwide. Of course, they didn't mention Samaritan's Purse as the catalyst, but it was the first voluntary disarming that happened. In God's providence, He knew by positioning our team in between those warlords, He could accomplish His greater purpose. And everyone on our team was kept safe.

Lambs among Wolves

When we left Afghanistan in 2007, Samaritan's Purse had operations in Kholm, Mazar-i-Sharif, and Kabul. With all we were doing there, we consistently asked ourselves, "How do we share Christ?" I had this idea in my head that talking about Him in Afghanistan had to somehow look different from, for example, talking about Him in a predominantly Catholic country, like Honduras after Hurricane Mitch. In Honduras, you could share Christ on any street corner. But in Afghanistan, you might get to share the Gospel *once* like that. Again, because of the animosity toward Christians in the Islamic world, simply expressing your faith is a huge risk. Yet, in reflection, we estimated that more than five hundred people had come to Christ and underground churches were started. Only God knows the potential ripple effects those believers have had in their homeland.

In 2021, when the US military evacuated in the collapse of the American position, if an Afghan had worked for American NGOs, like Samaritan's Purse, there was at least a visa path for them. Hundreds and hundreds of people wrote to us, folks that we knew to be believers who wanted out. Knowing the dire circumstances there, we helped as many as we possibly could. I reached out to Mark Morris, whom I spoke of earlier. A few years later, after our time together in 1991, he relocated to Memphis, Tennessee, to pastor a church and run a refugee program for Afghans. Hearing that he was working to get Afghan Christians out, knowing they could be executed, I offered our help. Amazingly, some believers felt called to stay, choosing not to come out for the sake of the Gospel and the people there.

Over those years of service, we built a twenty-five-bed surgical hospital that was very sophisticated for a medical facility in that part of the world. We drilled

Afghanistan/Pakistan region, 2003

wells and built schools. We helped 4,500 refugee families repatriate through a partnership with the United Nations High Commissioner for Refugees.

Afghanistan taught me that God can do miracles in and through our weakness. When we realized all the spiritual victories there, I remembered Jesus' words in Luke 10:2–3: "The harvest is plentiful, but the workers are few. Ask the Lord of the harvest, therefore, to send out workers into his harvest field. Go! I am sending you out like lambs among wolves."

In so many places around the world, I have witnessed "wolves" horribly ravaging "lambs." And I certainly understand what it feels like to walk into a room, such as in the home of an Afghan warlord, knowing I am being sent in as a lamb. But that is exactly when I have been able to experience the triumph of the Lion of Judah, who is forever worthy.

"Stop weeping! Look, the Lion of the tribe of Judah, the heir to David's throne, has won the victory. He is worthy to open the scroll and its seven seals."

Then I saw a Lamb that looked as if it had been slaughtered.... He stepped forward and took the scroll from the right hand of the one sitting on the throne. And when he took the scroll, the four living beings and the twenty-four elders fell down before the Lamb.... And they sang a new song with these words:

"You are worthy to take the scroll
    and break its seals and open it.
For you were slaughtered, and your blood has ransomed
    people for God
    from every tribe and language and people and nation."
        (Rev. 5:5–9 NLT)

Chapter 4

Anyone Who
Welcomes a Little Child

Bosnia
1992–1995
Ethnic Cleansing

I have a photograph I took in Sarajevo of a man and woman sitting at a bistro table on the small terrace of their apartment. They were calmly enjoying a cup of espresso in the morning. Outside their little sanctuary, the contrast was starkly brutal. Part of their building was destroyed, reduced to piles of rubble. Bullet holes and shrapnel marks scarred the remaining walls.

What you cannot see in the photo are the explosions going off nearby. Through the noisy chaos, the husband and wife sat out in the open, appearing to savor the day like nothing was happening. I was across the street when I noticed them and snapped the photo. As I watched for a moment in total bewilderment, the man made eye contact with me, smiled, and raised his cup into the air in a toast, as if to say, "Come what may, right here, right now, I will enjoy my coffee."

I also knew of people who went for a walk deliberately through areas of the city that were called Sniper Alley. While the name originally referenced the main road to Sarajevo that snipers focused on, it came to describe any area where gunmen would set up on a tall building to shoot at anything that attempted to move through a corridor. After a while, entire sections of the city came to be called Sniper Alley, a term used to quickly communicate potential danger. Because this threat was so prevalent, some of the residents would reach a breaking point of isolation and desperation and say, "You know what? I'm not standing for this any longer. I can't take it anymore. I'm going out." A family member might respond, "No, no, don't go," but then rethink the futility of their situation and add, "Okay, well, wait a minute. I'll come with you."

The terrace scene I photographed and the kind of conversations I heard about between family members depict a mysterious response unique to folks who become trapped in war zones. Life lived in such violent and volatile circumstances can take a strange toll and affect behavior in curious ways. I've witnessed this firsthand many times over the years.

In the early 1990s, most people knew of Sarajevo only as the home of the Winter Olympics in 1984. On TV, the city looked absolutely enchanting, covered with snow. The first time I heard about any political stirrings in what was then known as Yugoslavia was in 1988 while we were living in Ethiopia. My oldest son was in school with two brothers from there. At an event where students' families were visiting, I talked with the two teenagers and their parents. They told me about trouble brewing in their homeland and voiced concerns that a war might begin between the three primary ethnic groups—Serbs, Croats, and Muslims—and how Serb nationalism would fuel that conflict.

I knew about Marshal Tito, who had come into power in 1943 and, as premier and president, promoted socialism in government, defying the Soviet Union while also bettering the country's

Sharing baklava, 1995

relationship with the Western powers.[1] For years, Yugoslavia had been able to live in somewhat of a balance between the East and the West. Of the six republics, each had its own armed forces, while the manufacturing industry was compartmentalized. For example, all the aluminum and steel was created in one republic, while electrical and energy came from another. Even though all six were forced into becoming a "country," together, they found a very unique way of operating in a centralized economy.

That is, their system worked until March 3, 1992, when a referendum in Bosnia brought an overwhelming landslide vote of 99.7 percent declaring independence. The Socialist Federal Republic of Yugoslavia was broken up into five countries: Bosnia and Herzegovina, Croatia, Macedonia, Slovenia, and the Federal Republic of Yugoslavia, which later became Serbia and Montenegro.[2]

Allow me to give you more context on this conflict and, ultimately, the reason why Samaritan's Purse came to be involved there.

In 1992 when the Republic of Yugoslavia separated, the fighting began in Slovenia, and soon broke out in Croatia. Each ethnic group had its own portion of the former Yugoslavian army and refused to hand over their weapons to the Serbs. So fighting went from republic to republic, from Croatia into Bosnia. I saw that this was unlike other wars in that there was not a clear demarcation of sides or ideology. Sometimes, the Serbs would fight the Bosniaks alone, while, in other locations, the Croats would join them. Staying apprised of the unpredictable political affiliations was challenging because, at both the national and local level, change could happen quickly. Bosnia-Herzegovina seemed to me to be the historical line in the sand where the Habsburgs stopped the Ottomans. Consequently, Sarajevo was made up of three ethnic sectors—Muslims (identified as a nationality on ID cards and passports), Croats, and Serbs. Inside Bosnia, there was a section or territory and a government structure for each of the ethnic groups.

In May of that year, two days after the United States and the European Community (pre–European Union) recognized Bosnia's independence, Bosnian Serb forces with the backing of Serbia's President Slobodan Milošević and the Serb-dominated Yugoslavian army launched an offensive on the capital, Sarajevo. They attacked and forced out Bosnian civilians from the region in what was identified as ethnic cleansing, the expulsion of a group of people from a geographical area. Ethnic cleansing is different from genocide, which is the actual physical annihilation of a group. Definitions aside, atrocities including murder, rape, and torture are often used in ethnic cleansing, just as in genocide.

The war centered on resentment of economic disparities in the country, as well as ethnic hatred, causing everyone to suffer horribly. At that time, the Yugoslavian army was the fourth-largest in the world, so when it broke apart, they were well armed. Brutally armed, in fact. Speaking as an eyewitness, the conflict in Bosnia was hell. In Sarajevo alone, though initial estimates were much higher, final studies concluded that 100,000 men, women, and children were killed.[3] Between 1992 and 1995, approximately 2.2 million people were displaced from their homes, but still within the borders of their countries.[4]

Though the Bosnian government had tried to defend the territory with the help of the Croatian army, Bosnian Serb forces had control of most of the country by the end of 1993. Peace proposals failed when the Serbs refused to give up any territory. The majority of the Bosnian Croats had fled, with some able to remain only in small towns. The United Nations High Commissioner for Refugees launched a response to provide humanitarian aid to the thousands of victims.[5] That's where Samaritan's Purse came in.

Beliefs and Bullets

In August of 1992, just months after the war broke out, Franklin and I agreed that I would go to Croatia with George Hoffman, the man who founded Tearfund in England. He had left that NGO in the fall of 1991 and later had come to the US to meet with Franklin. They made a decision to launch what was initially called Samaritan International, essentially Samaritan's Purse United Kingdom. George had spent time in Croatia and had contacts there. For my first trip, I was glad to be able to follow his lead.

Right away, I could see that George was very tenderhearted and caring. Driving through the country, witnessing the brutality of war, I watched him walk through the ruins of cities as he empathetically took in the tragedy. His capacity to express the compassion of Christ made a lasting impression on me. George wanted people to know about Jesus. There was no divide between his word and deed, a quality I've not seen in many people. So many can show great enthusiasm and zeal in proclamation yet are not able to "go and do likewise," as Jesus instructed in the parable of the Good Samaritan (Luke 10:37).

Tragically, only a month after this trip, Franklin called me with the very sad news that after George had gone back to London to speak at a church, he stepped out in front of a bus and was killed. After being with him in a war zone, I was shocked to hear he lost his life in a peaceful city. It was such a heartbreaking end to a vibrant life. George was definitely a man with whom I wanted more time. But his legacy carried on because, while we were in Croatia, he had introduced me to many Christians there who would become our partners to eventually reach millions of people.

One of those relationships was with Ivan Vacic, who was leading the humanitarian efforts for a Christian publishing company based in Zagreb, Croatia, called Duhovna Stvarnost, which in English translates to "spiritual reality." When I began traveling into Bosnia with Ivan, we became good friends, moving in and out of the country through southern Croatia. The bridge had been blown up, so we had to cross the river on a ferry. On our first trip, Franklin was with Ivan and me. When we crossed back into Croatia, we made a brief stop in a town on the way. We began talking with a man who

Receiving flak jackets, 1995

was up on the roof of his house repairing holes. Suddenly, rockets started hitting our immediate area. I will always remember the man calling out as we were running, "Hey! Where are you going? There's work to be done here!"

Eventually, Ivan and I began to go deeper into the war zones. In our travels, we were able to identify only a handful of Christians in Bosnia. Most of the people had fled to escape the fighting. One place within the war zone was especially significant: a street that ran alongside a waterway in Sarajevo, where Archduke Franz Ferdinand of Austria-Hungary was assassinated in June 1914, triggering the events that led to World War I. We had driven by the historic site a hundred times before I realized its significance. That area was also inside one of the Sniper Alleys. Gunmen would shoot people who attempted to cross the hundred-foot bridge there, making more deadly military history in that spot.

I heard stories of men who would get up in the morning, kiss their wives and children goodbye, walk to the top floor of some abandoned building, grab a rifle, sit in the window, and shoot people. Instead of going to work, they went to war. I got to know a taxi driver who, in response to the constant threat, drove with absolute reckless abandon. She didn't drive; she flew. The woman stayed in a state of mind that I have seen in many people who've been forced to live in war zones. They do what they feel they have to do with a wanton disregard for risk. To her credit, she was simply trying to make a living.

Once, I was about two blocks from the market inside the center of Sarajevo when a mortar round struck, killing sixty people. Immediately, I ran to see how I could help. Folks who were just out shopping suddenly disintegrated in a heartbeat. Over time, all these accounts took an emotional and psychological toll on me. When you go back home, you don't get to just leave it. The trauma stays with you. (More on this later.)

The Bosnian conflict was the first time I became emotionally attached to the people—not a particular side, but the people as a whole. I knew folks who lost thirty to fifty pounds due to malnutrition. A woman would put on her best dress, only to see that it now hung off her frame. A man would put on his dress shirt and be able to get his entire fist between the collar and his neck.

In Sarajevo, I became dear friends (and still am today) with a neurosurgeon and would periodically stop by his apartment to bring him food. (Yes, a neurosurgeon who needed food—evidence that war affects everyone, regardless of profession.) When the war began, he was married to a Serbian woman who fled Sarajevo. He eventually remarried, to a woman whose husband had fled as well.

Because the war was causing so many horrific injuries, in 1993, I decided that Samaritan's Purse needed to send medical teams to help in the hospitals. Franklin suggested I contact Dr. Mel Cheatham, the head of clinical neurosurgery at University of California, Los Angeles, at the time, who was well-known around the world for his knowledge and skill. (Since 1992, he has been a board member for Samaritan's Purse.) He and his wife, Sylvia, agreed to join me. Dr. Cheatham assembled a full surgical team including a neurological anesthesiologist and operating room neurological nursing assistants. Dr. Michael VanRooyen, who at that time was an emergency room doctor at the University of Illinois in Chicago, also agreed to go with us. Mike would go on to Johns Hopkins and then to Harvard, eventually becoming the chairman of the Department of Emergency Medicine there. He also cofounded the Harvard Humanitarian Initiative. I was blessed and amazed that both Mike and Mel, being such highly distinguished physicians, made the trip with us.

The United Nations Refugee Agency (UNHCR) was working with the United Nations Protection Force (UNPROFOR) to provide assistance to humanitarian organizations. With our UNHCR credentials, we were able to fly directly into Sarajevo in heavy-lift aircraft built for going in and out of war zones. Upon deplaning, you had to run straight into a bunker that served as the terminal. (The airport closed down at 5:00 p.m. each day, and no one was allowed to stay there overnight.) The processing area was protected by several feet of sandbags stacked at least nine feet high. Never before or since have I been in an airport like that. You definitely knew right away you had entered a dangerous place.

I had made arrangements in advance through the UN channels for an armored personnel carrier equipped with steel tank tracks. We had to run out of the sandbag area and climb up into that vehicle. The carrier drove us to an abandoned ski lodge that had been used during the 1984 Winter Olympics. We spent the night there in any available bunk space with a couple hundred other UN peacekeepers. From our landing to arriving at our lodging, there were constant explosions and flying bullets. For personal safety, we all had to wear protective gear.

The next morning the armored carrier took us north to a large centralized hospital in Zenica, an area under attack from Serbian troops. It was one of the few hospitals in the country at the time with neurosurgical capacities. The majority of the patients there had been wounded in the war. Staying there as our base, on the second day, Dr. VanRooyen and I rode with the British military to a village called Nova Bila. There was a Catholic church there that had been converted into an emergency field hospital with about 120 beds. For the next two weeks, Dr. VanRooyen stayed and worked in Nova Bila, while Dr. Cheatham and the team were serving in the neurosurgical ward of the hospital in Zenica. We had to pass through an active war zone every time we drove between the two facilities. Making that journey almost every day, I knew how exposed we were and how very real the threat was.

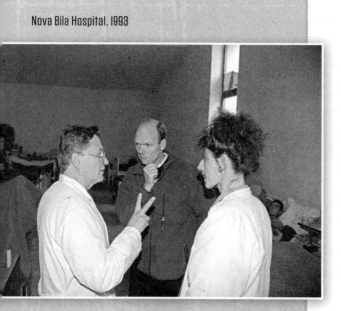

Nova Bila Hospital, 1993

In the final days of that trip, I escorted Dr. Cheatham and the surgical team to Nova Bila to help a patient with a life-threatening head wound from a bullet. Fractured pieces of his skull had been pushed down into his brain by the impact. This man's survival was completely dependent on Dr. Cheatham's team.

Performing the surgery in a garage that had been converted into an operating room, they were able to successfully extract all the bone fragments and repair his skull. That would have been a valiant effort in any environment, but especially in a war zone. Years later, I learned that this man recovered and was leading a normal life. On that trip, I learned so much about emergency medical responses, including what medical supplies are needed in war zones and how to work to save lives while under the constant threat and stress of war.

On the day of our departure, at the Sarajevo airport, we were waiting in the bunker. Explosions shook the ground, causing sand to vibrate out of the sandbags. As time passed, we became concerned because if the plane didn't come for us before dark and we were forced to leave the airport, we had no carriers or lodging arranged. Suddenly, a French soldier threw open the door out to the tarmac and screamed, "Run! Run! Run to the plane! Now!" Wearing combat helmets and forty-pound flak jackets, we all sprinted out of the bunker toward the plane sitting on the runway, climbed inside, and sat on the bench seats lining the walls. In that setting, the plane gives you a false sense of security because you're enclosed in metal, but those walls offer no real protection from artillery or rocket fire. The minutes waiting to begin taxiing out to the runway felt like an eternity before the plane took off. While we all got home safe and sound, everyone was deeply touched by what we had experienced God accomplish on a very dangerous medical mission to help people in Jesus' name.

But our time in Bosnia was not yet over, because knowing the plight of the people there would lead Samaritan's Purse to our most widely known outreach to the world.

A Loaves and Fishes Story

In December of 1989, the dictator of Romania, Nicolae Ceaușescu, and his wife were overthrown and executed, and their bodies were hung from a balcony at the palace. That change opened a window for the world to see the massive orphanage problem in Romania, particularly children with AIDS. Many were locked up like prisoners, and their treatment was brutal. Around that time in the United Kingdom, Margaret Thatcher de-socialized industry, and a lot of blue-collar workers lost their jobs. A group of unemployed men in Liverpool and Manchester saw the plight of those orphans and decided to use their new-found free time to take action. They began to mobilize collections and deliver gifts to children in Romania. As they brought more structure to their cause, they named this effort Operation Christmas Child.

Their simple concept was that participants would pack shoeboxes with small toys and hygiene items, then the organization would distribute them to children. Because they had become aware of our involvement in Bosnia, in 1993 some of those men in England asked us to join them. They needed financial help, and Samaritan's Purse's first gift was somewhere around $15,000, a lot of money to us back then. Many times, Franklin has told the story of when he promised the folks at Operation Christmas Child that we would contribute by providing boxes as well. But then, with so many projects going on, he forgot. In November, his assistant got a phone call from one of the founders, asking, "We wanted to see if you were able to pack some shoeboxes?"

Immediately, Franklin asked Paula Woodring, one of our staff members at Samaritan's Purse (who later became our Executive Vice President, Quality Control and Social Media), to take a shoebox to a local store, buy some items, fill it, and get the sample to our friend, Reverend Ross Rhoads, a board member and an adviser to Franklin, at his church in Charlotte, North Carolina. Ross was a true hero of mine—such an encourager and so smart. He agreed to hold the box up the next Sunday to his congregation, explain the program, and ask his members to participate. At that time, every night, the news led with stories from Bosnia, so the congregation was already aware of the situation. Ross would be offering members an opportunity to bless a child living in the war zone.

That Sunday morning, I drove to Ross's church to watch his presentation. Estimating there to be about 3,500 people in the sanctuary, I thought we had a good chance of maybe a third of the people filling boxes. About ten days later, I got a call from their church administrator. He was very direct with me, wanting to know why I hadn't warned them about what they would be up against with this project. He informed me that UPS was angry because they were not prepared for such a high volume of deliveries. Confused, I finally interrupted him to ask, "I'm sorry, but what are you talking about?" He blurted out, "Shoeboxes! We have shoeboxes everywhere! They're five feet deep across our gym floor! You can barely walk through there."

I had to see this for myself, so I drove there to take a look. As I walked into the church gym, I saw that the guy had not exaggerated. There was only enough space left for someone to walk through. I had hoped for a thousand or so boxes, but there were clearly *thousands*—plural—stacked high in there. I decided we could place them on pallets and then shrink-wrap as compact and uniform as possible to ship. We had already reached out to USAir, and they agreed to load a dozen pallets into the cargo bay of a 767 bound for Frankfurt, Germany, where they could be transferred to a truck and driven into Bosnia.

Mark DeMoss, who ran his own public relations firm and handled all our PR at the time, Paula Woodring, and I got on a call with a lady named Ann from USAir. Mark told her, "We are so appreciative of your company's support, but I think we may have a few more boxes than we originally thought." Naturally, Ann asked, "Okay, well, how many more do you think you'll have?" Mark continued, "At least ten thousand." That's when I chimed in, "Ann, I think it's going to take *two* planes." I could hear Mark's breath being taken away, concerned I was too direct with the lady. To their credit, USAir kept their word and agreed to fly every box on every pallet from North Carolina to Frankfurt.

On the Sunday before the cargo was to be transported to the airport, the church planned a prayer of dedication over the project. They had placed about a hundred boxes on the altar to represent the entire shipment. As I walked in to help, Ross said, "Kenney, a few folks are going to pray before the service. Please join us." As I followed the pastor down a corridor, I began to hear muffled organ music (at the time, I didn't realize that we were one floor beneath the organ).

When the prayer time was over, Ross said, "Kenney, come with me." We started walking up a ramp as the music and congregational singing got louder.

I asked, "Ross, where are we? What are we doing?" He smiled and answered, "Just follow me. I want you to say a few words." At that point in my career, I had rarely done any public speaking, certainly never in front of thousands of people. I was immediately very nervous. Likely knowing I might object, Ross decided to take the forgiveness-over-permission approach.

Suddenly, we were standing in front of the entire church! Because I had come there only to help load boxes, I was wearing jeans and a T-shirt. Ross motioned for me to sit down in one of the ornate throne-style chairs that you see on the platforms of formal churches. I was petrified and praying, *Oh God, help me. Please, help me. I don't know what I'm going to say.* After Ross got up and welcomed everyone, he introduced me. Standing behind the massive wooden podium, I gripped the sides with white knuckles and kept my speech short, mainly focusing on the need for volunteers after church. After I finished and thanked the congregation, I had to pry my fingers from the podium, and I could see sweat rolling down the sides from my handprints.

Having experience vetting things that had to go through customs, I knew each box would need to be inspected and then sealed with tape. My biggest concern was any toys that resembled some sort of weapon, like a water gun or rubber knife. Plus, we couldn't ship any food. Even though people had good intentions when they filled their boxes, there were some things we couldn't take a chance on getting through.

When the church service ended, I walked to the gym, and, to my surprise, there were already about three hundred people there. I was not anticipating that level of energy and excitement to help. People obviously wanted to be involved with this effort to bless kids on the other side of the world living in horrible circumstances. Reminiscent of Jesus climbing into a boat and going out several feet into the water to be heard by a crowd, I climbed up on a stack of pallets to be able to be seen and heard as I called out the instructions. "Hey, everyone, I need you to open the boxes, and if you see any food products, take them out. If you see a toy that looks anything like a weapon or is in any way inappropriate for a child in a war zone, please remove it."

As the volunteers began their inspections, I noticed that the majority of the boxes had UPS or FedEx labels on them. I asked a question I had missed up to this moment. *"Where* did all these boxes come from?" Looking at some of the labels, I saw they had come from all over the country. Realizing I had to add another step, I jumped back up onto a pallet and called out, "One more thing! Because we need to send an acknowledgment and thank-you to everyone who shipped a box, if there's a label, please cut the return address off and get it to me."

A couple of hours later, when all the shoeboxes had been inspected, sealed up, stacked on pallets, and shrink-wrapped, I had thousands of names and addresses. Everyone there that day enjoyed the experience and was blessed to be a part of the very first US-based Operation Christmas Child project.

And the final box count? 11,700!

The mystery of why so many boxes had been

Mostar, 1993

shipped to the church was solved when I found out that Ross's service was carried on the Bible Broadcasting Network across the United States. That's how the number grew from 1,000 to almost 12,000! Because my thoughts were always on what Samaritan's Purse was doing overseas, I never dreamed of such a strong domestic response. Driving back from Charlotte that evening, I called Franklin and asked if he could meet me at the office. I could not subdue my excitement as I told him, "I have never seen anything like this in my life! The people were absolutely electric. They *love* this idea!"

Miracles at Mostar

After USAir flew the pallets to Frankfurt, they were loaded onto trucks, driven to Zagreb, then broken down, put into smaller trucks and cars, and taken down to Mostar, a beautiful historic city about a two-hour drive southwest of Sarajevo. At that time, the Serbs were shelling the city. Amid the historic buildings and colorful apartment houses, snipers were everywhere. On my return to distribute the Operation Christmas Child boxes in Mostar, I brought a team of about fifteen people. Pastor Ross and his wife, Carol, came with me. A lady named Jean Wilson, who had worked for the Billy Graham organization in London and then with George at Samaritan International, was also with us.

Zagreb, Croatia, 1993

Our destination was the Mostar hospital, but on the way we came across a parked passenger train sitting in a train yard. Going aboard, we saw thousands of people packed into the cars. As we started handing out boxes to children, they all began to realize what the boxes were, and we saw the kids' responses. Our team was deeply touched by how a simple gift could make such an immediate difference in the life of a child. As we continued on through the city, we gave a box to *any* kid we saw.

To get to the hospital, I knew we would have to go through yet another Sniper Alley. Our team put on flak jackets with steel plates that weighed forty pounds. One of our members was a larger woman who couldn't get a jacket around her. With her safety being my utmost concern, I took mine off, put it across her back, and then laid the other over her chest. (My reasoning was if she got shot, Franklin would kill me! I could *not* let that happen.)

In our motorcade of seven small cars and one van, driving fast on curvy roads, we finally arrived at the hospital with no shots fired. There were about forty shoeboxes left in each car, and we unloaded and stacked them onto hospital gurneys to wheel down the hallways, starting in the pediatric ward. They had nailed up sheets of plywood over all the windows to block the snipers' view. Yet there were still bullet holes where they had shot anyway, likely to instill fear. One of the hospital staff alerted us to certain vulnerable spots where we would need to run across so that a sniper would not have time to aim and fire.

The most touching moment that day was with a child who was noticeably blind. His stare was obvious with his eyes sunk back in his head. Ross grabbed a random box and placed it in the boy's hands. As he assisted the boy in opening it, they found a Sony Walkman inside, a nice gift even by American standards at the time. That God had orchestrated for a blind boy to receive a box with a device that could allow him to listen to music was absolutely miraculous. That realization caused us all to get teary-eyed.

After that, we began to take notice of what I could only call little miracles coming together, where boxes appeared to be handpicked for certain children. This reminded me of Jesus' words in Matthew 7:11 when He said, "If you, then, though you are evil, know how to give good gifts to your children, how much more will your Father in heaven give good gifts to those who ask him!"

Seeing the destruction of human life in Bosnia created a much deeper compassion and empathy in me for the plight of children. When we first began to discuss Operation Christmas Child internally, the dire circumstances were not lost on us. We asked one another, "Now, wait a minute, these children are living in a war zone! There's an imminent threat on their lives every day, and we're going to give them a box with a toy in it? Is that really the *appropriate* thing to do? Is that the *best* thing to do?" We finally came to the conclusion that the end goal was to be a blessing to kids and allow God to use our efforts however He saw fit.

One Child at a Time

After navigating through a war zone with the constant threat of sniper fire, our entire team returned home safely. Right away, we started planning for the next year. In 1994, there was a law firm in Charlotte that was doing work for Samaritan's Purse. On a Sunday afternoon, one of their young attorneys, Todd Chasteen and his wife, Kim, had driven to Boone to see our offices. Franklin "just happened" to drive by and see them in the parking lot. Pulling in, he began a conversation where Todd shared that he felt called to our ministry. Franklin answered, "Well, I don't need a lawyer right now, but if you want to come to work here, you could help us with this new program called Operation Christmas Child." Todd left the firm and came to work with us, promoting Operation Christmas Child (OCC) in the US.

We established a base for the logistics aspect of OCC in Huntsville, Alabama. There was a freight company there at the time called Panalpina. We had reached an agreement with them to charter two of their planes: one to Zagreb, Croatia, and one to Kigali, the capital of Rwanda. Jim Harrelson, who had been running our work in Somalia since 1993, helped out, along with folks from our Canadian office. Needing a warehouse, I found a family—a mom and her two adult daughters—who owned one close to the airport in Huntsville. They smoked like freight trains and cussed like sailors, but they had good hearts and agreed to allow us to use their facility.

In figuring out the most efficient way to process the boxes, Jim and I got some portable metal conveyors in long connecting

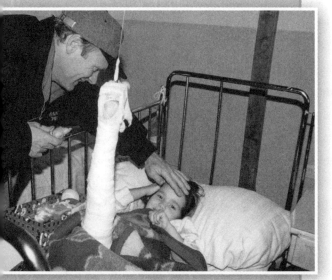

Sarajevo, 1994

sections covered with roller wheels on top. You could shoot a box down the entire length of the assembly line. Next, we taped pieces of cardboard on the floor with numbers to mark each position. On the roller tables, we wrote down the task at each station.

Once the logistics system was in place, we needed some people power. I went to the local radio station and explained the program on one of their shows, asking for volunteers. Once again, the response was overwhelming, and we were flooded with help. I'll never forget this one very nice Jewish lady who was an elementary school teacher. One day, I pulled her aside and asked, "Help me understand. Why are you helping us do this for Christmas?" Her answer was clear, "Because it's such a beautiful idea, and I love it." In fact, the only exception we made for volunteers under sixteen years of age was when we allowed her to bring her entire class to help. With her supervision, we had a bunch of little kids helping pack boxes for other little kids.

Todd had identified a list of sixty-seven potential partner churches and brought it to me. Looking at the list, I got nervous. I had seen what happened with *one* church in Charlotte, so what would almost seventy create? Would we be overwhelmed in our first official year? I read over his list and culled it to about forty churches. Just as we had experienced from the very beginning of this effort, the word spread organically from those churches. I mean, it spread like a wildfire in a windstorm! That December, we gave out 345,000 boxes!

In 1995, the group in England that had started Operation Christmas Child asked Samaritan's Purse to officially take over, and we agreed. The issues they had consistently faced were typical start-up problems that we had the systems in place to solve. While they had such an incredible idea, the challenge they faced was having no support base or distribution network. We had and were continuing to build a partnership with both individuals and churches in the US, and we had alliances on projects in other countries. Samaritan's Purse had the infrastructure for donors *and* distribution on an international level.

In our planning, Franklin's leadership added new vision to the program. In one particular meeting with a number of our folks gathered from around the world, he told us all, "I believe if we make OCC about Jesus, God will bless the work, and it could become the largest children's evangelism program in the world." In that moment, I realized how serious such an endeavor was and what it could mean for kids all over the world being brought into the Kingdom of God.

As Operation Christmas Child grew in 1993 and 1994, Franklin came to me and said, "We have got to put the Gospel in this program." That directive prompted us to design a three-by-seven-inch card with Bible verses on both sides in the Serbo-Croatian language that went into every box for Bosnia. Then, in 1996, we designed an illustrated book called *The Greatest Gift of All*. A decade later, as growth multiplied, we were also able to develop a discipleship program for those who received the Gospel called "The Greatest Journey."

In an increasingly secular global society, there is a major perspective difference between a humanitarian program and a ministry-based evangelical effort. But I saw the power of Operation Christmas Child's ability to break down those barriers when the French group Médecins Sans Frontières (Doctors Without Borders), a very large secular organization, sent a couple of their people to us in Bosnia after hearing about "these shoeboxes full of gifts for kids." With a medical operation set up in Sarajevo, they asked, "Hey, can we get some of those? We have children in the hospital where we're working." Two days later, they returned and asked for more boxes. I knew then that if a group like that was able to overlook our Christian message in favor of the benefit to the kids they were treating, we were onto something. What a blessing to see the spiritual "borders" truly removed to bless children.

In 1997, Jim Harrelson's influence and leadership grew the program to the point where Franklin decided it was time for OCC to be its own division. I was thrilled with that decision because God had definitely put the right person in place. Jim is a very detailed, organized, methodical thinker, planner, and doer. His skill set was perfect for the job.

Today, in every country where we work, we have OCC national leadership teams. While the number can change from year to year based on circumstances, we have a presence in 105 to 120 countries. Each team has its own evangelism plan for its country or region, along with a dedicated strategy. We're able to work together through what we call Global Connect meetings. Anywhere a disaster strikes in the world, we reach out to those OCC leadership teams first. Our partners in all these countries literally give us a global network to take action. While this has never been a church-planting effort, churches have started organically, and the program has led to the amazing work of translating Gospel resources.

Another unforeseen blessing is that we have people working for us today who came to Christ as a child after receiving a shoebox. Some of these were those who grew up in orphanages. Some serve in their home countries, while others have moved to the US. Over the years, millions of children and their family members have come to know Christ. Millions have also gone through the discipleship program. We have seen the fruit come back to us in adults who help us continue to multiply this simple approach of helping the children of the world. Samaritan's Purse has never been into numbers and stats, but in 2023, we were so encouraged to find out that we had collected and distributed over eleven million boxes.

From eleven thousand that first year to eleven million thirty years later!

Dr. Ross Rhoads with Ken, preparing to deliver shoeboxes, Mostar

Forever Family

Helping millions of kids over the years is incredible, but we always remind ourselves that those numbers represent individual children, each with their own unique story. One of the most miraculous stories that Franklin has shared many times is about a boy who told the folks trying to give him a shoebox that he didn't want it. The volunteer said, "No, here, it's a gift. Please take it. This box is for you." The boy kept insisting his answer was no. When they finally asked why he would not receive it, he answered, "Because I want parents."

After they finally convinced the boy to take and open the box, he found one of the items inside was a letter from the family in the US. Through a translator, the boy wrote back to them. After their correspondence continued, the couple ended up traveling to meet him, and, eventually, they adopted him. Through that simple shoebox, God granted that boy's deepest desire—to have a family. One of many miracles only our heavenly Father could have done, and, year after year through Operation Christmas Child, He continues to do.

"Whoever welcomes one of these little children in my name welcomes me...."

He said to them, "Let the little children come to me, and do not hinder them, for the kingdom of God belongs to such as these." (Mark 9:37; 10:14)

Operation Christmas Child
2023 Statistics

11.3 million shoeboxes packed by people from eleven countries

2.9 million decisions for Christ

5.1 million children participated in The Greatest Journey discipleship program.

Since 2009, 40.5 million children have enrolled in The Greatest Journey.

In January 2023, Samaritan's Purse celebrated the 200 millionth box given in Lviv, Ukraine, to a beautiful little girl whose parents had been killed in the war.

Scan the QR code below for more information.

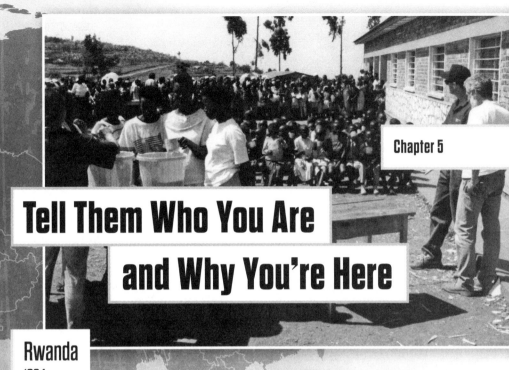

Chapter 5

Tell Them Who You Are
and Why You're Here

Rwanda
1994
Genocide

Disclaimer: This chapter describes some graphic scenes of brutality. My goal was to balance being honest about the evil in Rwanda while avoiding very real details that sound like the script for a horror movie. In short, R-rated scenes are told in PG-13 detail.

Over the years in honestly answering the question "Where do we get involved next?" I've realized that you could throw a dart at a world map and, if you hit a landmass, you would find some sort of humanitarian crisis. That truth is consistent with what Jesus taught us, recorded in the Gospels of Matthew, Mark, and John: "The poor you will always have with you" (Matt. 26:11). The same is true for the sick and brokenhearted. A major part of our leadership at Samaritan's Purse has to do with stewardship of our staff and resources, as we constantly ask, "Where do we feel like God is leading us to serve?"

In 1993, we had a small medical team in an area of southern Sudan called Ulang to treat people who had contracted a disease known as relapsing fever, spread by bites of infected ticks, fleas, and lice. It's called "relapsing" because a patient appears to get well and then the symptoms recur. We had chosen our site based on need, not necessarily permission. Technically, we were in what is called a "no-go zone."

About a month into our team serving there, they got caught in the middle of a cattle raid between the Dinka and the Nuer tribes and literally had to hide to escape the violence. The United Nations agreed to go in to extract them, but it wasn't a simple operation because it was a no-go zone. Everyone was safely evacuated to Lokichogio in Kenya, the logistics hub of operations for the UN's Operation Lifeline Sudan. Dozens of other NGOs were also based there while working in the southern part of Sudan. (An important note is that South Sudan was not its own nation until July of 2011. More on this to come.)

Several months later, in early 1994, we sent that team to do the same work at another location called Old Fangak. Within weeks, another cattle raid occurred between the same two tribes. Samaritan's Purse was able to get the group safely back to Lokichogio once again.

A Bridge to Cross

On April 6, 1994, while at home in Boone, I heard that an airplane had been shot down in Kigali, Rwanda. (I remember the date because that was my mother's birthday.) The president of Rwanda and the president of Burundi were killed, which unleashed what would come to be called the Rwandan genocide. In one hundred days, Hutu extremists, known as the Interahamwe, slaughtered approximately 800,000 Tutsis, which included anyone they considered their political opponents, regardless of ethnicity.[1] That number of murders in such a short time is staggering. For a sobering perspective, that would be like killing every resident of Boone, North Carolina, where I live, in less than three days.

Because we had moved the aforementioned team to our office in Nairobi, they were available. Whenever there is a humanitarian crisis in the world, while we have never been reckless, we do run to the fire. Samaritan's Purse has always intentionally gone into dangerous places, while also trying to recognize, understand, and mitigate the risks to protect the lives and well-being of our staff, very much like a First Responder, who has to constantly deal with danger while doing their job and work to avoid unnecessary risks so they can serve another day.

Considering the reports we were hearing of thousands of refugees attempting to flee the violence, I called our office in Nairobi and began discussions there, as well as with Franklin and our key staff members. We all agreed we had to do something. I recall telling everyone, "We've sent teams to Somalia, Sudan, and other parts of Africa in times of crises. Why not do the same for Rwanda?"

Primarily because I was still working in Croatia and Bosnia, I wasn't able to go to Africa right away. Deciding to send Jim Harrelson, who worked for us, I called Mike VanRooyen, whom I mentioned in the previous chapter. After getting Mike up to speed on the situation, I asked if he would like to go with Jim. He graciously agreed. The primary mission was to assess the situation and find out where the majority of the refugees fleeing Rwanda were going. (In Mike's 2016 book, *The World's Emergency Room: The Growing Threat to Doctors, Nurses, and Humanitarian Workers*, besides some very generous comments about me, he wrote that everything he learned he *shouldn't* do, he learned with me. I wear that quote as a badge of honor.)

Mike and Jim discovered the primary path of escape for Rwandans was heading south into Tanzania. Ten days later, when I was able to join them, we found out that the United Nations High Commissioner for Refugees (UNHCR) had been designated by the Tanzanian government as the agency in charge of anyone fleeing into their country. Since UNHCR was active with partners on the ground, it wasn't accepting anyone new. Yet everyone involved was overwhelmed by the sheer magnitude of the crisis. The strategic nightmare was that both victims *and* criminals were fleeing across the river into Tanzania. Hutus who had perpetrated attacks blended into the masses that were now trying to escape the approaching armies of the Rwandan Patriotic Front (RPF). One obvious differentiation was that few Hutus spoke English, while the majority of Tutsis spoke at least some English, if not fluently.

Mike and Jim had decided the best way for us to get involved was to partner with another NGO in an outpatient clinic ten miles away from the refugee camp where it was reported that as many as 250,000 people had amassed in a field. That camp was an absolutely wretched, horrible place. There was no drainage for human waste, and smoke from all the campfires hung in the air just above ground level like a dense fog. Later, there was confirmation that this camp indeed contained the majority of the killers who had unleashed the horror in Rwanda.

Hearing Mike and Jim's plan, I wasn't convinced, so I told them, "We have to do better. I want to go back and find a different way." By that time Mike had to go home, so after he left, Jim and I decided to try to meet with the camp director. When we arrived, the director informed us that she would not take on any more sanctioned partners. Samaritan's Purse wouldn't be allowed to work there in an official capacity. Yet with the landmass so large and the number of people so vast, Jim and I were able to assess the incredible needs of the people gathered there.

Deciding we had to get as close to Rwanda as we could, our next option was to go to the Anglican Murgwanza Hospital near Rusumo International Bridge that spans across the Kagera River connecting Rwanda and Tanzania. Dale Hamilton, a pilot with Africa Inland Mission (AIM AIR) who loves Jesus and was always dedicated to his mission, met us at the Karagwe, Tanzania, airstrip to fly Jim and me. The landing was very tricky on a grass runway right on top of a mountain ridge. With the hospital as our base, we would drive out during the day to continue to seek out the best path forward to serve the masses of suffering people.

One day, we drove to the Rusumo Bridge, about forty-five minutes from the hospital. Standing on the Tanzanian side, I saw a massive pile of machetes, scythes, and hoes that I would estimate to be about two hundred feet wide and five feet high. In the days of peace, those had been farming tools to clear land, break up the soil, and cut crops. Now, they were weapons to kill their neighbors. Before anyone could cross the border to safety in Tanzania, the border guards made them throw their weapons down. Another clear sign that both sides of this conflict—the guilty and the innocent—were fleeing the country.

I went up to a Tanzanian army guard and asked, "Can I walk out on the bridge?" He answered, "You can go halfway if I am with you." The first thing I noticed after reaching the middle was the smell. The air and the mist created from the water below reeked of a horrible stench—a smell I would soon realize was part of everyday life there. Looking out over the river, I could see a waterfall about two hundred yards away. That's when I saw them. Something so surreal and shocking. Bodies in various stages of dismemberment were coming over the falls and flowing down the river by the thousands. *Yes, the thousands.* Too many to count.

Rutare, May 1994

Right away I thought of the Holocaust—a mass annihilation of a people group born out of sheer hatred. It was one of the most gruesome sights I've ever seen in my career and, to this day, is still burned into my memory.

Looking across the bridge, I saw a small guard post with eight to ten RPF soldiers in military uniforms with red berets. I told the armed Tanzanian guard that I wanted to go over there to talk to them. His immediate answer was, "No! You can't do that. I can't let you go over there. We have to go back now." I pressed him, "But I want to go over there. I need to talk to those men. We came here to help *their* people." As I pointed back toward Jim, who was now speechless from seeing the bodies in the river, I stated, "I promise I'll come back, and I don't think you're going to shoot me." I turned and began walking the rest of the way across the bridge toward the Rwandan guards. The horror that I had just witnessed in the river *drove* me to go to their side. I knew we had to do *something*.

The Unaccompanied Minors reunification program, Kigali, early 1995

I have to tell you that I gained lifelong lessons out of that experience. One was to not be afraid to go over to "the other side" and ask questions. If you are trying to find answers, you *have* to go to the source of the problem. To get in, you have to *try* the door. And, if God opens that door, you walk through. Since that day, I have crossed over thousands more bridges, both physically and metaphorically.

I walked cautiously up to the soldiers on the other side. The one they called "Commander" was in his early twenties and told me his name was Innocence. (The irony of his name was not lost on me.) He spoke enough English and I spoke enough French that we could attempt a conversation. After I was able to express that we wanted to get into Rwanda to help their people, Innocence told me, "Write a letter stating what you want." We scrounged up a piece of paper and a pen, and, in basic English, I wrote down who I was and then stated that Samaritan's Purse was prepared to offer an EHK (Emergency Health Kit)— large cartons of medicine designed to provide general medical care to 10,000 people for ninety days. After I handed the letter to Innocence, he told me to come back in two days.

At the end of forty-eight hours, I returned to the bridge. The first thing I noticed was the Tanzanian guards weren't quite as tense as before, and they let me walk across with no questions and no escort. As I greeted Commander Innocence, he simply stated, "They are waiting for you in Melinde." I had no idea where Melinde was and I had no idea who "they" were, but I thanked him and left. This young man had done exactly what he said he would do without any form of danger or threat.

Why Are You Here?

We made arrangements for Dale, our pilot from AIM AIR, to take us back to Nairobi. Remember, this was 1993, so I had to find a store there that sold maps to locate Melinde, whose location was just a tiny dot in northern Rwanda. From Nairobi, we took a flight to Uganda and secured a vehicle to drive to Kabale. From there, we would make the twenty-two-mile (thirty-five-kilometer) trip to cross the border and reach Melinde.

One of the first things we noticed as we drove into Rwanda was the sudden and eerie absence of the sounds of life. No people. No insects or birds or barking dogs. No one was walking along the roads, much less driving. The unnatural silence felt so oppressive that we stopped talking. To offer an analogy, if on the bridge I smelled smoke, here I could feel the flames. While I have definitely had that experience since then in other parts of the world, this was my first.

Arriving in Melinde, we located the right place simply by it being the only area with any sign of life. There were a few huts, one of which was the "office" of the RPF's humanitarian coordinator. It was pitch-dark inside the twelve-by-twenty structure. I was surprised to see other people there waiting, including another American who was visibly impatient. When Jim and I introduced ourselves to the coordinator, a woman named Christine Umutoni, she said she had received our information. (I never got an answer, but I have always wondered how my letter, or at least the message I had written, managed to get from the bridge all the way to this primitive hut. Did someone read it over a radio or physically deliver it? One of the thousands of unanswered mysteries of my career.)

Christine told us to have a seat on a little bench against the wall. As the minutes passed, the impatient American, who I came to learn was with a well-known US NGO, grew more adamant about having to wait and finally exploded with, "I've been sitting here for two hours! I've come here to save lives! Don't you care about your own people?!" His Western entitlement, arrogance, and crass accusation has stuck with me all these years as a stark reminder of how you should *never* act in any country to anyone.

Christine glared at him, then just above a whisper, stated with total dignity, "Where have *you* been the last *twenty* years?" She enunciated *twenty* slowly for emphasis in a "How dare you?" tone.

As I sat stunned by her sobering response, the man, clearly humbled, sat back down in silence to wait. As Christine got up and walked out of the hut, I noticed she was rubbing her forehead. I motioned to Jim for us to follow her. Outside, I asked, "Do you have a headache?" She nodded yes.

"Then would you like some medicine like an ibuprofen or Tylenol?" She nodded yes.

We invited her to sit in our vehicle as I gave her a couple of tablets and some water. After taking them, she asked, "Why are you here?" (I couldn't help but contrast her question to me with her question to the other American.)

"We want to provide medical care to the people in your country. We're just looking for a place."

Without hesitation, she said, "Okay, let's go." She motioned for us to start driving.

Because there were roadblocks everywhere, having her with us was a game changer. After a while, we came upon another vehicle. A woman got out and waved us down. Her accent seemed to be French, but she was actually from Tunisia. We stopped, and I got out of the car to speak with her. My only explanation was that she must have seen two foreigners in the car and assumed we were humanitarian workers.

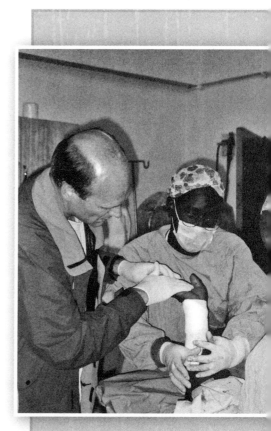

Kibogoro Mission Hospital

She began to tell me that she worked for MSF—Médecins Sans Frontières (Doctors Without Borders)—and they had set up a fifty-five-bed hospital inside a Catholic church in Byumba, Rwanda. She cautioned that they would tell me no help was needed here but that was not true. I appreciated her honesty and candor. When I expressed our plan to help, she told me about a place called Rutare where thousands needed help immediately. I could see that she obviously truly cared about the people. I also believe that, through her, God answered our prayers of where we needed to go. Being "randomly" flagged down led us to the best spot to help the most people. We asked Christine if she could take us to Rutare, and she agreed.

Driving down into a valley surrounded by hills and mountains, we saw masses of people gathered. We estimated there were about 10,000 with nothing but the clothes on their backs and the things they could carry. Refugees flee because of insecurity as they consider conflicting thresholds of risk and competing interests of their loved ones, their property, and their perception of danger. In this particular situation, the RPF instructed displaced people to go to this camp. I believe they felt the area was safe. Also, once a local population finds safety in an area, word spreads like wildfire (this was true even back in the days before the internet and social media). The RPF had secured Rutare and the northern part of Rwanda as they came in from the southern part of Uganda. Regardless, there's always incredible confusion and chaos where tens of thousands of people are moving and fleeing for their lives.

Kigali, 1995

Christine located the "camp manager" and introduced us. After talking, we made a commitment to return with as much help and as many resources as we could. This was a Friday midday, and we promised to come back by Monday at 8:00 a.m. We drove back to Melinde and dropped Christine off, and I went to Nairobi to mobilize our staff, while Jim went to Mbarara to start working on getting trucks for transporting supplies. One of our mission partners, AIM AIR, stepped up for us in a big way by providing three planes—an old DC-3, a Bonanza, and a MAF King Air to fly cargo. The plan was for them to land on the airstrip in Mbarara Sunday afternoon. Jim would be there with the trucks for us to move the four and a half tons of supplies to Kabale, Uganda, and then into Rwanda the next morning by eight as promised.

Franklin was on his way back from Russia and decided to take a detour and go with us on the trip. Franklin, our team, and I flew out Sunday around noon to Mbarara and then drove to Kabale. Jim had made arrangements to rent two floors of a hotel for Sunday night where some other NGOs were also staying.

Go Make Some Big Decisions

In the thirty-five-plus years that Franklin and I have worked together, we've shared a room only this one time. It was very small with two twin beds with maybe a foot and a half between them. There was a tiny bathroom with no door. As we were about to go downstairs to dinner on that Sunday night with our team, Franklin was reading his Bible when he looked up at me and said, "Buddy, I'm going to tell everybody who we are." I knew that everyone on our team knew who we were, so I responded, "Well, Franklin, it's a public restaurant." He continued, "I want them *all* to know who we are. I want them to know about Jesus." To be transparent, I confess I felt a little awkward about that idea.

As we sat down at the long table with our twenty team members, Franklin stood and began to address everyone, with the entire restaurant of at least fifty other people listening. He gave his clear signature Gospel presentation, closing with, "This is why we've come to Rwanda. We want everybody to know that by believing the Gospel of Jesus Christ, they can be forgiven of their sins and receive eternal life." I learned such a valuable lesson from witnessing that moment: never, ever hide who you are. The truth is, I can't speak like Franklin. In fact, very few can. But, in my own way, from that day forward, I have always made sure people know who we are and why we're there.

As promised, Christine met us Monday morning to get to Rutare by 8:00 a.m. After we arrived, we unloaded the trucks, set up, and got to work. We had no idea at the time that, within just two weeks, the population of that camp would swell to more than 125,000 people. We delivered babies and treated severely malnourished children. And, of course, there were those who had come in with machete wounds that somehow survived the brutal attacks. Our team dealt with all manner of injuries, illnesses, and, unfortunately, death. With such a massive number of people, supplies of food and water were heavily strained. Christian Solidarity International, a group from Germany, helped incredibly by bringing us a five-thousand-gallon stainless steel water truck.

After days of surveying everyone in the camp, we identified 930 unaccompanied minors—930 children whose parents were dead or had been separated from them in an escape. The realization that these were kids who had no one got to me emotionally, so I knew I had to take action on their behalf. I decided to go to Kampala, Uganda, to try to get help.

From a pay phone there, I called one of my best friends, Mitchell Minges, and told him, "These children have lost their families. They're sleeping on the ground, and we don't have enough food for them." Mitchell responded, "Kenney, I'll give you $50,000. Now, you go make some big decisions." Next, I called Franklin, who was now back in the States, and told him about the children. Immediately, he answered, "Absolutely. You go get whatever they need."

Yet again, I learned another valuable lesson. Sometimes you need to make big decisions quickly based on the magnitude of the need and the belief that God will provide. He was so clear in the Gospels about His love for children and, in James 1:27, His desire that we take care of orphans. In Kampala, I was able to buy truckloads of supplies, such as food, blankets, beds, and cooking equipment.

Saving Lives amid Death

The camp was up in the mountains about fifteen to twenty miles from Kigali, so we could hear the gunfire and shelling in the distance. By the middle of July 1994, I could tell the fighting was starting to decrease. We had rented a house back in Kabale, Uganda, to use as an administrative base with space for four people to stay at one time. I decided to go back there before going to assess the circumstances in Kigali. My first morning, I was sitting in the living room when a man came walking in from one of the bedrooms and introduced himself as Dr. Paul Chiles. (I previously talked about Paul in the 2001 story about Afghanistan, but this situation in Rwanda was the first time we had met.) He asked, "So you're Ken Isaacs, huh?" I said, "Yessir." He continued, "I've heard about you." Because of the nature of everything we had to deal with in Rwanda, we had not organized quite the way we typically would. The chain of command wasn't made as clear as usual, but that hadn't been a problem thus far. So when Paul arrived, he *assumed* he was in charge. But I *knew* I was in charge.

Applying eye drops, southern Rwanda

Realizing the dynamic, I said, "Dr. Chiles, because the fighting is subsiding, I'm going to go to Kigali today to assess the needs there."

"No, I'm not going to let that happen. It's not safe. There's a roadblock every three kilometers."

"Well, I think it is safe enough now, so I'm going there today."

Again, he pushed back, getting a bit stronger in his tone, "I'm *not* going to let that happen."

I raised an eyebrow, looked him in the eye, and stated, "Dr. Chiles, I think the *only* decision you'll need to make today is if you're going to come with me or not."

A bit shocked at me being so direct, he gave up and announced he was going with me. After that exchange, Paul and I have been lifelong friends; he's one of my dearest friends in the world.

As Paul and I began our drive to Kigali, like he said, there was an RPF checkpoint every three kilometers. For this trip, the RPF had assigned a soldier named Johnson to go with us and act as our guide. At each stop, he would talk to the guards to let us through. I had brought along a batch of black baseball-style caps with a patch that read "Samaritan's Purse International Relief." When the soldier would agree for us to pass, I would smile, take off my hat, and give it to him as a gesture of goodwill. Then I would put on another one from the batch. I ended up giving away a *lot* of hats that day.

When we drove into Kigali, the city was a ghost town, but it was also in chaos with shooting and shelling still going on. We heard explosions close by that would shake the ground. Dead bodies were lying randomly in the streets. The most vivid memories of coming into the city were driving by roadblocks where a large pile of bodies of people who had been hacked to death would be stacked up. Blood was everywhere. The scenes were surreal, otherworldly, apocalyptic.

Don Norrington with Ken, working in orphan care, Rutare

Soon, I was able to locate the United Nations building, but it appeared to be deserted. Ironically, though, I was able to find Kate Farnsworth, whom I had met at the US embassy in Ethiopia back in 1988, and here she was in Rwanda. Kate became somewhat of a legend for her travels and front-line assessments. Charles Petrie, whom I had met in Somalia in 1992, was in control of the office. He had been assigned as the United Nations

Humanitarian Coordinator for Rwanda. With all of that group staying there, Kate invited Paul and me to join them.

Charles had something I had heard of yet never seen before—a satellite telephone (SAT phone). They had mounted the dish outside on a little terrace. Fascinated by this device, I asked if I could call the Samaritan's Purse office back home. Now, to paint the picture clearly, there was the occasional bullet flying by, so to talk, I lay down behind the block wall of the balcony out of sight. The occasional *ching* sound could be heard as a bullet ricocheted off the building.

I called the office, and when they got Franklin on the phone, he asked, "Where are you?"

"I'm in Kigali."

"How? What are you calling me on?"

That was the question I was waiting for. "It's the coolest thing, Franklin. They have a satellite here, like six feet in diameter. I'm calling you on that phone."

Then he asked, "What are those sounds I'm hearing?"

"Bullets! Those are bullets flying around."

Not exactly a comforting picture for your boss, while you're trying to assure him of your team's personal safety in the city. After we talked, though, he was supportive of us working toward providing medical care in Kigali.

Over the next few days, we drove around the city trying to determine the best thing for us to do to help the most people. I met a man from the Belgian Red Cross who told me the Central Hospital of Kigali, the largest in the region, was no longer usable because of the number of dead bodies inside. I decided to go see for myself and assess whether anything could be salvaged. The entire place was a horrible atrocity, an absolute killing ground. Here, I had a close-up view of what I had seen from a distance in the river.

After surveying the facility, I sent word for some of our team members to meet Paul and me. About five days later when they arrived, we organized ourselves according to the necessary responsibilities, such as logistics, hiring new staff, and providing direct medical care. But, first, we all began the difficult task of cleaning up the grisly sight. There was already a mass grave dug outside the hospital, so we started taking bodies out to bury them there. The stench of death literally hung in the air. As I said before, there are some details I have chosen not to share, so just know what I am telling you here, regarding what we had to deal with, was just the tip of the iceberg.

This Is My House

For our team of thirty Americans and Canadians to be able to serve in shifts at the hospital, I knew I had to find a place to live close by. I not only needed a large house but, for protection, I also wanted a compound. As I began to drive around and look, I saw looters going through neighborhoods, loading up everything of any value they could find, literally going door to door stealing out of people's houses. And the majority of those homes had dead bodies in them.

I was finally able to locate a home that had a solid wall surrounding the perimeter. If we were to run out of room inside, there was space to set up tents in the yard. There was also enough room to park all our vehicles inside the walls. Walking through the house, I discovered a couple squatting there that had a newborn baby. There was another guy with them who had way too much electronic equipment, leading me to correctly assume that the two men were looting and storing the items in the house. But the dead far outnumbered the living. My count of corpses reflected the size of the house—twenty-one. Dried blood was caked on the ceiling, walls, and floors in the rooms where people had been murdered with machetes. It's hard to imagine having an infant in such a place.

Before I could address the looters and start the cleanup, I knew I needed some sort of official permission to occupy the property. Driving back to the center of town, I located a compound that looked like a military unit. There was a woman in charge there known as Major Rose, who would later become the mayor of Kigali. After I introduced myself and explained who I was with and how we wanted to help her city, she did an amazing thing. With a green pen in English cursive on a card, she wrote (showing her exact spelling, punctuation, and line breaks):

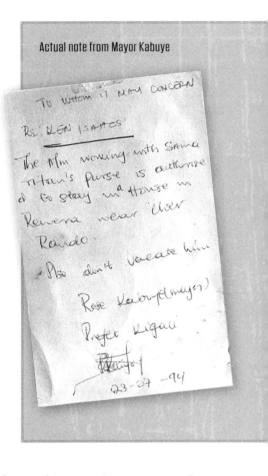

Actual note from Mayor Kabuye

To Whom It May Concern
Re: Ken Isaacs
The man working with Sama-
ritan's Purse is authorise-
d to stay in a house in
Remera near Chez
Rondo.
Plse don't vacate him.
Rose Kabuye (Mayor)
Prefect Kigali
23-07-94

In December of 1996, that card was presented to me as a beautifully framed gift. Years later on July 12, 2013, a lady who had worked with us in Rwanda dropped by my office and taped a note to the bottom of that frame. She wrote, "Dear Kenney, I'm in Boone today visiting SP. I fondly recall the details in Rwanda from 1994 to 1999 when I worked between SP and the Free Methodist work in Kiro and Kigali. I recall your hard and effective work in guiding and supporting the volunteers. Many thanks again for your dedication and service for our wonderful Lord. The Lord is so good and has been to me. I recently remarried and my name is now Harriet Boladar Davenport. Thanks for all that you do.

God bless you, keep, protect and guide you. —Harriet." Every day when I'm in my office in Boone, I see that card from Rwanda as I turn the light on and off. I believe that speaks to the gravity that my time there had (and still has) in my life.

At the time, I called Major Rose's handwritten note our "lease." With as much official paperwork as you can get in a situation like that, I walked back into the house, found the two men, and said, "You have to get out of my house and take your stolen stuff." (In circumstances where you aren't quite sure who you're dealing with, you have to be authoritative and no-nonsense.)

One man pushed back, "This is not your house!" That's when I showed them both the card and said, "It *is* my house. I have permission to be here. You need to get out." One of them asked, "But where are we going to go?" That's when I had an idea, especially in light of the woman and the newborn baby. "Well, the Belgian Red Cross gave me permission to use another house that won't work for our purposes. You can go there." I decided to write my own "lease" for them that said, "To the extent that I have legal authority in this house at [address], I hereby give it to you so you and your family can relocate there." After I signed it, they appeared to be satisfied, loaded up their loot, and left. That situation well illustrates the level of lawlessness that was going on in Kigali at the time.

I was ready to attempt to make the house habitable, but whenever there are that many corpses left exposed for days, vermin, as well as starving abandoned dogs, are going to be attracted, which was definitely a problem we had to quickly address. Just as we had witnessed at the river and the hospital, people had been killed in anger and hatred by machete—you can imagine the scene. An intense level of spiritual darkness saturated the atmosphere. Yet one of the most intriguing aspects about our team was that none of us were afraid. Cautious? Yes. Fearful? No. The fact that everyone was a strong Christ follower who felt a calling to be there definitely impacted our resolve. For the first several nights, we all stayed in the living room as a group. We weren't armed, but we did keep anything we could find that might be used as a defensive weapon close by.

Two ladies, Bethany Bransford and Helen Liko, were the primary team members who helped me get the bodies (and severed body parts) out of the house and buried. Bethany graduated from Johns Hopkins as a nurse and married Edward Densham. Both were raised as missionary kids in Kenya, and, today, Edward is the International Director of Projects for Samaritan's Purse. Bethany remains active in overseeing and directing teams that go all over the world to do cleft palate and cataract surgeries. They both worked in Sudan in 1998. Helen was an older woman from Arizona. Both Bethany and Helen served with us in places and situations where others wouldn't go.

Once all the bodies were buried, we had to try to scrub the blood off the floors. I crushed up swimming pool chlorine tablets and mixed them in five-gallon buckets of water. While the chemical smell was overpowering, at least it began to somewhat mask the horrible stench. Helen, Bethany, and I got down on our hands and knees and scrubbed the concrete floors and then the walls. Mix, scrub, and rinse; mix, scrub, and rinse; over and over. Even with all that work, we never did fully succeed in getting rid of the odor or removing all the discoloration from the concrete.

Once we got the house purged and cleaned the best we could, we designated one side for the ladies and the other side for the men. That first morning, ready to begin to try to live as normally as possible, while everyone was eating breakfast, I read a Scripture passage to the team that I felt the Lord had told me to share—Psalm 58, where David cries out to God for protection and encouragement, as well as judgment and justice.

> Do you rulers indeed speak justly?
>   Do you judge people with equity?
> No, in your heart you devise injustice,
>   and your hands mete out violence on the earth.

Even from birth the wicked go astray;
   from the womb they are wayward, spreading lies.
Their venom is like the venom of a snake,
   like that of a cobra that has stopped its ears,
that will not heed the tune of the charmer,
   however skillful the enchanter may be.

Break the teeth in their mouths, O God;
   LORD, tear out the fangs of those lions!
Let them vanish like water that flows away;
   when they draw the bow, let their arrows fall short.
May they be like a slug that melts away as it moves along,
   like a stillborn child that never sees the sun.

Before your pots can feel the heat of the thorns—
   whether they be green or dry—the wicked will be swept
      away.
The righteous will be glad when they are avenged,
   when they dip their feet in the blood of the wicked.
Then people will say,
   "Surely the righteous still are rewarded;
   surely there is a God who judges the earth."

Today, in my Bible, at the top of that page, you can see where I wrote, "Revealed to me in Rwanda 1994." I cannot do justice to how powerful those words were to each one of us gathered together that morning in Kigali, where you could feel the presence of darkness all around you.

When Franklin returned for another visit to the hospital, one of the morning shows of a major US network asked him to do a live interview. They told us to meet a small crew at the outdoor football stadium where 4,500 people had been murdered. Franklin would be live just after 7:00 a.m. eastern standard time. While we were waiting for the broadcast to begin, he wrote two words on a piece of paper and slid it toward me: "Please pray."

We huddled together nearby and asked God to give him peace and the words to say. When the interview began, the anchor said, "So, Franklin Graham, we understand that you're in Rwanda. Tell us what you're seeing there." She asked, so he answered honestly. He told about how we had first gone to the hospital and found people with their throats cut, people that had been butchered with machetes, and how blood was everywhere. As I heard Franklin be honest about the dire situation from where he was sitting on the other side of the world from the interviewer in New York, I knew there were Americans watching who were eating their breakfast about to walk out into their normal lives of safety and freedom. Maybe

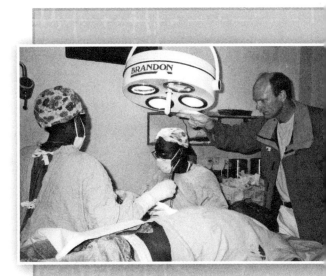

Southern Rwanda

the average Smith and Jones families were startled by what Franklin said, but he simply spoke the truth about the tragedy of Rwanda.

As we treated survivors at the hospital, we were told so many horrifying firsthand accounts of the atrocities. The Interahamwe and the Hutu government that had been in power worked through an administrative control structure called Nyumba Kumi, where every ten households had a designated leader, a system much like Cuba had under the Castro regime. This allowed them to keep track of every citizen, where they were and what they did, under meticulous surveillance and scrutiny. If they felt suspicious of anyone getting out of line, officials would get on the radios and order the killings of individuals, entire families, and even large groups.

Here's one example I heard: When the killing began, a Tutsi woman's husband disappeared. Not knowing if he had been murdered or ran away, she was alone with her seven children. The government leader for her community decided to make an example of her family to instill fear. Every week, he called all the people together, brought out her seven children, and ordered that she choose her next child to be killed. Then they forced her to dig the grave. After all her children were murdered, the leader raped and impregnated her. When she was in her last trimester, her husband returned. Later, they somehow managed to reunite and reconcile. A miracle of forgiveness and restoration amid unimaginable and unspeakable evil.

Coordinating logistics at Kigali Airport

The May 16, 1994, cover of *Time* magazine printed a quote from a missionary that read, "There are no devils left in Hell.... They are all in Rwanda."[2] I certainly understood those words. But I figured if Satan was going to loose his demons there, then we needed to be right in the middle of the battle, to respond by caring for the hurting and dying in the name of Jesus.

When the hospital had been attacked, all the medical staff either were killed or ran away. So as we rebuilt the facilities, we also had to restaff. Our US

World Medical Mission team went into overdrive to find more doctors, nurses, and staff. Some Rwandans who returned to the hospital said they were trained but had no paperwork. Of course, we had to sort through and vet those people to be certain. The original hospital had six hundred beds with two hundred of those designated as a VIP wing in a separate building. The Australian military had come in and was running that section. The idea was that those patients with resources would pay to get a higher level of care and attention, which could then subsidize the other half of the hospital.

Miracles in the Madness

From 1996 until 1999, Jim and Nancy Klein served with us in Rwanda. During those years, we helped the Ministry of Health reestablish its capacities to a basic level of functionality. Besides reopening Central Hospital in Kigali and restaffing it, we also built a nurses' training center and a chapel on the grounds. One particular story that we highlighted on the Samaritan's Purse website shows the amazing grace that some people discovered, even while struggling with survivor's guilt.

In 2004, the tenth anniversary of the Rwandan genocide, the Kigali Genocide Memorial was inaugurated. Several years later, as Alex Nsengimana visited the memorial for the first time, he looked out over a rose garden planted in remembrance of the one million people who were killed in Rwanda. His focus was on the large photos of murdered children. Their corresponding plaques offered two things: (1) each child's favorite toys and things they loved to do and (2) their cause of death, using words such as *bullet*, *grenade*, *club*, and *machete*. The contrast is difficult to process, especially when talking about young kids.

Reading those details and seeing their photos, Alex stated, "I look into their eyes and read what they wanted to be when they grew up.... I could have been one of them. And if I live my life with bitterness and unforgiveness, I'm not giving them justice. I'm just wasting my life.... They are my fellow brothers and sisters that never got the chance to go on to fulfill those dreams.

I would like to fulfill their dreams, live their dreams, so that they didn't die in vain."[3]

As a child in Rwanda, Alex had received a shoebox through Operation Christmas Child. That gift led him to a strong faith in God and eventually to a calling to plant a church and minister to the people who killed his family. In 2003, he came to the US to study and graduated from Crossroads College in Rochester, Minnesota, with a pastoral leadership degree. Afterward, he returned home to visit the village where he grew up and distributed OCC shoeboxes to the children there. But another much tougher ministry had to take place for Alex—offering forgiveness to his uncle's murderer, a man who had been their neighbor and friend. Through his faith in Christ, Alex realized that to truly be free, he had to forgive those who killed his family.

Like so many survivors of horrible, senseless tragedies, for a long time, Alex wondered why he was spared. Yet his conclusion was, "I want to be back in Rwanda so I can share the ministry of forgiveness because that's the only thing that has continued to heal me…. Christ loves them just as much as He loves me. He doesn't love me any more, and He doesn't love them any less."[4]

Besides witnessing the power of personal forgiveness from folks like Alex, I learned many lessons in Rwanda, such as the importance of trying to reappropriate and restore material things for the glory of God. On one of my explorations around Kigali, I found an abandoned technical school with a massive campus—twenty-five acres with forty buildings. After walking through and finding no one there, I took rolls of yellow caution tape and roped off the entire area.

Now, remember those 930 orphaned children in the camp? We moved them all into that school and ran a program for them there. For the next two years, we were able to reunite 896 of them with either one or both of their parents or extended family members. The remaining 34 children were placed in a permanent orphanage that was run by the Belgian Red Cross. Jack and Jennifer Norman from Canada took that work to heart. They were a very sweet, hardworking couple who loved those children and did a great job of caring for them. Even amid so much madness, God did so many miracles in Rwanda. I met people there with whom I still have close relationships today.

In 1994, I was finally able to return home to stay for a while. That was the first time I had difficulty transitioning back, and my wife was incredible through that season. Not until 9/11 would I learn about PTSD—post-traumatic stress disorder. No matter how tough we may be or what type of personality we have or how called we are in our faith, as humans, we cannot witness such horrific scenes without having a psychological, emotional, mental, and spiritual reaction to horrors that God in His creation never intended for us to face.

I had another reminder of this at Christmastime in 2004 when I decided to go see the newly released movie *Hotel Rwanda*. I had no idea how emotionally devastating that film would be to me. Because I was there. I saw, I smelled, I felt the evil that had been unleashed. And while I will never be able to forget it, I trust and believe two of the most powerful words in Scripture that can change everything, that can make the impossible possible: *But God.* This truth, found in words like Joseph's in Genesis 50:20, echoes throughout history in the battle between Heaven and Hell.

You intended to harm me, but God intended it all for good.
He brought me to this position so I could save the lives of
many people. (Gen. 50:20 NLT)

Chapter 6

Will I Die Tonight or Tomorrow?

Zaire
1996
Detainment/Interrogation

In 1996, with our team continuing the work at the Central Hospital in Kigali, Rwanda, I was traveling in and out of the country as needed. I know this sounds archaic today, but our most reliable form of communication there was short-wave radios. One day, an urgent call for help came in to our office on one of the frequencies. I heard and responded to the man, who said he was a missionary in an area of Zaire he identified as Kishungu. (Today, Zaire is called the Democratic Republic of the Congo.)

He reported that Rwandan refugees were pouring into his area. His estimation was 60,000 men, women, and children. I knew right away that these were part of the 2 million that had fled across the border into Zaire. There was also a massive cholera epidemic with thousands of people dying every day. Eventually, I learned that the missionary on the radio was Jim Lindquist. Rwandans were coming to his mission station, trying to flee this horrible situation.

Following the plane crash that had killed Rwanda's president and the geno-cide that had begun against the Tutsis, the military commander of the Rwandan Patriotic Front (RPF), Paul Kagame, responded by leading a force of 10,000 to 15,000 soldiers to fight the Hutus. Kagame's forces were able to retake Kigali in July of 1994. Right away, the military leader's power and influence began to translate into political power. (In 2000, he was elected the president of Rwanda and is still in office as of 2025.)[1]

The government the RPF had begun to establish was saying that these refugee camps were an existential threat to their country's security, and they wanted the people to return to their homes right away. But the dynamics became challenging when the many humanitarian organizations based in eastern Zaire were arguing that it was still not safe for anyone to leave the refugee camps. Many of the camps were supplied by NGOs but manipulated and controlled by the Interahamwe. What Jim was experiencing was a spontaneous gathering of people fleeing the larger camps because they feared for their lives.

The government's position was that if Rwandans were confident the threat was over, they would voluntarily go home. In my experience, I have seen that, regardless of location in the world, anytime you have a sudden mass displacement of people, they vote with their feet—to stay or go, and what direction to go in. The vast majority of the refugees were hunkered down and staying put in camps like Jim's.

What a Difference a Day Makes

To answer Jim's request, I had our office in Nairobi purchase a large quantity of medicine, enough to fill the 208 Caravan airplane we owned. To deliver this cargo into Zaire, as well as try to assess the other needs there, I brought along Dr. Paul Jones and, a name you have come to recognize by now, Dr. Michael (Mike) VanRooyen. Both men were in Rwanda working with our team.

Our pilot was Curtis Wilkerson, who was tall and lanky in his build, quiet and thoughtful in his demeanor. While this was my first time working with Curtis, I would quickly discover that besides being great at flying, he could always figure out a way to get things done in situations that would prove too difficult for other pilots. I came to appreciate how proactive he could be in tough circumstances. (Curtis and I would go on to fly several missions together in dangerous and challenging parts of the world.)

I took all our passports to the Zairean embassy and right away noticed that the personnel there were very edgy. They were nervous like something was wrong, but I had no idea what or why. Along with the normal fees, I paid the expediting charge to get them back the next day. For those refugees in Zaire, I knew time was critical.

After being in Africa so much, I knew that Zaire could be a very corrupt place, especially for Americans trying to get in and out of the country. To pay the duties, taxes, and any other possible "charges" to get the medicine into Zaire, I brought along $10,000 in cash—a hundred brand-new one-hundred-dollar bills. I hid the money in a place I most suspected would not be inspected. From Genesis to Revelation, I placed individual bills throughout my Bible, which was ragged and worn from years of reading, as well as

Michael VanRooyen, airport attendant, and Ken, Kigali, November 1996

from being carried tens of thousands of miles around the globe. If someone were to scan through the Scriptures, along with the stories of Moses, David, Isaiah, Jesus, Peter, and Paul, they would randomly and repeatedly see Benjamin Franklin's tight-lipped stare.

As soon as our passports were ready and in hand, Paul, Mike, and I headed to the airport in Kigali to meet Curtis at the plane. Kigali International had easy customs and relaxed immigration officials, so we were able to walk right out to the edge of the runway where Curtis pulled up and parked to refuel.

Standing at the plane, I began to have the distinct sense, that unexplainable feeling the Lord gives, that Dr. Jones didn't need to go on this trip. While he was the oldest, in his sixties at the time, that wasn't the reason. Somehow, I just knew he wasn't supposed to come with us. Confident in my decision, I said, "Hey, Paul, why don't you go on back to the house? There's really nothing for you to do on this trip. Mike and I will drop the medicine off, do a quick assessment of the needs there, and likely be back tomorrow." Paul had no objection, took the car, and left Kigali International to go back to our base, only about two miles from the airport.

The Caravan had no extra passenger seats. While the plane did have a cargo bay below, because we had so much medicine, the majority had to be in the main compartment, with us sitting in front of it, behind Curtis. Around four in the afternoon, we landed at the airport in Bunia, Zaire. As we taxied off the runway, which was only a grass strip, an immigration official came running out to the plane, screaming in French, obviously upset. He immediately began to question why we had come. Though it was difficult to communicate with the language barrier, I could tell he was demanding we pay a fine of one hundred dollars a person. While he gave no explanation, I saw it simply as an assertion of authority and an opportunity to make some money. With no argument, I pulled out three crisp, new one-hundred-dollar bills (somewhere out of Psalms, I think) and gave them to him.

Pilot Curtis Wilkerson making final checks at Kigali Airport before flight to South Sudan

He then told us to hand over our passports and come back the next morning to give him time to sort everything out. From there, we got back in the plane to continue on to our planned destination, which was Nyankunde Missionary Hospital. After the short fifteen-minute hop, we touched down on the Mission Aviation Fellowship (MAF) grass landing strip. Upon Franklin's request in 1989, Carolyn and I had visited there so I could assess what it would take for Samaritan's Purse to build a hospital at this location. I also knew there was a guest house on-site.

That evening at dinner, Pat Nixon, a doctor, was among the dozen or so people gathered. I had gotten her name from Jim on the radio. She was our point of contact to figure out how we could get the medicine to the camp. As we talked, I sensed some tension in the air that didn't have anything to do with our mission. But, in the course of our conversation, we soon discovered the source of the problem. What we had no way of knowing had happened was, after we had taken off from Kigali earlier in the day, the Rwandan Patriotic Army (RPA) launched a full-fledged war against the border regions of Zaire. Their attack was consistent with their multiple expressions of concern and warning about the refugees, as well as about those that controlled the camp being an existential threat to the national security of Rwanda.

Pat and the others had heard the news not long before we arrived. We had flown in on the very day of an invasion, and no one had any idea what this meant or what was to come. Whether there was an official declaration of war or not didn't matter; the outcome was the same. This news also explained why the folks at the embassy were on edge and the airport immigration official angrily questioned our purpose in Zaire. The same man still had our passports, along with information that we had flown in from Rwanda on the day of the attack. Everyone's nervousness should have tipped me off that a need for deeper investigation was warranted. Here was yet another very valuable lesson for me: You must pay attention and be alert to the specific dynamics around you—what you feel, what you sense, the invisible, the spoken, and the unspoken.

After the meal, we decided to press on with the mission and determine who would go to Kishungu. We also discussed the complex political dynamics in the region involving the refugees and the attack by the Rwandan army. Pat was helping us coordinate the entire response as she had been maintaining radio contact with Jim. After a couple of hours of planning, we set the time to meet at the MAF hangar for 7:00 a.m. to leave and deliver the medicine. Then together, we prayed for God's protection, wisdom, and guidance.

But little did we know our plans were about to radically change.

Backs against the Wall

Around six thirty the next morning, Mike, Curtis, and I were walking to the hangar where our plane was parked outside in the grass when we saw a truck loaded with a dozen heavily armed Zairean soldiers drive into the village. Jumping out, shouting in French, they started calling out the name of the man they had been ordered to find: James Isaacs—the name on my passport.

After confirming everyone's identities, they grabbed Mike, Curtis, and me and led us inside the MAF airplane hangar. Immediately, they split us up and began to interrogate us individually. Their attitude and tone were clearly designed for intimidation. I was taken into a small room that had no windows, so the space was very dark. Several of the soldiers came into the room and motioned for me to sit down on the other side of a small table with my back against the concrete block wall. They stood between the table and the door as one man sat down across from me. It didn't take long to figure out he was an intelligence officer, a military interrogator.

Because my passport had a stamp showing I had recently come through Entebbe, Uganda, they paid particular attention to me. That's why *my* name was called out. Using the timing of our trip, along with our confiscated passports, the military had arrived at the interesting conclusion that we must be American spies sent into their country. If that were to be true, it would have to somehow mean that the United States had prior knowledge of the attack between two African nations and wanted to get involved covertly.

And also that the planeload of medicine was just part of an elaborate ruse to throw them off our trail. But obviously, the surprise attack for Zaire, after all that had gone on in Rwanda, created a great deal of paranoid suspicion and speculation.

While the national language was French, the interrogators spoke Lingala, a Bantu language of Central Africa. One of the MAF personnel who spoke fluent French and English came in to act as an interpreter. The interrogator's questions were translated from Lingala into French and written down, and then the translator would read them and ask me in English. I would give my answer, and he would translate into French, which was also written down, then converted to Lingala. The tedious process of translating and documenting through three languages created a very formal interrogation.

About three hours in, exhausted, I stood up to stretch my legs. Truth be told, I was trying to claim some control over my situation, and I wanted to see if they would allow me that. While I said nothing and made no aggressive moves, I knew that standing was an act of assertion. Immediately in the darkness, I got my answer when I heard gun bolts pull back and bullets rack up. Slowly, I put my hands out and sat back down. Quickly humbled, I thought to myself, *Okay, I won't be standing up again.* The soldiers' response assured me that I was not going to make any movements without their orders.

After several hours of nonstop back-and-forth, around midday, they let us know we were going to take a break and be allowed to have lunch. While we were eating, I noticed one of the soldiers had a paratrooper's pin on his uniform. (In November 1994, after Rwanda, my best friend, Mitchell Minges, knew I had been through something horrible, so he made arrangements for the two of us to go skydiving. After ground school, I jumped that first day, and a week later we went back and jumped again. While Mitchell never jumped again, I have continued through the years, and I've made 350 jumps. I found the exhilaration to be very cathartic.) Using the little bit of elementary French I knew, along with hand signals, I let him know I was an experienced skydiver. While I was just trying to make a personal connection to break the tension, that exchange backfired. Divulging my hobby gave them one more piece of evidence—namely, if I jumped out of planes with a parachute, I *must* be a spy. Realizing their conclusion, I decided not to volunteer any more information and, like a witness on the stand, simply answer the questions being asked as simply as possible.

Ed Morrow and Ken with a local pastor in Yakasu, 1998

Back into the interrogation, they would hammer me for a while on some specific line of questioning, then bring Mike in and send me out. When they would bring me back in, they would send Mike out. While they did interrogate Curtis early on, I think they quickly decided he wasn't involved and was "just the pilot." They were clearly scoping for any conflicts or discrepancies in our stories.

Later in the afternoon, the interrogator slid over a paper with writing on it and motioned for me to sign. I reminded him that I couldn't read French and I wasn't about to sign anything I didn't understand. Showing his irritation, the interrogator allowed the page to be translated into English. I was very surprised to hear it was a true and accurate account of what I had answered in response to his questions. So I signed the paper.

From there, the focus shifted to the part of my story where I had spoken to Jim Lindquist on a shortwave radio transmission from Rwanda to Zaire. They informed me that our communication was illegal. At that point, a soldier escorted Pat into the room. Knowing that she spoke French, he began to question her directly. With this totally new pattern, I realized what was happening. They were asking her the exact same questions they had asked me, comparing answers. Answers I had given in an account that I had just signed to create a legal document. If Pat's story turned out to be at all different from mine or it appeared that either of us were lying, we were all in deep trouble. I could see the possible dilemma shaping up in the room. I had no reason to lie. Pat had no reason to lie. But we all know that eyewitnesses can tell a slightly different version of the exact same scene.

Now, I want to be abundantly clear that what I am about to share with you I have never experienced before or since. As I've said, my ability to speak French was minimal, extremely basic. But, as their conversation began, my only possible explanation for what I experienced was that the Holy Spirit allowed me—in the moment—the ability to understand fluent French only for His purposes, our protection, and His glory. Somehow in some way, I began to comprehend their conversation—perfectly—every word the interrogator and Pat spoke. Again, I have no explanation for what happened apart from God's providence.

In Acts 2:7–12 we read,

> Utterly amazed, they asked: "Aren't all these who are speaking Galileans? Then how is it that each of us hears them in

our native language? Parthians, Medes and Elamites; residents of Mesopotamia, Judea and Cappadocia, Pontus and Asia, Phrygia and Pamphylia, Egypt and the parts of Libya near Cyrene; visitors from Rome (both Jews and converts to Judaism); Cretans and Arabs—we hear them declaring the wonders of God in our own tongues!" Amazed and perplexed, they asked one another, "What does this mean?"

Of course, that first sermon in Acts was all about getting the Gospel out to people who had come into Jerusalem and would be returning home to nations far away. But the Holy Spirit, who knows all languages, gives the ability of both speaking and understanding as He sees fit. As a disciple of Jesus, in a room where I was only there in His name to minister to the Rwandan refugees in Zaire, I was given a similar gift *once*, in the moment. It was a gift that was as practical as it was mystical with God as its Source.

As I listened intently, I could tell Pat's story lined up with mine. She offered no details that were different from mine. That temporary understanding brought peace and relief to my heart and mind. By the next morning, the soldiers seemed to be satisfied that all our stories were in sync. I was very grateful that they never did a search of our belongings, because they would likely have found the cash dispersed throughout my Bible.

But the nightmare wasn't over yet.

The next morning, the soldiers began a different accusation. Now, they had suspicions that the medicine we brought into their country was poisoned. After ordering us to unload the cargo from the plane, the lead interrogator informed us (translated into English), "Today, you're going to fly us back to Bunia in your airplane, and we're going to put you in jail."

Ultimately, the medicine was put to good use at the Nyankunde Missionary Hospital, but the soldiers' goal was obvious: they were not after the medicine; they were after us.

From Bad to Worse

To comply with their orders and transport the dozen soldiers, after they all sat down on both sides along the walls of the main cabin, I took a rope and double-cinched it to the metal tie-downs in the floor to create a makeshift seatbelt for them. I deliberately pulled the rope down hard across their midsections to make them as uncomfortable as I had been while trapped for twelve hours between a table and a wall. As I pulled tight, they said nothing. I assume because they wanted to be secured well in a plane that *our* pilot was flying.

Moving supplies in Yakusa, 1998

Feeling some level of control, I decided to go one step further. I told them they couldn't keep their guns with them on the flight and would need to let me stow them away. Let's just say that did *not* work. They did not agree. In fact, they raised their rifles, pointing at me, like "You just try it, buddy." My hands went up in surrender as I backed off to go sit down.

So Curtis, Jim, and I, with our captors tied down to the floor of the plane, flew to Bunia. But another man had decided to make the trip with us, and the soldiers had agreed he could come— a Zairean ophthalmologist named Dr. Tony Ukety. Tony was an unsinkable optimist with a great sense of humor, always laughing, smiling, and high-fiving people. It didn't take me long to realize why Tony had wanted to ride along. As soon as we were in the air, he started a conversation with the soldiers, trying to convince them that all visitors to Zaire should be treated with respect and that taking us to jail, especially as foreign missionaries, would be a mistake. By the time we landed, Tony had worked out a compromise with them.

Ian Campbell, the mission director in East Congo for Africa Inland Mission, had a home in Bunia. They agreed to take us there. Upon arrival, they locked us in. While I never stepped foot outside to know for sure, I always had a feeling there were soldiers standing guard around the house. Fortunately, they did allow Tony to come and go as he pleased. Meanwhile, Ian was there on his shortwave radio organizing the evacuation of all the missionaries in the area, which was a sizable group. He was also adamant that we should never try to open the door. The longer we were there, the more gunfire we heard. There was a definite sense that the instability in the town was increasing. While we were clearly under house arrest, we also knew that essentially being in hiding there offered at least some protection from the threats outside.

History has proven the Rwandan concerns about the Interahamwe's manipulation of the camp populations were accurate. The killers were intimidating, abusing, and executing people as they saw fit. They were also manipulating the entire population through their control over the food and supplies that were coming into what truly were massive camps. The vast majority of the people were victims of the killers'

exploitation. In the days following, as the Rwandan government began its appeal for its citizens to return to their homes, the estimated 1.3 million Rwandans who had fled into eastern Zaire eventually came back voluntarily. The remaining estimated 400,000 had either gone to be with family members in neighboring countries or were directly involved in the genocide and wouldn't return for fear of facing justice.[2]

At Ian's house, Mike and I shared a small bedroom with two twin beds. That first night, around two o'clock in the morning, there was sudden automatic rifle fire close by. Mike jumped up and called out, "What was that?!" Being more accustomed to the sounds of war, I tried to encourage him, "Lay back down, Mike, and keep your head *below* the window. There's nothing we can do. Just relax."

Much like my team had experienced in Rwanda, we weren't fearful, but we were definitely concerned about what was to come.

Moving supplies in Yakasu, 1998

Over the years, I have made many notations in the margins of my Bible. Some of them are a reminder of the country I was in and the circumstances. Curtis, Mike, and I would sit around the kitchen table, praying and reading Scripture out loud to one another. We were able to draw strength from God's Word, reminding ourselves that so many of His faithful followers had experienced threats while He protected them. Held prisoner in Ian's house with gunfire outside, on November 23, 1996, in the margin beside Isaiah 43, I wrote "Will I die tonight or tomorrow?"

Do not fear, for I have redeemed you;
   I have summoned you by name; you are mine.
When you pass through the waters,
   I will be with you;
and when you pass through the rivers,
   they will not sweep over you.
When you walk through the fire,
   you will not be burned;
   the flames will not set you ablaze.
For I am the LORD your God,
   the Holy One of Israel, your Savior. (vv. 1–3)

Another passage we read repeatedly was Isaiah 38:16–19:

You restored me to health
   and let me live.
Surely it was for my benefit
   that I suffered such anguish.
In your love you kept me
   from the pit of destruction;
you have put all my sins
   behind your back.
For the grave cannot praise you,
   death cannot sing your praise;
those who go down to the pit
   cannot hope for your faithfulness.
The living, the living—they praise you,
   as I am doing today.

We meditated on and prayed those passages, along with many others that spoke peace to us in our circumstances. The three of us also wrote letters to our wives, making a pact that if any one of us was able to get out, we would take the letters back and deliver them to each home. While we were praying in faith, we had to prepare for anything. Scripture is clear that both mercy and martyrdom can be God's answer.

As morning blended into afternoon, into night, and into the next day, every morning, Dr. Tony would come to visit, always smiling and trying to encourage us. But one day when he walked in, I immediately noticed a drastic change in his usual upbeat countenance and demeanor. Deeply concerned, I asked, "Tony, what's wrong?"

"Ken, it's bad. The soldiers informed their superior officers in Kisangani about you. Their general knows they are holding three Americans that they suspected to be spies, and they also know you have an airplane. We have to get you out of here!"

Over the radio, Ian had also heard reports that six hundred troops and their family members were in military trucks, having made it to Beni and headed to Bunia. This news obviously created tension and put pressure on us all, as well as the local population, because the Zairean army had a reputation for brutality to their own citizens.

Desperate Measures

Hearing this news, we all felt the very real impending threat. Knowing I had to take action quickly, I did something I have done only this one time. I took twenty-five one-hundred-dollar bills out of my Bible—$2,500—handed them to Tony, and said, "You have to find a way to get us out of here because they will kill us when they get here." Tony took the cash and headed out the door on a mission. He ended up having to make a number of trips back and forth to work out a plan, and, ultimately, I had to use a total of $7,600 of the original $10,000 I had brought to pay taxes on the medicine. What became very apparent was that Tony's decision to come with us on this trip was one of the many ways God was watching out for us. And my intent for the money to be used for taxes was replaced with divine intervention to allow us a way to try to get free.

At 6:00 a.m., right around sunrise, Tony bolted through the door in a panic. "You've got to come with me *now*! *Right* now!" We all ran out of the house, constantly looking around for soldiers, following Tony down narrow alleyways through the maze of masonry block buildings. These structures all looked the same with their gabled roofs, curved arches over the windows, and shutters open against the walls. Several blocks away, he led us into what appeared to be some kind of office.

Inside, we stood in front of an obviously frustrated man seated at a desk whom Tony had likely paid and negotiated a plan with. He pushed a piece of paper across the desk toward us, as the sound of gunfire started up again. Outside, I knew the neighborhoods were quickly disintegrating into conflict.

The man told us in English, "Sign this." Hurriedly, Curtis stepped up and signed the page. Then Mike. As the only one who still needed to sign, I asked,

"What does this say? What am I signing?" Mike looked at me, surprised, and, in desperation, stated, "Come on, man, just sign the paper!" As calmly as possible, I responded, "Mike, they may kill me, but they will *not* kill me because I confessed to something I did *not* do."

I looked the man behind the desk in the eye and said, "I need you to tell me what this piece of paper says. You have to translate it." Though he was even more irritated now, for some reason, he did what I asked. The bottom line of the document stated that we would be *legally* deported because we were confessing we had entered Zaire *illegally*.

As I signed the paper, I said, "Okay, I'll take that. You can legally deport me." While we had certainly not entered the country illegally, I was not going to, as they say, die on that hill. *Literally.* Now we had to try to make our way back to the house where we had been imprisoned to get to the SUV Tony was driving ... without getting shot.

We ran for our lives, the sound of gunfire no longer muffled by the block walls. Safely back at the house, we grabbed our backpacks and piled into the vehicle with Tony behind the wheel, flooring the gas to escape. That drive felt like an action sequence from a movie with the sounds of automatic rifles going off as we sped through the streets. With the sun now up, the fighting was growing more intense.

Pulling into the airport, we drove out onto the runway, right up to our plane. Curtis jumped out and began to refuel while Mike threw our backpacks into the open door of the plane. I looked over to see a man walking toward me. I recognized him as our lead interrogator and stared at him, wondering why he was here and waiting to see what he was about to do. Let me remind you that this was the same man I had spent many grueling hours with, having to go through a translator to communicate. That's when I heard him say:

"Mr. Ken! I see you are leaving us."

Obviously, his arsenal of tactics included hiding the fact that he understood *everything* Mike and I had said. Not once had I seen any indication that he had understood us. Realizing that all along he spoke flawless English, I maintained my game face.

I responded, "Yessir. I am leaving."

"I just wonder, How do you like Zaire?"

"Oh, Zaire is a beautiful place. I love it here."

"Well, thank you. I would like to come visit *your* country one day."

I reached into my wallet, took out my business card and a pen, and wrote down every phone number to reach me. "Here's my card. If you get to America, call me." I have to admit, after my offer of hospitality, there was definitely some sarcasm in my words as I continued.

"I want to congratulate you on the professionalism you showed when you interrogated me."

"Well, thank you. It was your CIA that taught me."

"Ah, well, you did a very good job."

Suddenly, he switched gears. "I have a favor to ask of you, Mr. Ken."

"What would that be?"

"You see that man over there, that brown man?" he asked as he pointed.

I looked to see exactly who he described—a brown man standing alone. "Yes, I see him."

"He's an Egyptian military adviser. He has a wife and two daughters. When the army comes here, they will kill him. I want you to please take him out of the country."

"But I can't do that. We have a policy. We're not allowed to take anyone in our airplane that is not staff."

At that point, I realized the true nature of the interrogator's small talk and his making nice, so to speak. He was trying to lead up to this request. He began to plead with me to save this Egyptian man. While I have experienced this sort of circumstance many times over the years, I always marvel anytime there is a clear and sudden shift in power dynamics. When the officer was holding me at gunpoint, he controlled when I could speak and when I could stand up. Yet now here we were with me about to board a plane to leave, legally discharged from his control, and he was practically begging for my help.

He made one final attempt. "Please, Mr. Ken. He has two daughters. If you don't help, he will be killed."

I had clearly seen how he thought and how he negotiated, so I decided to follow suit. I looked at him and said, "Okay, but it will cost you two hundred dollars." Ironically, he reached into his pocket and pulled out two brand-new, crisp one-hundred-dollar bills. Immediately, I recognized the money, some of the same bills I had brought into the country and had to give to Tony to try to buy our way safely out of the country.

As he handed me my own cash back, I nodded in agreement, and we escorted the Egyptian adviser onto the plane. Within minutes, Curtis had us safely off the runway and in the air. We flew to Entebbe and turned the Egyptian adviser over to immigration. Because of the urgency of his escape, he didn't have a visa. We left him there in good hands to sort out his situation diplomatically.

In retrospect, I have to wonder, because the Lord obviously knew the interrogator spoke English, did that have something to do with me being given the ability to understand his and Pat's conversation in French? Did the Spirit allow me such understanding at a critical moment because they were using covert tactics? As I have said before, this was yet another of the many mysteries I have experienced in my years of relying on God's provision and protection.

Later that night, finally safe and sound, very relieved and grateful to be alive, we had a celebratory dinner. Mike, Curtis, and I had survived our kidnapping hostage-interrogation house-arrest high-speed-escape spy adventure in Zaire. All because I had answered a call for help from Jim Lindquist to get medicine to Rwandan refugees. (Just in case you're wondering, no, to this day, I have never met Jim.) From there, we traveled back to the Samaritan's Purse office in Nairobi.

Later we found out about a saving grace that had delayed the Zairean army from reaching our location. Due to heavy rains, the roads had become very muddy. What would have normally been a two- or three-day trip for a truck convoy turned into ten days. That extra week of travel allowed many people to escape Zaire and, frankly, saved the lives of many people, including us, the AIM missionaries, and Dr. Tony Ukety, who decided to walk to Uganda. Often, we cannot see the power of prayer until we look back on a crisis. From all the hours that Mike, Curtis, and I prayed His Word, I believe God heard and answered.

But there are two important follow-up stories left to tell.

Didn't See That Coming

Back in Nairobi, a man named Lauren Fast, who was head of the Africa Inland Mission, along with one of his coworkers, came to see me at our office. After a two-hour conversation of answering their questions and discussing my experience in Zaire, I was not clear on why they had come and what they wanted from me. Yet, sitting almost knee to knee, I walked through the details of what had happened to us there.

Strangely, after they left, I noticed I felt better. And I didn't understand why. As I have referenced before, after 9/11 when I was at Ground Zero in New York City, I learned about PTSD for the first time. In 2001, looking back on that visit in Nairobi with Lauren and the other man from AIM, I realized they had training in debriefing and processing trauma. Unbeknownst to me, they were guiding me through what I had experienced in Zaire. Part of what they communicated was the understanding that all my feelings about my ordeal were perfectly normal and that I should allow for the fact that I had survived a traumatic experience.

Several years ago, when I was back in Nairobi, I ran into Lauren in a store. I was able to thank him for coming to talk with me that day. I told him that, even though I didn't realize it at the time and he never told me what he was actually doing, I would always remember that somehow, some way, I felt better, more complete, and more whole after spending time with them.

The second and final story to share proves there are times in our walk with God when we realize some detail may have been the actual story all along. In 2018, I was the American candidate for the director general of the International Organization for Migration. This intergovernmental organization, created in 1951, advocates for humane and orderly migration to benefit both migrants and society. As part of the UN system, it follows the principles in the Charter of the United Nations with an emphasis on human rights and respect for migrants' dignity and well-being.[3] I spent five months of that year traveling internationally, talking with hundreds of government officials.

At the African Union in Addis Ababa, Ethiopia, I was meeting with ambassadors, foreign ministers, and ministers of interior from countries all over the world. The ambassador from Egypt came up to me and, after a gracious introduction, said, "Mr. Isaacs, my country owes you a debt of gratitude."

Surprised, I asked, "For what?"

"In 1996, you helped get an Egyptian man out of Zaire. He is alive today, safe with his wife and two daughters, because you agreed to bring him out. The government of Egypt would like to thank you."

That's when the memory came rushing back of standing on that runway in Zaire, after escaping our own horrifying ordeal, having our CIA-trained interrogator point at this man and plead with me to put him on our plane. The surprise of that story and the ambassador's gratitude for saving what was obviously a very important man to them was so emotionally moving that I was speechless as tears welled up in my eyes. The fact that his story made it back to their government and the ambassador had connected it to me twenty-plus years later was amazing. Following that event, when I was in Geneva, the Egyptian ambassador there also thanked me. He was fully aware of what had happened as well.

Bringing medical supplies, 1998

Zaire, now called the Democratic Republic of the Congo, is huge geographically with unimaginably thick forests. If you fly over parts of the interior at ten thousand feet, the terrain below looks like solid clumps of florets sprayed with mist, separating areas of the country. This divide allows little to no infrastructure, supply chains, and open markets to connect the wealthier western side and the more rural, landlocked eastern side. Today, the war in the eastern side of the Democratic Republic of the Congo continues. An estimated six million people have died with savage attacks, mutilations, rapes, and torture still happening. In my opinion, this massive destabilization of the region that began with the genocide is still prevalent today because of the evil in that region that controls so many lives.

Today, among my photos from the past, are some that were taken of Curtis, Mike, Paul, and I standing in front of the plane at the Kigali airport, just before we boarded for takeoff. When I look back on those pictures, I see how determined and carefree we were with no idea how close we were about to be to a very different outcome. Right after they were taken was when I felt that Paul didn't need to go, which is exactly why those photos have always had a profound effect on me. While the old saying "A picture is worth a thousand words" is indeed true, sometimes they create just as many feelings and emotions.

God does indeed work in mysterious ways and, just as Ephesians 3:20 tells us, does "immeasurably more than all we ask or imagine," far more than we can understand this side of Heaven. Over the years, I've also been continually reminded of the sheep's response to Jesus in His parable in Matthew 25, when they asked Him, "Lord, when did we see *You*?" (see v. 37).

Whether helping a refugee in a camp in need of medicine or an Egyptian man caught in war who needs a stranger to invite him onto his plane, we may not know the significance of what we did, but we must always stay mindful to say yes to those things that Jesus places in our path and calls us to take action on in His name.

> Then the King will say to those on his right, "Come, you who are blessed by my Father; take your inheritance, the kingdom prepared for you since the creation of the world. For I was hungry and you gave me something to eat, I was thirsty and you gave me something to drink, I was a stranger and you invited me in, I needed clothes and you clothed me, I was sick and you looked after me, I was in prison and you came to visit me." (Matt. 25:34–36)

Chapter 7

To Go into the No-Go

South Sudan
1993
Persecution

In 1993, Samaritan's Purse began to work in very remote areas of South Sudan. Originally a region of Sudan and later its own nation, it has long been one of the poorest places in the world. We had come because the people were suffering from tribalism and a lack of infrastructure, healthcare, and education. The Arabic Islamist government, based in Khartoum, added to the problems for the people in the south as it persecuted and even enslaved them because of their race and religion. From then to today, the war in Sudan has always had many different layers exacerbated by great political strife.

At the time, there was a United Nations program called Operation Lifeline Sudan (OLS) that coordinated humanitarian assistance to meet the needs of the Sudanese who were suffering because of the war. The program had three members—the UN, the government of Sudan (GOS), and a rebel group known as the Sudan People's Liberation Army (SPLA). UNICEF and the World Food Programme were the primary leaders and coordinators of OLS. This arrangement was unique because UN agencies typically only engage with formal governments and not rebel groups trying to break away from or overthrow the government.

The OLS would often agree that entire regions of southern Sudan would be classified as "go zones," while others were classified as "no-go zones." The government of Sudan was known for manipulating this process for the purposes of prosecuting their war by attacking civilians. An NGO would have to submit its proposal of intervention and then, only after securing permission from the OLS, could you enter into any designated areas. So even in a go zone, you could ask but they could say no.

We began hearing reports that the Sudanese government was openly bombing civilians who had gathered to get food or other types of humanitarian assistance. These were the go zones that had been approved where active food distribution sites brought in hundreds, up to thousands of people, coming for help. The government obviously knew the distribution times and locations and was targeting its attacks to kill people and create terror among them. Clearly, this war was inflicting serious suffering on the innocent. We were also hearing about the persecution of Christians. (There are many well-documented atrocities of war and human rights violations in Sudan over decades.)

As we were learning about the problems in this nation, I couldn't help but ask, "If the government is bombing in go zones, how much worse is it in the no-go zones?" The mounting evidence was causing me to want to *go* into a *no-go* zone. (By now, you probably aren't surprised by that statement.)

Allow me to offer some brief historical context here: Sudan has a long, complicated history of colonialism, tragedy, and misery. Through generations, there have been tribal and ethnic issues that have led to a deepening hatred. An ongoing theme has been oppression from whoever is in power, whether

Franklin Graham with Ken at a South Sudan state dinner, immediately after South Sudan declared independence, July 9, 2011

the former colonials or the Islamist government. In 1956, Sudan won its independence from British and Egyptian rule. The British had divided the south roughly into three areas—the Episcopalians, the Presbyterians, and the Catholics. The point was to give these denominations designated authority and allow for their missionaries to come in and work among the people.

Over the years, Sudan has had recurring civil wars between the north and the south. The Arabs in the north continually tried to convert the people in the south to Islam through the mandatory application of Sharia law to everyone throughout the country. These efforts led to tremendous brutalities and human rights abuses. The government in the north was involved in slavery and trafficking, bombing schools and churches, depriving the population of economic growth, and generally making life absolute hell for the people. In 2005, the Comprehensive Peace Agreement (CPA) was signed, and in January of 2011, a referendum was set to establish South Sudan's self-determination. Voters overwhelmingly chose independence. Seven months later on July 9, the Republic of South Sudan declared its freedom from Sudan.[1]

Under the Radar, through the River

One day in early 1997, a letter came to Franklin from a missionary in Africa. After reading it, he handed it over to me. Right away, I contacted this man, whose name I won't mention for his protection, and after talking, I agreed to go with him into South Sudan.

A town in Kenya that you will recognize from the chapter on Rwanda, Lokichogio (often called Loki for short) was the coordination center for all humanitarian activities going into Sudan. Because so many NGOs had their facilities there, the runway was a constant drone of C-130 and Il-76 cargo planes taking off and landing between airdrops of tons of food. Loki reminded me of the scene in *Star Wars: Episode VI—Return of the Jedi* where Jabba the Hutt held court, because you had people from all over the world flying into a region about the size of Texas to deliver humanitarian assistance. There were people who were there solely to make some big money through the various rebel and military factions, as well as missionaries, NGOs, and UN staff. Loki was one of the most unique sites I've ever witnessed.

Because the authorities knew about anyone who flew out of there, as well as their destination, I wanted to find another way to get in, off the radar, figuratively and literally. Roger Winter, a wonderful man with a lifelong love for South Sudan and its people, connected me to the director of national security in Uganda. I was seeking unofficial permission to fly from his country into the southern part of Sudan, inside a region where the civil war was being fought. (Roger was absolutely fearless, and I learned so much in my time with him.)

The pilot I wanted for this trip was Curtis Wilkerson, my Zaire adventure buddy. In May of 1997, Curtis and I, along with my new missionary friend and two other Samaritan's Purse staff members, met in Entebbe, Uganda, to fly into South Sudan. Our destination was a town called Maridi. There was an airstrip there, and the missionary had sent word by shortwave radio to the crew that we were coming. But before leaving, we had to solve a dilemma. We didn't actually know the safest way to navigate our flight through a war zone. Would flying high be suspicious and cause us to show up on radar? Or would flying low keep us under the radar yet make us susceptible to ground fire? We played out all these scenarios and questions in our discussion.

We finally decided that flying low was the least risky of our two options. At times we were only three to four hundred feet above the ground. We also flew at a slow speed, trying not to appear aggressive or threatening to anyone watching from below. As the airfield in Maridi came into view, we could see there were barrels lined up in the middle of the grass landing strip, which obviously hadn't been mowed in quite a while. The grass and weeds looked at least three feet high.

While we circled the area a couple of times, several men came running out to move the barrels off the strip. Although we were concerned about the height of the grass with our small plane, Curtis was able to land safely. With the plane idling, the four of us grabbed our gear and jumped out. As soon as we shut the door and were clear of the wings, Curtis turned around and took off. Just to remind you, there were still no cell phones. We had no SAT phone, no way to communicate with the outside world. As the sound of the plane faded away and disappeared on the horizon, there I was on some remote dot on the map in Africa, a situation that was becoming quite familiar to me by now.

Through prior arrangements made by the missionary, there was a heavy-duty cargo truck waiting for us under the authority and control of a group of SPLA fighters. In the NGO world, people give a lot of attention to staying clear of combatants. While I don't necessarily seek them out, I also recognize that anyone in a position of authority has been appointed by God. In Romans 13:1–5, Paul states:

Food airdrop for famine response in Sudan

Let everyone be subject to the governing authorities, for there is no authority except that which God has established. The authorities that exist have been established by God. Consequently, whoever rebels against the authority is rebelling against what God has instituted, and those who do so will bring judgment on themselves. For rulers hold no terror for those who do right, but for those who do wrong. Do you want to be free from fear of the one in authority? Then do what is right and you will be commended. For the one in authority is God's servant for your good. But if you do wrong, be afraid, for rulers do not bear the sword for no reason. They are God's servants, agents of wrath to bring punishment on the wrongdoer. Therefore, it is necessary to submit to the authorities, not only because of possible punishment but also as a matter of conscience.

Living in the United States, I know this is a passage that many Westerners may choose to conveniently ignore, but, from my own experience, whether you're in Sudan, Bosnia, New York City, or anywhere else attempting to serve people, you must recognize authority. And as I had learned in Afghanistan, if there are guys with guns, it's a good idea if they're your friends. Because men with guns represent authority, I'm going to talk to them in a respectful way and treat them like human beings.

Food airdrop for famine response in Sudan

The soldiers took us from Maridi to a place called Kotobi, where the Episcopal Church of Sudan had a compound. There, I met Reverend Geoffrey Kayanga, a man who would teach me two random but unforgettable points of knowledge. First, I learned more from him than I ever did at school about the US Constitution. Second, he showed me how to recognize a satellite in the night sky. The reverend called it "watching Sudan TV" as we would sit in the darkness, amid the sounds of all sorts of wild creatures in the bush, intently scanning the sky filled with what appeared to be millions of stars. Suddenly, he would point up and excitedly say, "There's one, Ken! See it? See that one star that looks like it's moving? That's a satellite!" My eyes would follow his outstretched arm and finger until I saw a small, steady, bright light moving slowly across the sky.

Another man I met who would prove to be vital to our mission there was Scopus Lunjin, the area representative for the South Sudan Relief Agency, the government entity that coordinated humanitarian interventions. (I use the word *coordinated* loosely, simply because they were doing the best they could with limited resources.) I began to hear Scopus and Geoffrey talk about a place that had just been liberated from the GOS by the SPLA. They said there was an old, abandoned missionary hospital in a town called Lui. Intrigued about the potential of a place someone had once deemed a good spot for medical care, I asked if we could go there.

After Scopus had made the arrangements, we began our drive over the dirt roads. I had yet to see anything paved or even graded. Passing through many of the small villages and towns, we saw only mud huts. On our drive to Lui, when we got to Mundri at the Yei River, the men wanted to make a stop. Pulling up to a building, Scopus led us inside where he introduced me to a man named Baxter, who called himself a nurse medic, although I had no idea of his medical training. He took us to an area where he was treating thirty to forty men who were bleeding and wounded from battle injuries.

Surveying the obvious suffering in the room, I said to Baxter, "Please tell me what's going on here." In desperate frustration, he called out, "We have nothing! Nothing!" I noticed that he was washing out bloody gauze and hanging it outside on bush limbs to dry. Because they had no more, he was reusing it. The scene was heartbreaking. Since this was only an assessment trip for us, we had brought no supplies to leave with them. But seeing the conditions here told me we needed to try to find a way to bring help to this area as soon as possible.

Leaving there, we had to cross the river. The bridge had been blown up as a defensive move to keep the government of Sudan from coming to the other side. As in much of Africa, rivers in South Sudan have high and low seasons. This was in May, normally the low season, but there was still more than five feet of water at the deepest point. In addition to challenges like crossing the river, we had to deal with extreme heat as each day of our trip reached 110 degrees Fahrenheit. Taking our only way forward, as we drove into the river, because the truck had no top, I moved to the back, reached up to grab a roll bar and pulled myself up as high as I could to try to stay dry. Even though the chassis was several feet off the ground, the water was washing in and rising higher on the floorboard.

Fortunately, we soon began to come up on the other bank, and the water started receding from the truck. Back on dry ground, we had thirteen very long miles to go at our maximum speed of twenty miles per hour. There were also huge potholes and washouts in the road that we had to constantly navigate around. I had no idea at the time that there were land mines planted throughout the area. That's the kind of information it's hard to know if you really want to find out in advance or not. As the old saying goes, "Ignorance is bliss."

Following in the Footsteps of Faith

Surviving the drive, we finally arrived in Lui. While we were told there were about a hundred people left in the village, it felt abandoned. I never saw more than a dozen people the entire time we were there. There were only four abandoned structures—a girls' boarding school, the old missionary hospital that looked more like a large hut, a church, and a house that had been used as a military command post by the GOS. Tall elephant grass surrounded these structures. You could tell the church by its steeple, rising up through the vegetation.

Just past the house, the SPLA had a deep defensive trench dug with a large recoilless rifle still in place. Looking over into the trench, I saw the bodies of soldiers still lying right where they had been killed. We were also warned that there were land mines all around the area. Lui had only been liberated and reclaimed in the past ten days, so that news explained the absence of people.

Near the church, I found the very simple, humble headstone of Kenneth Fraser, a doctor from Scotland who had come to Lui with his wife, Eileen, in the early 1920s and died on January 10, 1935. Below his name and a cross, an inscription read, "He preached unto them Jesus." What an amazing legacy for any of us to leave on this earth. (There is a book about him called *The Doctor Comes to Lui*.)

After the Frasers arrived, he engaged with some of the locals to help him build a simple house. During construction, the tribal chief's wife was attacked by a lion and was barely alive. They brought the woman to Dr. Fraser as his very first patient, and he prayed for God's help and healing because, if she died, this would gravely affect his ability to help the people, as well as their response to the Gospel. He was able to save her life. One interesting detail in the story was that when he used chloroform as an anesthetic, the people thought when she later woke up that he had resurrected the chief's wife from the dead. God's blessing allowed Dr. Fraser to quickly gain favor with the people to start treating patients, and they eventually built the large hut we could still see that acted as his makeshift hospital. Between 1921 and 1934, the Frasers documented 41,000 patients.[2]

A couple of hundred feet away, I could see the thatched roof of the old hospital, which, like the church, had elephant grass ten to fifteen feet high all around it. I was warned not to go near

Lui, May 1997

that area because of the likelihood of land mines. Hearing the stories of Dr. Fraser's work, seeing the hospital where he served, and reading the inscription on his headstone, I felt like something very special had been revealed to me. I sensed I had been entrusted as a follower of Christ to once again make an investment here in Lui.

After being in South Sudan for about a week, we had to travel back to Maridi to meet Curtis at the landing strip. But before leaving Lui, I met with Reverend Geoffrey and Scopus under the shade of a large tree to discuss the great needs we had witnessed from the effects of the war and to evaluate how Samaritan's Purse could most effectively serve the people. As is often the case in so many places like this, the immediate need was to treat the injured to try to save lives. With Geoffrey in agreement, Scopus asked, "We would love for you to please come and reopen a hospital here. Would you consider this?"

The abandoned girls' boarding school had classrooms and bunk rooms. While there was no furniture left, the space would work well. We made the decision that this building would be the best suited to convert to a hospital. But before any refurbishment could begin, we would have to have the surrounding area de-mined. I told them that as soon as I got back home, I would ask Franklin if this was something he felt we could effectively take on and, if so, when we could start. I promised to let them know as soon as possible.

Ken with Mike VanRooyen, Lui, May 1998

Back home in Boone, I told Franklin all about my experiences in South Sudan, emphasizing my time in Lui and what I had learned and witnessed about the work of Dr. Kenneth Fraser, the missionary. I told him about Geoffrey and Scopus's request to open a hospital. Franklin knew me well enough to know that on the way home I would have come up with a proposal for how to make this work.

He asked, "So, what are you thinking?"

"We open two wards, one male and one female, thirty beds in each for ninety days."

"What do you think that's going to cost us?"

Having calculated my itemized estimations on a table napkin, I responded, "I think we can do it for $100,000."

Franklin gave the go-ahead to begin what we knew would be a long process.

I'm Trying to Help

Upon my return to Lui, the area around the hospital project was being de-mined when a device exploded, seriously injuring a man named Morris. Doug Crockett from Canada was helping me at the time. Hearing the explosion, Doug and I ran to Morris to get him to the hospital. His leg had to be amputated, and then it had to be cut shorter because of the growing infection. Sadly, he contracted lockjaw, the only case I have ever seen, and died in the operating room. Not long before he passed, he told me, "Ken, I'm a believer in Christ, and I know where I'm going when I die." I will always remember Morris for his bravery and calm demeanor in the face of such a horrible death.

When we completed the conversion of the boarding school to the hospital, there were about one hundred beds with two operating rooms. We had designated October 20, 1997, as the day of dedication for the facility. As we were getting ready that morning, a troop of soldiers made up of three hundred of the best-trained, best-dressed, most heavily armed SPLA fighters I had ever seen came through Lui. They were led by General Pyiang Deng, who had decided to come take a look at what we were doing. After we were introduced, I made it clear to the general that even though this was not a military hospital, he could bring his wounded troops to us and we would treat them. But also, after taking notice that his armed soldiers hovered around him at all times, acting as a very serious personal security detail, I told him that I never wanted anyone to bring a gun into our compound.

That's when I had an idea. I said to General Pyiang, "Today is the day we were going to open the hospital. Would you like to cut the ribbon as we dedicate the facility to God's glory?"

Understanding that I was honoring his authority, he answered, "Yes, Ken, I would like that."

As General Pyiang started to walk through our gate, he stopped. He looked at his men and said, "Half of you put your guns down here and come inside with me. The others stay out here." He heard and respected what I had said about the guns. He set the precedent from that day forward that no weapons were allowed in the compound. We never had to enforce that rule ourselves. In fact, someone painted a small sign and hung it on the wall that read: "No smoke. No gun. No arrow." That creed, which still hangs in the hospital today, became the law of the land.

Lui became yet another place in the world that displayed the platform of our witness and the quality of our work. Before opening the hospital, I had bought supplies in Uganda and Kenya that we had shipped in containers over land routes. There were a lot of stories of surviving battles, rescuing people, and seeing God's hand at work in amazing ways. One such situation was a night that Mike VanRooyen, Doug Crockett, Baxter Kayanga, and I drove from Lui to Tindalo to pick up three wounded female civilians from an aerial bombardment.

After we arrived, although we searched, we never located the women, but we did discover some injured soldiers. Back at the hospital in Lui, like always, with no hesitation at all as to who they were or what side they were on, Mike began treating the wounded soldiers. He consistently lived out the story of the Good Samaritan. If his actions could speak, they would say, "Hey, look, this wounded person is a human being. Injured or shot, no matter who he or she is, I'm going to help." Yet another example of word and deed finding balance. Watching Mike jump in to save anyone in need has always stayed with me.

In my work, I came to learn that the Geneva Convention was created for the purpose of treating wounded combatants. Henri Dunant, a young evangelical Christian, had organized the convention in 1864. He did so after writing a book called *A Memory of Solferino*. The bottom line is, in war zones, any wounded combatant is a patient, a protected class of people. (Dunant is considered a cofounder of the Red Cross and won a Nobel Peace Prize in 1901.)[3] There is a similar dynamic within law enforcement in the United States that says after a police officer shoots an offender, he or she must then stop and render aid to try to save a life. This is the same principle—the combatant becomes a patient.

Another lesson came on that trip to Tindalo. On the way back that night with six wounded guys in the back of our vehicle, at one o'clock in the morning as we came up over a rise, we saw a truck stuck in a steep anti-tank trench. There were at least eighty Sudanese pushing on it. The problem was that half of them were pushing on the front and the other half were pushing on the back, unknowingly working against each other.

I got out, walked over to the truck, and, ignoring them all, knelt down to look underneath. Right away, I saw the issue. The truck was high-centered, meaning the middle of the frame at the bottom was sitting on the ground. I started digging out the slimy, sludgy

John Garang and Ken at New Site, 1999

mud underneath with my hands. As I was down in the muck, somebody tugged at my shirt, and I heard a Sudanese voice ask, "What are you doing?"

Without stopping, I simply stated the obvious, "I'm digging your truck out."

He reached down, grabbed a big handful of my shirt, and pulled me up so that I was looking him in the eye. In a much more aggressive tone, he stated, "No! I'm asking you what are you doing! You are in a war zone in the middle of the night. You are laying in the mud, *and* you're not from here. *What* are you doing?!"

Without flinching, I repeated, "I told you. I'm trying to help you get your truck out."

In that strange encounter, that man and I had a moment of clarity and communication. When he saw I couldn't possibly have any agenda other than to help, we actually ended up becoming friends. Turned out he was a senior official in the SPLA hierarchy, a relationship that would be advantageous later, one that God would use to open other doors, one that, had I not stopped to help, we would never have realized.

Ken helping a wounded soldier, Tindalo, 1997

In our years at Lui, we treated people who suffered from animal attacks, snake bites, tropical diseases, and various illnesses and injuries. As I have told you at the close of every chapter about every world crisis where we became involved, God blessed us in so many ways that we didn't anticipate or couldn't have predicted when all we were trying to do was be faithful to His call.

In 2007, we had to pull our team out of the hospital due to an increase in violence and turn it over to the Sudanese staff. While all the local tribes respected us for how we helped the people, the fighting was reaching a point where we could no longer risk someone getting hurt or killed. Over time, we significantly expanded the existing hospital incrementally as a series of additions, ending up with around 150 to 170 beds. We also added a lab, a chapel, and a patient waiting area. The hospital continues to this day, but at a much lower level of medical care staffed by local practitioners. Over the years, we have maintained a supply chain of materials going to them—evidence that the hospital in Lui is still very much a part of Samaritan's Purse's legacy in Sudan.

As we came out of our work there, God opened more doors for us. We established special relationships with people such as Dr. John Garang, the leader of the independent movement for South Sudan. Later, Franklin, Gary Lundstrom, and I were invited to meet multiple times with President Omar al-Bashir in Khartoum, a city that was heavily sanctioned and declared a state sponsor of terrorism. At the consistent urging of Franklin, President George W. Bush joined the effort to end the war between the north and the south. Dr. Bill Frist, who was also a senator, and Dr. Richard Furman, the cofounder of World Medical Mission, went there with us many times to treat patients. All these vital relationships opened doors for us that continue to allow Samaritan's Purse to minister in South Sudan today.

One of the major accomplishments there and in the Nuba Mountains was the reconstruction of 514 churches that had been destroyed by the government of Sudan during the Islamist attacks. About 120 of those churches were built in the mountains, where the people truly are free to worship and speak their minds. But, unfortunately, that is an oasis of peace in a desert of cruelty. While the rebuilding of those churches took six years to carry out, we saw new energy and encouragement in the spiritual blessings of every one of those communities.

As It Is in Heaven

Through my experience in South Sudan, I learned the valuable lesson of going where needs exist, not necessarily where permissions enable. There are times when, as Christians, we will be called to *go* to the *no-go* zones, to run to the fire, whether across the globe, across town, or across the room. When we read the Gospels and survey the life of Jesus, He consistently looked beyond the limitations and boundaries that the Pharisees, Sadducees, and the culture had set and ventured into the no-go zones of His day. Healing on the Sabbath, talking to the woman at the well, having dinner in the homes of "sinners," and, as a rabbi, washing His own disciples' feet are great examples of how He didn't just push the boundaries but blew completely past them. Why? To "love the Lord your God" and "love your neighbor as yourself" (Matt. 22:37, 39). Each time I came to the realization of lessons such as these, I committed to them as principles to live by and conducted myself accordingly.

Over my first decade of working in various nations of the world, the places where I witnessed the kingdoms of this earth meet the Kingdom of God, I saw there are actually no dividing lines between the secular and the sacred. To God, everything He created and ordained is sacred. As we go into all nations in His authority, we should treat people with respect and dignity because they have been fashioned in His image, which is exactly the way the Good Samaritan treated the wounded man. That also means there is no division between humanitarian and ministry aspects. Again, word and deed together.

Governor Malik Agar of Southern Blue Nile and Governor Abdul Aziz la Hilu in the Nuba Mountains, 2000

For Samaritan's Purse, when we have responded to a need in the world, God has granted us access, and then, by helping people, by being transparent, by being honest, by being responsive and fulfilling our commitments, we have earned respect from the people and His name has been glorified.

With what shall I come before the LORD
    and bow down before the exalted God?...
Will the LORD be pleased with thousands of rams,
    with ten thousand rivers of olive oil?...
He has shown you, O mortal, what is good.
    And what does the LORD require of you?
To act justly and to love mercy
    and to walk humbly with your God. (Mic. 6:6–8)

Lui Hospital. 1997

My Seventeen-Month Detour through Washington, DC

In February 2003, I received a call from Roger Winter, who was being promoted to assistant administrator of the Bureau for Democracy, Conflict, and Humanitarian Assistance, the agency containing the humanitarian response assets of the United States Agency for International Development (USAID). Roger was leaving the Office of Foreign Disaster Assistance and asked if I would consider taking over the role.

I talked about Roger in the previous chapter, but I had been introduced to him in 1997 when I needed to connect with someone in Washington about South Sudan. Surprised at Roger's call, I realized the honor of being considered for the prestigious position. After a visit to Washington to discuss the details with Andrew Natsios, the administrator of USAID, as well as much thought and prayer, I turned him down. But, two months later, the offer came back a second time. While Franklin was supportive, he expressed he didn't want me to leave. Eventually, Carolyn and I came to a peace about accepting the offer, a huge step of faith for us to leave family and friends in Boone.

After obtaining the necessary security clearance, on August 15, 2004, I began my new job. Keeping our place in Boone, we bought a townhome in

Alexandria, Virginia. During my service in Washington, the only domestic disaster I was involved with was Hurricane Katrina, specifically the devastating flood in New Orleans. Part of my responsibility was to regularly brief Secretary of State Condoleezza Rice with updates. Along with the always exemplary work of the US military, many at USAID, the Federal Emergency Management Agency (FEMA), and the State Department gave their heroic and tireless efforts to the victims of Hurricane Katrina.

I took the lead in the United States' humanitarian assistance inside Sudan, making multiple trips there. In December of 2004, I was involved with the US's response to the tsunami that killed 225,000 people in Indonesia, Sri Lanka, India, Maldives, and Thailand.[1] I worked closely with the Department of Defense, State Department, and National Security Council and developed a great working relationship with then Brigadier General John Allen (who later became a four-star general), as these entities impacted hundreds of thousands of people.

Tsunami relief supplies, Jakarta Airport, 2005

That said, I soon learned that Washington, DC, is complicated, diluted, and highly inefficient. While I understood politics and complex power struggles, I wasn't prepared for the politicization of humanitarian response. I would define modern politics as the competition for power and influence, from the White House down to the interns. Life is about competition for budget and resources. There may be a nice, neat flowchart on paper, yet, often, there are few clear lines of authority.

Secretary of State Colin Powell briefing embassy staff with Jeb Bush, Jakarta, Indonesia

By the end of August 2005, with Carolyn standing within earshot, I called Franklin and said, "I feel like I need to come back to Samaritan's Purse." He responded, "Well, then, come on back." Hanging up the phone, I sensed peace flood back into my heart. Carolyn was ecstatic because, for a while, she had wanted to go home to Boone.

In January of 2006, back at Samaritan's Purse, I realized that Washington was absolutely God's will to give me a detour to learn, grow, and expand my knowledge and experience for His glory along with the greater benefit to others. When I resigned at Samaritan's Purse, I was the International Director of Projects. When Franklin and I talked, we decided my new position, the one I still have today, would be Vice President of Programs and Government Relations. I put to use everything I had learned in Washington, improving our response to crises around the world. I had gained an inside perspective on governmental processes and figured out how we could adapt those. For example, I learned the acronym DART—disaster assistance response team. We could create and engage a DART for any need, from a famine to one of Franklin's events, providing management from our headquarters while deploying teams in the field.

Today, we have approximately 2,700 people on our DART roster with roughly 50 percent being medical personnel, including surgeons, doctors, and nurses, as well as those who can set up and operate an emergency field hospital. The other 50 percent include administrators, finance personnel, logisticians, and operations personnel, among others. Our Operation Christmas Child office has 400,000 volunteers annually with 3,500 of those being full-time. Our North American Ministries office has 12,000 to 15,000 volunteers involved in projects like building churches in Alaska or homes after tornadoes and hurricanes and working with wounded vets in Operation Heal Our Patriots.

If you're interested in becoming involved in a Samaritan's Purse DART, I invite you to reach out to us because, if we don't have mobilized ministers like you, we simply cannot do what we are called to do. Whatever you do for a living, whatever skills or gifts you may have, we have a way you can serve. Whether you contact us or not, please accept my challenge to find your place where God wants you to serve Him and minister to people in His name.

I tell you the truth, anyone who believes in me will do the same works I have done, and even greater works, because I am going to be with the Father. (John 14:12 NLT)

To learn more about how to join our DART roster,
scan the QR code with your smartphone:

Jane Graham, Franklin Graham, Ken Isaacs, President George H. W. Bush, Barbara Bush, Carolyn Isaacs, President Jimmy Carter

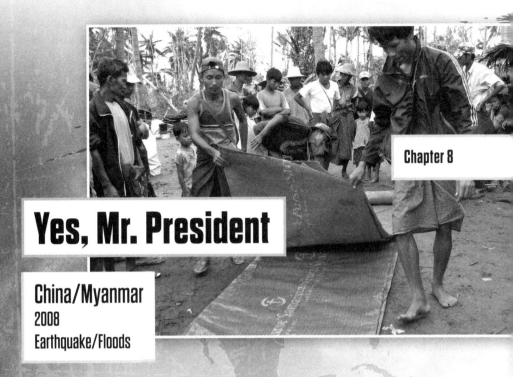

Chapter 8

Yes, Mr. President

China/Myanmar
2008
Earthquake/Floods

On May 12, 2008, a magnitude 7.9 earthquake hit southwestern China with the epicenter in Sichuan. Eighty percent of the structures in that region were flattened, causing 90,000 people to die or be declared missing; 375,000 were injured in collapses or by falling debris. Millions were displaced and homeless.[1] The destruction of the roads caused many of the remote villages in the mountains to be impossible to reach.

Only ten days before this earthquake, on May 2, Cyclone Nargis caused a severe flood in Myanmar (known as Burma until 1989). Twelve-foot walls of water accelerated by high winds surged through villages. In the Irrawaddy Delta, an estimated 138,000 people were killed or declared missing.[2] In the same region of the world, two massive disasters struck that literally impacted millions upon millions of people.

Providentially, at the time, Franklin was in China speaking at a series of engagements, back when the nation was more open to religious activities than it is today. Immediately following the earthquake, Franklin called me. Realizing the severity of the tragedy in China and also talking about the devastating floods in Myanmar, we made the decision to respond to both disasters as soon as we could pull the resources together.

After receiving the contact information for a senior diplomat from the government in Myanmar who was stationed in the US, I went to visit him. (I am intentionally withholding his name and location to protect his identity.) He was very welcoming, gracious, and kind, clearly wanting to help Samaritan's Purse help his people. Historically, politics in this nation has been extremely hard-edged and complicated with those involved being wary of one another. After giving me the names and numbers of about a dozen people, he told me there was a way to receive a visa upon arrival.

Cyclone Nargis damage, Irrawaddy Delta, Myanmar, 2008

Calling the numbers, I was able to reach someone in Myanmar. He was very suspicious and direct with his questions, asking, "Why are you coming?" "What is your purpose here?" and "Why do you not get a visa in Bangkok like others?" I explained that we were coming to bring relief supplies to the people in Irrawaddy, distributing them in cooperation with local partners. Confirming what the diplomat had said, the official told me they would give us visas upon arrival.

With seven tons of relief supplies, after touching down in Yangon, we were told to wait in the airplane. After about an hour, they allowed me to go into the airport to speak with the immigration staff. Right away, they said we would need to leave because we didn't have our visas. Politely, I informed them that I had spoken with a senior member of the government who told me and my coworker that we would be given visas on arrival. After another two hours, the immigration official came out and gruffly told me we would get our visas.

The reason I'm sharing this story is because the list of names given to me by the senior diplomat proved to be very helpful to the successful completion of our relief mission. To this day, I believe that Myanmar diplomat I spoke to in the US was a Christian and there is some sort of secret society in the government there that is supportive of Christianity. Regardless, I'm thankful, once again, that God put someone in my path to open the necessary doors to carry on our mission and ministry.

We had already formed a DART to respond to Cyclone Nargis that was in Bangkok procuring emergency supplies to send to Myanmar. We then formed a second DART with a plan to respond with a chartered 747 loaded with emergency relief supplies from our US warehouse, including plastic tarps, water purification equipment, cooking pots and pans, and blankets for China. As that plane was being readied to leave, I took a commercial flight to Bangkok and met with our DART there. We developed our plans, and, after chartering a Russian cargo plane and locating the necessary suppliers, we bought the same types of items to fly into Myanmar that we were taking into China.

Arriving in the Irrawaddy Delta, we were able to partner with local churches. We ended up sending seven planes there with each one carrying seven to eight tons of emergency supplies. After setting up a distribution network, we were able to quickly help many thousands of people by delivering necessities to them. Seeing that all our systems were up and running there, I left Myanmar, flew back to Bangkok, and then on to Sichuan, China, where I met the first DART that had just recently arrived from the US. On my first trip to China in 1997, I had found the people to be very open, surprisingly warm, and friendly, so I knew the sort of welcome we would receive.

The first night we stayed in a modest hotel in Sichuan where my room was on the sixth floor of a twelve-story building. Right after I checked in, a

6.6 magnitude aftershock occurred. I could hear people screaming, running out of their rooms and down the hallways. Everyone was trying to get out of the building for fear it would collapse. I distinctly remember the drapes over the windows in my room swinging at least a foot from side to side. But I was so exhausted from severe jet lag that I decided I would just sleep. I remember thinking to myself, *I'm not going to run. I don't think the building's going to fall. And if it does, I'm ready to go.*

The next day, as we began to explore the devastation, we met volunteer teams from various Baptist groups serving there. I recall people from Texas, Mississippi, and Tennessee. The leader of our team was Mark Eller, who at that time was reporting to me as our Director of Projects. Our team, along with Mark and me, drove far up into the mountains to the earthquake epicenter zone where we witnessed so much destruction and chaos. At Hanwang, we saw what would become an iconic landmark after the earthquake—a five-story clock tower whose hands stopped right at the moment the disaster struck—2:27 p.m.[3]

Because the majority of buildings had collapsed, there were literally thousands of people sitting around on the ground. There was a different level of danger in the mountains because aftershocks could also cause huge rockslides. Using my background, I began putting the water filtration units together. When the people realized we were going to help produce clean water, they were thrilled with us.

Fortunately, the Chinese government provided us with unhindered access to the survivors, allowing our planes into their country. From a diplomatic relations and humanitarian standpoint, everything went extremely well. I was also able to meet some Chinese Christians who had driven to the epicenter in their own vehicles from other parts of the country to help. They had several carloads of Chinese Bibles to distribute. The degree of outreach they showed inspired me as they didn't simply share God's Word but also provided supplies, like blankets, food, and pots and pans. In a disaster of that magnitude, certain basic necessities are needed, such as items for preparing food, something to carry water in, tarps, and blankets. I continually saw supplies like these arriving spontaneously from the population.

Have You Been There?

Just after I got back home, a friend who was the humanitarian adviser on the National Security Council for President Bush called to ask, "Hey, Ken, would you like to come to Washington and take part in briefing the president on the response to the earthquake in China? We're going to hold the event at the Red Cross International Headquarters, just down the street from the White

House." Although I was very nervous, I agreed to go. The date was less than a week away, and this would be my first time meeting the president.

The day before I left for Washington, my friend called to inform me, "Hey, Ken, I just want to let you know that you're going to be one of four people called on to make comments and remarks to President Bush. An aide will bring you a note to make this request a few minutes before the president comes in the room, but I wanted to give you a heads-up now so you can be thinking about what you may want to share."

Relief food for Cyclone Nargis victims

I thanked him for his thoughtfulness to tell me that the next day I was scheduled to speak with the president of the United States! As I mentioned previously, I had briefed Condoleezza Rice during my stint as the director of the Office of Foreign Disaster Assistance, but this was clearly another level up. I immediately went into panic mode as I had no idea what I would say. As my thoughts began to race, my brain was screaming, *Incoming! Incoming!* and all my internal anxiety alarms were going off. Even though I had walked into a lot of rooms to speak with or negotiate with men who could end my life with one word, the idea of speaking to the president of my own country felt very different, invoking a sense of panic in me.

When I arrived in Washington, a car picked me up to take me to the Red Cross building. When I entered the large conference room, I saw there were fifty-plus people there. President Bush's entire cabinet was present with the secretaries of the various governmental departments. Sitting next to me was the deputy CEO of Chevron. One of Bush's cabinet members led the first part of the meeting, which lasted about an hour and a half. That time allowed everyone to share their experiences about China and get to know one another. Just as my friend had said, an aide walked into the room, came straight over, and gave me a handwritten note that said:

Ken:

When the President arrives, you will be called on to talk about what Samaritan's Purse has done in response. Please keep your comments under 2 minutes.

Thank you.

When President Bush finally entered the room, he went around the table to meet each one of us. As I shook his hand, I found him to be a very pleasant, easygoing guy. Regardless of your political leanings, back then, our presidents had a larger-than-life "it factor" about them. There was a presence about Bush I could sense right away. When I told him I was with Samaritan's Purse, he asked, "How's Billy doing?" (referring to Reverend Graham).

"Well, he's doing pretty good, Mr. President. He's getting on in years, but he's doing well." (Remember, this was 2008.)

President Bush smiled and responded, "All right, well, you tell Franklin I said hello."

Community well, Irrawaddy Peninsula, 2008

"I will, sir."

Turning to walk to his seat, he stopped, turned back around, looked at me, and said, "You tell Franklin I haven't forgotten about South Sudan." I was amazed at his memory and the connection he made so quickly after having just met so many people.

As the president called on the first of the four that had been asked to speak, the head of the US Chamber of Commerce, Bush asked, "Have *you* been to China? Do you have any Americans there?" His answer was no.

The second person called on was a representative for Habitat for Humanity.

Again, the president asked, "Have *you* been to China? Do you have any Americans there?" The answer was, "No, sir, but we're going there as soon as possible."

By this point, as my turn was coming up, I felt like the walls were closing in on me. For many years, I have had a natural tremor in my left hand. A doctor told me it was nothing to be concerned about, so I've just had to learn to live with it. But, when I get nervous, the shaking gets worse, and, as a lefty, I can't even read what I've written when my hand is shaking like that. Attempting to jot down notes, while listening carefully to the others' comments, I asked myself, *What am I going to say?!* Glancing down at what I had just written with my shaking hand, I couldn't even read my notes.

But then that's when the thought hit me with great clarity. I was the only one in the room who had been on the ground in China to witness the devastation that the president had invited us all into this room to discuss. Samaritan's Purse *did* have Americans there, and I *could* speak firsthand from my experience of the past few days. I didn't need to figure out what to say to him; I just needed to give him straightforward answers.

When Bush called on me to speak, to head off the questions I knew he had, I stated, "Mr. President, I have just come back from China. I have fourteen Americans there right now. So I would like to share my observations with you." Immediately, he leaned in and focused with great interest, then soon began asking penetrating questions: "Where were you?" "What did you see?" "What's going on there?" "What can the United States do to help?" "What's Samaritan's Purse's plan?"

To one of his questions about the severity of the aftermath, I answered based on some restaurant-napkin calculations that my team and I had compiled after talking with hundreds of people in China. I told the president, "There's a school of thought on the ground there that the homeless population could be as high as 15 million people."

After the president had thanked me for sharing my information, I glanced up at the clock in the room. He had talked to me for well over ten minutes, far beyond the aide's requested maximum of two minutes. After speaking briefly with the fourth person, Bush gave his closing comments, stating to his advisers and the NGO leaders that he wanted to help the Chinese people. His words were very positive and affirming of how he hoped the US could build on its relationship with China.

After he had finished speaking, a group of reporters was ushered into a roped-off area across from the conference table. When President Bush was asked by a reporter for a statement about the earthquake in China, he shared, "I've received information today that makes us think the earthquake may have caused as many as 15 million people to be homeless there." Hearing the president give the information I had just told him was very surreal. I couldn't believe it. But, immediately, I thought, *Oh my goodness, talk about the power of words! You have to be really careful what you say. Especially in a room like this. I had no idea I would be indirectly quoted to the press!*

Today, on the wall in my office, I have a framed photograph of that moment when I met President Bush for the first time. We're both smiling as we shook hands. Above the picture is a signed letter from him on White House stationery with the gold presidential seal that reads (in the exact wording and spacing):

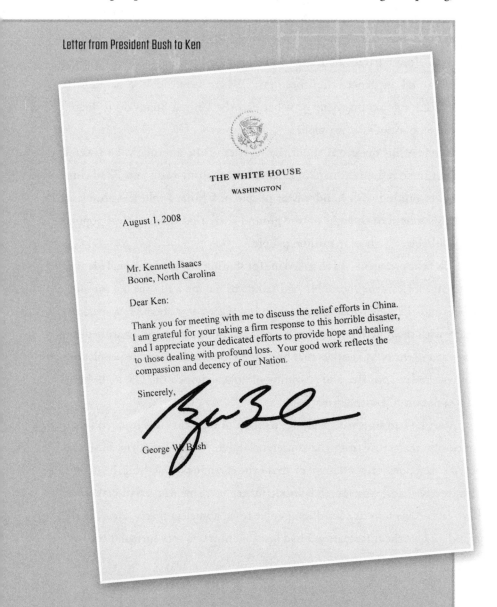

Letter from President Bush to Ken

THE WHITE HOUSE
WASHINGTON

August 1, 2008

Mr. Kenneth Isaacs
Boone, North Carolina

Dear Ken:

Thank you for meeting with me to discuss the relief efforts in China. I am grateful for your taking a firm response to this horrible disaster, and I appreciate your dedicated efforts to provide hope and healing to those dealing with profound loss. Your good work reflects the compassion and decency of our Nation.

Sincerely,

George W. Bush

On the back of the frame, I taped the note from the aide that included, "Please keep your comments under 2 minutes."

About two weeks later, I received an invitation to a reception at the embassy of China. They asked if I would give a fifteen-minute speech, and I accepted. At the event, there were more than four hundred people in the room. I had the privilege of talking for almost a half hour with Lieutenant General Jack Panter, whom General Allen had introduced me to in 2005. At that time in 2008, I was warmly received at the embassy, even while speaking as a Christian from a humanitarian perspective. In my speech, I expressed appreciation for how China had graciously opened its doors to allow us to help their people during a time of such tragedy and suffering. Today, the relationship with China is much more tense and the country is closed to Christian organizations.

A Time to Weep, a Time to Laugh

To close with a positive example of my experience with the people I met following the earthquake, as I walked through the streets, I saw thousands milling around everywhere. Trying to avoid going inside any structures because of the aftershocks and fear of collapse, people were cooking pots of food on the sidewalks, in the roads, and in the dirt. As I talked with a crowd of people through an interpreter, someone brought me some soup.

Looking into the bowl, I could see there were some tiny, round, wrinkly bits, smaller than a blueberry, in the broth. (They're called Sichuan peppercorns, and they are a mainstay spice used in cooking in that region.) What I didn't know and hadn't been told was that when you bite into one of those peppercorns, the juice released in your mouth creates a numbing effect, similar to getting an injection of novocaine, that lasts about two minutes. As soon as I bit into one, part of my mouth went numb. When I began to drool some broth out of the corner of my mouth, the people that had gathered around to watch my reaction were howling, laughing at me.

While I was the recipient of their inside joke, moments like that one were special amid a people who had suffered a great tragedy, and most of them had no idea when their lives would be able to return to normal again. Just as I had experienced in so many other parts of the world, whether we were providing clean water, medical care, or food or sharing laughter, I knew the reason I was there and Samaritan's Purse had responded. Governments and politicians may be hostile toward one another, but when people are in great need, anyone who is willing to help can become a friend.

Looking at his disciples, he said:

> "Blessed are you who are poor,
>> for yours is the kingdom of God.
> Blessed are you who hunger now,
>> for you will be satisfied.
> Blessed are you who weep now,
>> for you will laugh." (Luke 6:20–21)

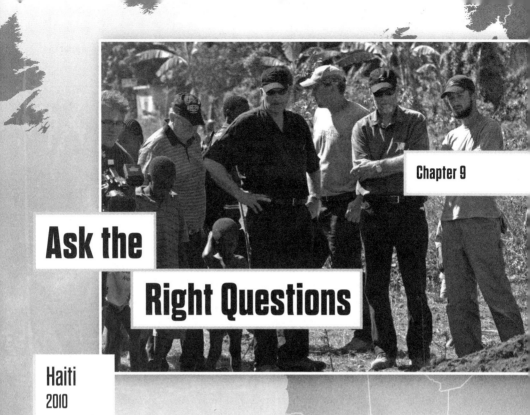

Chapter 9

Ask the

Right Questions

Haiti
2010
Earthquake

Disclaimer: This chapter describes some graphic scenes of deaths and injuries. As in the chapter on Rwanda, my goal was to balance being honest about the devastation while being cautious in describing the horror of human suffering I witnessed.

After leaving work on January 12, 2010, I went to the gym. While I was running on a treadmill, the TV mounted closest to me was on CNN. Suddenly, a breaking news report caught my attention as I saw video clips of chaos and destruction. The anchor stated that at 4:53 p.m. eastern standard time, a magnitude 7.0 earthquake struck Haiti with the epicenter being fifteen miles southwest of the heavily populated capital of Port-au-Prince.[1] (Haiti shares the island of Hispaniola with the Dominican Republic, about seven hundred miles southeast of Florida.)

While I knew the devastation a 7.0 earthquake causes, the TV report showed collapsed buildings and smoke coming up out of piles of debris. Moved by those images, I jumped off the treadmill, ran to the locker room, grabbed my clothes and bag, and sprinted to my car. Because the gym is only about a mile from our office, I was back there within minutes. Not long after I arrived, everyone on our team who worked directly with me had also heard the news and began to show up. The looks on their faces revealed that they, too, understood the severity of the tragedy.

Immediately, we began organizing a DART and getting ready for Samaritan's Purse's response. Even though at that time we didn't have the infrastructure we do today, we were able to get a team on the ground in Haiti within twenty-four hours. We coordinated with Mission Flights International to schedule transportation with their DC-3s.

Stephan Tchividjian, Billy's grandson and Franklin's nephew, called me and said, "Ken, I've located a campground that houses visiting church groups that come to Haiti to do mission work. I think you might be able to rent the camp." Right away, I got in touch with Global Outreach, a missionary agency that gave me the contact information for the camp. After reaching the manager in Haiti, he told me there were sixty-six acres with a fenced compound around several houses including a dormitory-style building with a cafeteria. Other than a couple of missionary families' homes, Samaritan's Purse rented the entire facility for a full year. Besides using it to house and feed our team, we also stored huge quantities of supplies there. Fortunately, we already had quite a few existing relationships with NGOs in Haiti. The primary medical mission group we had worked with there was called Baptist Haiti Mission. We were able to place doctors right away to do trauma surgery.

After landing at the airport in Port-au-Prince and driving into the city, I was immediately struck by the massive crowds of people everywhere. The chaos was disorienting. Having spent so many years in dozens of countries in Africa and arriving in so many places right after a natural disaster had occurred, while

I recognized the poverty I was seeing, I was also trying to discern how much of it was normal and how much was caused by the earthquake.

As we drove into the city, we saw that the crowds of the living were displaced by the stark reality of the number of dead. We saw dozens of dump trucks lined up, loaded with the bodies of people who had been crushed, being transported and dumped into massive holes dug out by excavators. The scene was like something from the apocalypse, and to this day, those images are still vividly burned into my memory.

Surveying the devastation, the thing I wanted to know was what was in the minds of the survivors. What were *they* thinking? On the way to Baptist Haiti Mission, we went through the most impoverished and densely populated area of Port-au-Prince called Cité Soleil, considered to be one of the most dangerous places in the Western Hemisphere because of gangs. I noticed that the walls of a compound surrounding a church had fallen down, and I felt like I needed to stop. Looking around, I found the pastor, Leon Dorleans, and told him I wanted to hire at least two dozen people who could work together. I asked if he could help me, and he agreed.

Back on the road, after we arrived at the mission, the extent of the deaths and injuries the earthquake had caused became clear. Homes and buildings everywhere had suddenly collapsed, crushing those inside. Because of the poverty and the economy, the majority of structures are not built to withstand an earthquake. One thing I learned later was that the sand most often used in Haitian concrete has a very high level of salt, which causes corrosion on the rebar inside the concrete, creating structural weakness.

The injuries we witnessed were absolutely horrific. The doctors and surgeons were amputating limbs to try to save lives. The bodies of those pulled out of the wreckage and those who had been killed from debris that fell onto their cars were as shocking and grisly as anything I had ever witnessed in any disaster. The horror there reminded me of Rwanda, but a major difference was the Rwandans were silent because they were traumatized by what they had done or had been done to them or their loved ones. The Haitian people were openly grieving, weeping, and expressing their emotions of sadness, fear, and anger.

Later that night, as we left the mission to go back to the camp, we saw corpses stacked up on the side of the road like cords of wood. Literally, miles and miles of bodies, numbering well into the thousands. Also lined along the roads were tens of thousands of people who had nowhere else to go, huddled tightly together in groups around lit candles, their only source of warmth. Meanwhile, the ground was still shaking and rumbling. Randomly, you would hear the sound of another building or home collapsing. You

82nd Airborne, 1st/325 representative with Ken and Paul Saber

could also hear people trapped inside structures calling for help, along with the cries and moans of loved ones outside, searching for family members who were trapped or dead.

During that drive in the darkness, a realization struck me: *everything* I had witnessed throughout the day since I had arrived at the airport was the result of the earthquake's devastation. Immediately, my heart dropped, and I felt guilty for having questioned or even thought that any of this could be "normal." Today, all these years later, recalling that moment of clarity quickly brings back the deep emotion I felt.

Because of the constant threat of aftershocks, I never wanted to stay inside any building. I had my own tent and always slept outside on the ground, away from any structures. The aftershocks and the constant rumbling of tremors affected all the survivors as they relived their terrible experience with uncontrollable fear of another devastating quake.

Surveys and Shelter

Still shaken by what I had witnessed on my first day, I was motivated to provide the leadership needed to move forward, and our team went to work with a strong sense of intentionality. A couple of days later, as I had requested, Pastor Dorleans put together a group of his members that were ready to go. They were picked up and brought to our compound where I divided them into twelve pairs—two to a team. The primary language of Haiti is Creole, derived from French during France's occupation of Haiti from 1697 to 1804. Haiti's independence made it the first country to be founded by former African slaves.[2] We created a survey in Creole with questions like:

- What are your biggest challenges right now?
- What are your greatest needs?
- How many people are in your family?
- How many of your family members died?
- How many of your family members were injured?
- Do you own or rent your house?

During the day, the teams went out to talk to people and then, in the evenings, would return to translate the information they gathered into English. As I listened to the interpreter, I tried to process the common issues they found in the population. Each time we conduct these surveys, the facts that come out are very interesting. For example, about 90 percent of the people in the Port-au-Prince area rented their houses. That made sense because the level of poverty created obvious obstacles for ownership. And no renter was going to build back rental property, and no relief agency was going to build back a landlord's house, for obvious reasons.

Renters not only had lost the roof over their heads but also had no land to even set up a temporary shelter, creating a double conundrum. The most important aspect of these evening meetings was the dialogue between the team members. They were gaining insights into their own culture and better understanding the problems of the people. Since these citizens were also victims of the earthquake, their realizations were as fascinating and informative to me as the information we received from the surveys. Those hours of dialogue were truly invaluable.

As each day passed, we customized the questions to drill down into certain subjects. One topic I wanted to explore was the influence of social culture versus the influence of the law. The download that night was very clear: Haitians primarily live by social culture with the law having very little to do with their lives and decisions. This information shaped my thinking in that the government was not going to offer land for us to build any sort of emergency housing on.

After five to six days of gathering survey answers and processing the info, we were able to confirm what we had seen, which was, of course, the need for clean water, food, shelter, and emergency medical care. We also realized that prevention of any outbreaks, such as cholera, was going to be important so we could try to head off a secondary crisis. While those findings might appear to be obvious, again, it's important to hear directly from the people who have been affected.

Assessing the needs and knowing what Samaritan's Purse does best, I decided the number-one objective for us was shelter. People were literally sleeping out on the streets with an estimated 1.5 million homeless from collapsed structures. Camps were spontaneously popping up everywhere. We would drive past an area where a camp had appeared that, literally, was not there the day before. Every time, we would stop and hand out as many tarps as we had with us on the vehicle.

Because of the dire circumstances, time was of the essence. The obstacle wasn't constructing shelters but, as the surveys had revealed, finding available land. *What* to build was much easier to figure out than *where* to build. I decided to come up with a tripartite agreement with the three parties being the mayor of a local community, the homeowner, and Samaritan's Purse. The key would be to not ask for permission to occupy the land permanently; rather, we would request residency for thirty-six months.

Here's how the plan would work: If the approved beneficiary living in a temporary house left, then the local mayor could take over that residence. If the beneficiary found a permanent location for the house, he or she could disassemble the materials and move, vacating the land. All the parties seemed to understand and have confidence that this could work to everyone's benefit. And, hopefully, three years would allow time for the local economies to recover to some degree. Once we locked in on that strategy, we had a lot of mayors sign up with us. Many of them expressed that they wanted to help their people but didn't know how or didn't have the means.

The next step was to set up a system of prefabrication, utilizing a US supply chain of pressure-treated dimension lumber, specifically two-by-fours. Franklin became very involved with us in devising a simple, basic house plan of twelve feet by twelve feet. The roofs would be nine feet high at the front and slope to eight feet in the back for drainage. The plan was designed to minimize the number of cuts made. As we set up what was essentially a house-building plant, other partners got involved with us, from local churches to NGOs.

I am very pleased to tell you that 15,030 houses were constructed and set up! That is a lot of two-by-fours! While these homes were spread over many communities, the final number was essentially like building an entire town from scratch.

The local survey is an important tool we use to this day. As I write this chapter, there are people in Colombia and Sudan involved in gathering information and making assessments. Another great lesson I learned from this is not to assume anything. Go talk to the people. These are their homes and their lives. While our eyes may correctly tell us that people need shelter or clean water or heat, the question is, "*How* do they perceive they need it?" Particularly as Westerners, we may correctly identify the generalized need but miss how to meet that need in a practical and cultural way for that population. We have to realize the societal aspect and understand how people relate to the need.

As in this example in Haiti, it was easy to say that we needed to build shelters, but the how and the where were critical to finding the right solution. While we must offer solutions quickly, we need our responses to be targeted and accurate. After two hundred or so interviews, you start to discover trends, some that can surprise you. "What would I want in this situation?" is the wrong question when you are in a different land with a different culture. The question must be "What do the people believe they need?"

We see this same dynamic in Mark 10 when a man named Bartimaeus, who was obviously blind, cried out, "Jesus, Son of David, have mercy on me!" (v. 47). After calling the man to come to Him, Jesus asked a really interesting question, "What do you want me to do for you?" (v. 51). Now, how many people do you think might have been puzzled or confused, maybe even angered, by that question? What might you have thought? But Jesus wanted the man to state his need, for Bartimaeus to be specific about what he wanted. He answered, "Rabbi, I want to see" (v. 51), and verse 52 gives us the outcome: "'Go,' said Jesus, 'your faith has healed you.'" Immediately, Bartimaeus received his sight and followed Him. As with all the Lord's encounters with people, there are powerful principles for us to learn in this story as we minister to people in His name.

A Welcome Liaison

While driving through the city center one day, I passed what appeared to be some sort of temporary US military installation. There were huge rolls of razor wire strung out and stacked for protection in the area surrounding the property. I stopped and got out to speak to the soldiers. After successfully being allowed past the first two rows of wire, I asked the guard in charge if I could speak to a senior officer. I was led to a captain, who might have been twenty-five years old, sitting in a tent. After we had introduced ourselves, he began telling me about their mission, speaking in a confident, rapid-fire, staccato fashion.

When he was finished, I said, "Captain, I've been doing this for a long time. Let me tell you what I think you're going to run into here." I then began to

Working with the 82nd Airborne 1st/325

explain how the world of NGOs and the UN worked in international disaster situations. I told him about a sort of pecking order called a cluster system coordinated through the UN for access to assets. There's the health cluster, the shelter cluster, the logistics cluster, and so on. One day of the week, everyone involved in a particular sector meets to talk and coordinate.

It became obvious as I spoke that the captain knew none of this, because he grabbed a pad and pen and started writing furiously, trying to keep up with me. That caused me to wonder whether I was the first person from a relief organization he had spoken with since he and his troops had arrived. As I was wrapping up my brief lecture on humanitarian protocols, I heard the ding of my cell phone with a text message.

Looking at my screen, I saw that my old friend, Ramiro da Silva, one of the senior leaders in the World Food Programme (WFP), sent: "Ken, I just got here. I'm at WFP headquarters. Can you come?" (Ramiro and I met in Khartoum when I was the director of the Office of Foreign Disaster Assistance—OFDA—and had become good friends.) I stood and said, "Captain, good to meet you. I've got to go." As I turned to walk away, he asked, "Hey, Mr. Isaacs, where are you staying?" Because many places in Haiti have no actual address, I explained where the compound was mostly by giving him landmarks.

I went to the UN headquarters where WFP had its office. When I located Ramiro, he said, "Ken, we've been meeting about the best way to get a lot of food distributed quickly. But, because people are nervous and afraid, we also have to stabilize the situation." While I knew the desperate need, I offered my honest answer, "Ramiro, I don't want to get involved in food here. I even told my staff before we came that we were not doing food." My reasoning originated from when I was at OFDA. I had seen how involvement with food in these circumstances usually turned into riots. I didn't want our team anywhere near such a threat. In fact, I had directed my staff, "Stay away from food, and don't talk to anybody about food."

But, never say never, right? As Ramiro has said (a quote I've shared many times), "A proper disaster response is much like dealing with a war. You make your plan, and then when you encounter the enemy, sometimes you need to adjust." He had a way of both calming me down and convincing me, so after all my explanations and protesting, I agreed to take a look at his distribution plan.

Ramiro led me into a large tent where I was surprised to see military leaders from countries around the world—Brazil, Ecuador, France, England, Israel, and Canada, as well as the US. A large map was rolled out on a table with the city of Port-au-Prince divided into sixteen zones. For example, Distribution Point 16 was Cité Soleil, where the dangerous gangs were. As I looked closer at the map, specifically DP 16, I saw the church where I had met the pastor and hired the survey crew. In that moment, I sensed that God had directed me to that church for a larger purpose. I knew I was supposed to go against my initial directive to my team and help Ramiro and these other nations distribute food with Cité Soleil as our specific focus. Confident in God's leading, I told him, "Okay, I'll do it. We'll help."

I knew distributing food was going to be complicated regardless of the method. The WFP's plan was to give out daily vouchers to women only, not to men. The idea was that women had to feed their families, and the hope was that this method would reduce corruption, since we knew the vouchers would quickly become a temporary currency. For example, someone with access to a copier could mass-produce fake vouchers. The decision was made to give an allotted number of vouchers to every mayor in Haiti, delivered as late at night as possible to reduce the number of fake ones that could be produced by morning. Each day, we made changes to the vouchers to avoid corruption, such as the color of the paper, the font style, and even the actual paper used.

Around six thirty that evening at the camp, the local guards I had hired to protect the compound gates came and got me. They said there were some US military soldiers out front asking to see Ken Isaacs. As I walked out of the gate, Lieutenant Colonel Patrick Hynes introduced himself. His sergeant major and driver were with him in a Hummer. They asked if they could come into the compound to talk, so I invited them in.

Once inside, I said, "Gentlemen, dinner's ready. You're welcome to eat with us." We all grabbed a plate and sat at the end of a table for privacy when Hynes got straight to the point, "You came and talked to my captain today. You're the only person any of us have spoken with that seems to know what needs to be done here." As I was hoping that wasn't necessarily true, he continued, "Would you be open to allowing me to place a liaison officer here in your camp?"

"What do you mean?" I asked. "What is that?"

In military fashion, he explained, "Well, in short, your words that hit the liaison officer's ears will be words spoken in my ears."

Knowing how much I appreciated working with the US military when I was the director of OFDA, I agreed, "All right. Sure, that would be great."

Hynes then said, "The officer I want to send is a woman. She's a captain and West Point grad. She's religious like you. I'll send a private and sergeant with her."

In one of the rooms, we used some large blue tarps to cordon off private sleeping quarters for her. Early the next morning, the captain, sergeant, and private arrived. From there, two platoons of soldiers from the First Battalion, 325th Regiment of the Eighty-Second Airborne Division got involved in our work with their Hummers and M16s. I knew from my time in Washington that the US military gets busy and gets things done. And Lieutenant Colonel Hynes's group was no exception. They were on board with literally anything I wanted to do.

Working with the 82nd Airborne 1st/325

The food distribution site in Cité Soleil was set up at a major three-way intersection. Even though the soldiers had been on tours in difficult and dangerous places like Afghanistan, they had never experienced an assignment like this before. Around five thirty every morning, there would already be several thousand women lined up waiting to get food with their vouchers in hand. The soldiers guided the long line, while also watching all the men hanging around the area who were trying to figure out a way to get food by conning or stealing. We led the women to a gate and then behind a concrete wall where the food was given out. Several times, we had to customize our entry and exit points, depending on how it had gone the day before.

I was stationed at the actual handoff of food to the women to look at the vouchers, watching for any discrepancies or anything suspect. Unsurprisingly, I found quite a few counterfeit vouchers. Because the majority of the people were in such a desperate place, I wanted to separate the innocent from anyone trying to take advantage of the situation. The US military's involvement was the perfect help we needed in such an extraordinarily chaotic situation, all for the purposes of humanitarian assistance. We could not have accomplished the food distribution at Cité Soleil in such an organized and uneventful manner without the soldiers' help.

Watch My Six

One day, I saw a guy back a Hummer into an alleyway. Curious, I went over and asked what he was planning. He said he was going to give away wind-up-powered shortwave radios for people to be able to hear the news. Deciding to share what we had learned, I said, "Hey, when you start giving out those radios, you're going to have a mob on you." Sitting inside his heavily armored vehicle with four-inch-thick glass, he dismissed me, "No, it won't be a problem." I asked, "Well, how many radios do you have?" He told me he had a case of thirty-six units. As I looked around, there had to be 3,000 to 4,000 people in the vicinity.

Trying to warn him, I said, "Once people start realizing you're giving something away, they'll start pressing in and you'll be trapped on three sides.

If it goes wrong, you won't have a way out." He looked at me with a bit of a smirk and said, "Sir, there is nothing in this theater that can penetrate my armor." When he started giving out the radios, within seconds, he was surrounded by a huge mob. He ended up throwing the entire box down on the ground, jumping back in his armored car, slamming and locking the door. After a while, once the radios were gone and it was obvious he had no more, the crowd backed away and he was able to drive out. In circumstances like those, desperate people do not follow the rules of normalcy. Anywhere in the world where there is dire need, you have to assume and plan for the worst-case scenario for everyone's safety.

Almost every day, we had shipments of supplies coming in from ports in southern Florida. There was a team there receiving and loading literal shiploads of resources, led by the tireless efforts of Richard and Karen Todd. We had secured a landing on the coast that belonged to a concrete factory. One day, we were at the dock waiting on the boat to come in to unload the supplies we needed. Now, when I say "we," remember there were US soldiers accompanying us everywhere we went. We received word that the boat had come into the wrong port and it was going to be another two hours until arrival. So we left to go back to the camp to eat.

When we returned, there was a new supervisor at the dock, an official with Haitian customs. When I told him through an interpreter what we were there to do, he said, "Well, I'm not letting you in." Trying to be diplomatic, I continued, "Look, I know the boat is coming, and you know the boat is coming. Please, just let us in." When the answer was another firm no, the sergeant major with us, who happened to be from New Jersey with a definite northeastern accent, jogged up to me and asked, "Sir, do we have a situation here?!" I simply said, "Yes, we do."

With a single hand motion from him, in seconds, there were two dozen armed soldiers standing around this lone customs agent. The sergeant major said through the interpreter, "Sir, I believe we have a misunderstanding here.

We need immediate access to this port." Hearing the translated words and seeing the looks on the faces of the soldiers, he said nothing else but turned and opened the gate. That kind of quick resolution rarely happens in the humanitarian relief world because you do not and cannot project that kind of force. But those soldiers were simply doing *their* job, which they did every day with great dignity.

A similar story involved one of the local mayors who had a well-known reputation for corruption. We found out that he had been giving food vouchers to his "girlfriends." I use quotes because that term should be interpreted loosely as a description of his relationship with apparently dozens of women. As I gathered more intel on this guy, I heard that he carried a gun and would use it. I told Lieutenant Colonel Hynes, "I need to go visit one of the mayors to discuss a problem with the vouchers. I'll be fine. I can just go and talk to him." Hynes was insistent about his men accompanying me, "Sir, trust me. We should go."

Within minutes, several Hummers of soldiers and I hit the road to visit this mayor. We pulled up to a small nondescript building, and I walked in with a roomful of American military muscle behind me. Very calmly and politely, I asked, "Mr. Mayor, how are you today?" Because he spoke a little English and I spoke some basic French, we were able to communicate enough without a translator. He invited me in to sit down across from his desk. As I pulled up a chair, the soldiers filed into the office behind me. There were now more men in the room than there was air to breathe.

While I spoke as if the soldiers weren't there, the mayor's eyes darted back and forth between me and them. I calmly explained what I had discovered about him handing out vouchers to his girlfriends. I reminded him of the purpose and agreement of the food program and asked for his compliance. He owned up to his transgressions and assured me that he would handle the vouchers properly from that day forward. I thanked him for his honesty and cooperation, stood, and we shook hands. As I turned to leave, all the soldiers filed out of his office behind me to go back to the Hummers. That projection of power through military presence was absolutely overwhelming. In this situation, the soldiers didn't have to say a word or do anything. Just being in the room was all it took to turn the tables.

Following that visit, we went back to Baptist Haiti Mission. The US military had brought in helicopters for us to start evacuating survivors to our doctors, who were working in the two operating rooms. Those rescue missions went on for a while, as people would discover a new survivor who had been hurt in a structure collapse. For some, enough time had passed that gangrene had set in. Many were found after having managed to crawl out from under debris, with injuries ranging from severe cuts to bone breaks.

During the Eighty-Second Airborne's time in Haiti, besides their direct support of our efforts, they were involved in logistical support and security for other NGOs and their personnel. The soldiers also helped secure any relief site and provided transportation for supplies and people, even in the remote mountainous regions where survivors were cut off from getting help. When they received reassignment orders and had to leave Haiti, they conducted a small but gracious ceremony to thank Samaritan's Purse for our work and cooperation with them. (One of my fondest memories is watching the Super Bowl with those guys.) Lieutenant Colonel Hynes and I continued to stay in touch. After Haiti, he returned to Afghanistan as the executive officer for senior commanders there. Numerous times, I witnessed a Haitian asking the soldiers not to leave. Not only was I very thankful for their service, but the Haitian people were as well.

Taking Authority over Darkness

Much like I talked about in Rwanda, in Haiti, I could constantly sense the presence of spiritual darkness, of evil. The practice of voodoo is prevalent throughout the country and, oddly, has been mixed in with some Catholic practices. A common sound at night in many areas is the distant beat of drums and chanting as ceremonies take place. To the west of Port-au-Prince, along the coastline, there are two towns—Grand-Goâve and Petit-Goâve. We had rented a compound in that area from a Canadian mission group. The wall around the perimeter of the house had fallen down, and the house had cracks in the walls, but it was still livable.

One day, I was out in the yard talking on my cell phone to my son when I saw a strange man walking around our perimeter. He was wearing sunglasses, had chains around his neck and bracelets on his wrists, along with what appeared to be an empty liquor bottle that had some sort of solid object in it. He was mumbling to himself, shaking and rattling the bottle as he walked. Taking all this in, immediately, I felt something demonic.

I have had spiritual experiences around the world that testify to the truth of demons' existence. I got the sense that this guy was attempting to cast voodoo spells on us. (I'm sure word had gotten around the area about us being a Christian organization.) Based on Scripture, I knew what I had to do. I told my son, "I can't believe this is happening right now. Wait just a minute. I've got to go rebuke this situation."

I walked straight out toward the man, got in his face without touching him, and firmly stated, "In the name of Jesus Christ, I rebuke you! I order you to leave this property and leave us alone!" He looked totally bewildered, as if he didn't know who he was or where he was, like he was waking up from some sort of trance. His arms went limp with the bottle still in his hand, then he turned around, and walked off through a banana tree grove. He never said a word, and I never saw him again.

Another similar situation occurred at a different base of operations in a place known as Jax Beach, nicknamed for Jacksonville Beach, Florida. The earthquake had caused a building there to turn over, to fall totally out of the ground, and flip over on its front. Our plan was to turn the property into a much larger compound where we could park our heavy equipment and use it as a base for our construction operations. After I was able to negotiate a monthly rent with the landlord, we brought in a big D6 dozer and some heavy trucks to do debris removal. A roadway that was big enough to accommodate the large equipment also had to be constructed.

On the property next to Jax Beach, there was a small building. Whenever I walked near that structure, the closer I got, the more darkness I felt. Finally, I decided to go inside to look around. Sure enough, there were two altars where some sort of animals had been sacrificed. I knew right away that this was a voodoo temple where ceremonies had taken place, and, by the looks of things, they had been done recently.

I brought the team together that would be based there and explained the situation. All fifteen of us joined hands in a circle and prayed that any demon, any force of darkness that had been invited there, would be rebuked, that its hands would be tied and its eyes blinded, and that Jesus would be the only name present and known on the property now. That prayer was a very emotional moment for us all as the feeling of darkness left and a palpable presence of light and glory surrounded the space. After we said "amen," I felt uplifted and knew the spiritual threat was gone. We claimed Jax Beach in Jesus' name and worked from there for the next two to three years. Every day as we would come and go out of the driveway, we would pass by that temple, but we never felt troubled again by a sense of spiritual oppression.

But, as Jesus warned in John 10:10, "The thief comes only to steal and kill and destroy." To accomplish these, he comes in many different forms. The last item on our list of the local survey findings was the concern of possible disease outbreaks. Dr. Tom Wood, a trusted epidemiologist, had expressed concern about cholera shortly after the earthquake, primarily because of the lack of sanitation. Sure enough, by October of 2010, the first case was realized, ironically brought in by some UN soldiers.

Dr. Tom went into what I have often called his Sherlock Holmes mode, and, through ground-level surveys, he was able to identify and locate the first patients. After traveling up the river and locating all the junction points, he made predictions about where the disease would spread next. He was 100 percent accurate and gave us a two-week window so we could prepare cholera treatment units. Even with the advance notice and the treatment centers, there were over 820,000 confirmed cases, causing the worst outbreak in recent history with an estimated 10,000 deaths.[3] Just as the nation was starting to get its footing, another tragedy occurred. While many died, ultimately, Dr. Tom's work helped save an untold number of lives.

Matters of Life and Death

About five weeks after I got to Haiti, Carolyn came to visit. On her fourth day, she got a call from her sister that Johnny, her older brother, had died suddenly of a heart attack. He was, of course, family, but I had also worked with him in the Wrights' well-drilling business. Right away, we flew back home. Afterward, Carolyn and her family were devastated, so I returned without her. While I was away and later after I left, Don Norrington kept the programs running in the very same way he did anywhere else he has gone for me. I first met Don back in 1984. In 1994, while in Rwanda, I went to see him and offered him a job, and he came to work for Samaritan's Purse.

Besides the one trip back home, I worked in Haiti for a total of three months. Another project we were involved with there was an orphanage, a small row of humble wood-frame houses. They had collapsed or been damaged in the earthquake. The original name was the Lamb Project, and we were asked to help build a new facility. When Greta Van Susteren and her husband, John, came to Haiti right after the earthquake, they surveyed the damage and took time to look at the work Samaritan's Purse was doing. She became emotionally attached to the orphans there and obviously cared deeply for the Haitian people.

Franklin wanted to honor her because she had been such a great friend to us, so the orphanage and the academy that were built were named the Greta Home and Academy. The home cares for orphans, while the academy is a community school of higher standards, consistently turning out students with some of the highest marks in the entire nation. One student has competed multiple times in international chess championships in foreign countries.

In the aftermath of the earthquake, there was an overwhelming amount of pain and suffering among the people. Besides the initial earthquake, three aftershocks followed that registered at 5.9, 5.5, and 5.9 respectively. Because the country has long been deemed the poorest in the Western Hemisphere and with so much of the population living in remote, rural areas, the death tolls ranged from 200,000 to 300,000, as reported by the Haitian government. However, there was such a rush to dispose of the dead because of the sheer number of bodies that the actual numbers will never be known.[4] Based on the horror I witnessed firsthand there, I would agree with their government's estimations.

Throughout the Haiti response, Samaritan's Purse was involved in the safe distribution of food, water, and medical supplies, as well as in the establishment of field hospitals, clinics, and distribution centers. I was amazed at the outpouring of generosity in service and loving professional care given by a multitude of volunteers. Some came for two weeks, while others ended up becoming full-time staff, but we were never short of people. There was a huge wave of volunteers with over three hundred on the ground right after the earthquake. In October, when cholera struck, we had another enormous swell of personnel who stepped up, willing to put their lives in harm's way to help others in Jesus' name. Seeing the body of Christ move in such a powerful way with gracious intentionality was deeply moving.

In my travels, I've seen so much terrible tragedy caused by the state of sin and evil in the world, but simultaneously, in those same places, I have been blessed to be among the people that God created and placed in those nations. As things seem to get increasingly worse by the decade, we have to remind ourselves constantly of the apostle Paul's truth in Ephesians 6:12:

"Our struggle is not against flesh and blood, but against the rulers, against the authorities, against the powers of this dark world and against the spiritual forces of evil in the heavenly realms," against the one Revelation 12:10 calls "the accuser of our brothers and sisters." So wherever we are on the planet, as we work to bring healing and salvation to people, both physically and spiritually, we must remember *everyone* is made in the image of God, as Genesis 1:26 tells us. For that reason, we keep our hearts encouraged by passages such as the one below from Paul's words to the church at Philippi.

But one thing I do: Forgetting what is behind and straining toward what is ahead, I press on toward the goal to win the prize for which God has called me heavenward in Christ Jesus. (Phil. 3:13–14)

Chapter 10

Like God Had Punched the Earth

Japan
2011
Earthquake/Tsunami

On March 11, 2011, an apocalyptic natural disaster struck Japan, causing a cascade of devastation.

First, a magnitude 9.0 earthquake hit at 2:46 p.m. off the northeastern coast of Honshu, Japan's main island. Secondary quakes and hundreds of aftershocks followed, registering in the 7s. (For comparison, the one that struck Haiti was a 7.0.) To date, the initial event is considered one of the most powerful earthquakes to be recorded since recordkeeping on earthquakes began in the nineteenth century.[1]

Second, the tsunami it triggered had waves more than thirty feet high that reached the shoreline within thirty minutes and traveled as far inland on the eastern side of the nation as six miles. With little time for evacuation, people scrambled to reach higher ground on land or in buildings. Thousands drowned in the flood, and, when the water began to recede and flow back, countless victims were swept out to sea.[2]

The third wave of devastation involved the damaged nuclear reactor in Fukushima, which was constructed on the coastline thirty feet above the ocean. When the plant lost power, the cooling systems failed, and the cores overheated. The result was the release of dangerous levels of radiation, prompting evacuations of more than 150,000 people.[3] The International Atomic Energy Agency placed this incident in the same category as the Chernobyl crisis of 1986.[4] The earthquake's epicenter was only eighty miles east of Sendai. Fukushima is just south of there, and the capital city of Tokyo is only 137 miles south of the reactor.

And, lastly, as if matters couldn't get any worse, because it was wintertime, a cold front swept in bringing snow and ice to the northern part of the island.[5]

One important detail to add regarding the measurement of earthquakes is that the Richter scale is based on what is known as a base-10 logarithm, meaning each number between 1 and 10 is ten times greater than the previous number. For example, a 7 is ten times greater than a 6, and a 9 is one hundred times greater than a 7. So you can see, while the Haiti earthquake was obviously devastating to that nation, the disaster in Japan was terribly severe.[6]

To this day, there are videos on YouTube of massive waves hitting the shoreline, sweeping away ships, boats, buildings, homes, and cars, including a news report that shows the tsunami waves hitting the Fukushima nuclear plant.[7] The violence of the crushing waves is difficult to process. Large ships were carried inland; some were too heavy to wash back out with the receding water. The *Kyōtoku Maru* sat on dry land for two years before finally being dismantled and removed.[8]

With the thirteen-hour time difference between Japan and North Carolina, I heard the news early that Friday morning. As reports with live footage were released, the entire world watched the destruction on TV. At our staff devotions, Franklin led us in prayer for Japan. After the meeting, I went straight to him and said, "I really feel like we need to go over there." He responded, "Kenney, Japan is the second-largest economy in the world after us. There's nothing we can do to help."

His answer was based on what I also knew. It's not that you don't want to help, but it's figuring out how. As I learned in Washington, it's very difficult to create an emergency response in a first world country. There are so many laws, regulations, codes, and requirements designed to protect people that finding a pathway to help is a daunting, if not impossible, challenge. You have no choice but to fully comply with the government. Even still, I immediately began to provide guidance to our staff to set up an incident management team for an assessment. While I was as aware as anyone of the obstacles, I was compelled to try to find some way to respond.

By Friday night, the news reports were offering more details of the devastation. Saturday, I couldn't stop thinking about how the Japanese people must be suffering. Several of our team met in our command center to learn more about the devastation, but it was such a desperate situation that we felt helpless. By the time I got up on Sunday morning, I felt like God was telling me, "You've got to go." Over the years, I have seen that if He calls us to go, then He has already made the way. Isaiah 40:4–5 tells us,

> Every valley shall be raised up,
>   every mountain and hill made low;
> the rough ground shall become level,
>   the rugged places a plain.
> And the glory of the LORD will be revealed,
>   and all people will see it together.
>   For the mouth of the LORD has spoken.

I called Franklin around nine o'clock. "God has just put it on my heart that we have to go there." His response was immediate. "Kenney, He put it on my heart too, and you're the one to do it." In Franklin's and my many moments of spiritual agreement and clarity, time and again I have experienced the beauty of Jesus' words in Matthew 18:19, "Again, truly I tell you that if two of you on earth agree about anything they ask for, it will be done for them by my Father in heaven." Like hearts and minds don't have to be in the same room for God to speak the same word.

By Sunday afternoon, I was on a plane headed to Japan.

Access and Answers

I called a few specific people to help, including my old friend, Dr. Paul Chiles, who agreed to meet me in Tokyo. We also connected with a philanthropist from Chicago who had a history of foundation work in Japan, mainly focused on the preservation of its gardens, cultural centers, and art. He made an official introduction for us and arranged a meeting with some high-level Japanese government officials. They invited Paul and me to the Office of National Intelligence in Tokyo. I don't think the location of our meeting had anything to do with a suspicion that we might be spies as much as it did with their lack of knowing how to relate to NGOs. (After my experience in Zaire, I had to consider these dynamics.) With other countries beginning to offer help, it was not lost on me that these government employees were now in the same shoes I had been when I was the director of the Office of Foreign Disaster Assistance (OFDA) after Hurricane Katrina struck US shores.

The normally crowded and bustling city was a ghost town, much like a hundred other places I have been in after a major disaster. Walking into the building, we noticed the lights and heat were off. They told us the power in Tokyo had been reduced to about 30 percent of normal capacity. The officials were fully focused on their emergency plan and doing the best they could with what they had. To this day, I applaud them for being so gracious to us with all they had going on in their world. When we told them we had a 747 loaded and ready with emergency supplies and showed them the packing list, they agreed we could come into the country and waived the usual import and duty bureaucracy. When our plane landed in Tokyo, OFDA was running logistics for the US military, flying in humanitarian resources. I knew the logistician coordinating the work, which always proves to be a benefit, especially then, as Samaritan's Purse was bringing in so many emergency supplies.

While I stayed in Tokyo, Paul and our team members who had since flown in secured two vans and began driving to Sendai. As far as we knew, they were likely in the only vehicles on the road as they went up the east coast. While the highway was heavily damaged in numerous areas, they managed to arrive safely. There were a number of very gifted people on that team who created a strong cohesion and sense of purpose to begin to assess, plan, and execute. They were met by Micah Lawrence and his wife, Ayeko. Micah was Scottish but had been raised in Japan because his parents were missionaries. They were referred to Paul to work with us, and both were excellent additions to our team.

Everywhere the massive tidal waves had struck, there were two common sights. One was that the massive wall of water's destructive force had literally scrubbed the ground clean in every landscape. When the water

Inspecting supplies at the airport in Tokyo

pulled back, there were only residual foundations—no walls, no roofs, and very little scrap material left on the ground. Trees and telephone poles were gone. But unrecognizable debris was everywhere. One very surreal photograph I took was several miles inland of a Mercedes sedan sitting on top of a three-story building. The car washed in on the waves and, as the water receded, remained there. For anyone who was not able to make it to higher ground, with that much water moving that fast at that height, there was little to no chance of survival. Early on, the loss of life was difficult to estimate because of the number of missing people, with totals ranging from 10,000 to 30,000.[9]

When I was done and ready to leave Tokyo to join the team, I had several people with me, so we took the train. Micah drove to pick us up at the station and take us to the house that Paul had worked out for us to stay in once we arrived in Sendai. The house was owned by a Christian family who had fled the area. (On the drive, Micah had informed me that only about 1 percent of the population identified as Christian.) They told him we could use their home until they returned, and we were able to move about twenty-five people from our DART there. As per our usual protocols, we designated an area for the ladies and another for the men. While it was a nice house, all the bedrooms were upstairs. At first, everyone wanted to be near the front door in case another earthquake or aftershock required a quick escape. So we all slept on the floor in sleeping bags with no electricity or heat, and the daily weather brought a damp cold. Now the first step was accomplished—a place for the team to stay. The next steps were to figure out where and what to eat, where to get water, and then what the needs were that we could meet.

Like ants on an apple, everyone on our team was "running their feelers" to get info and answers. Because we didn't have any connections or experience in Japan, we needed to hear from the authorities. We decided to go out and talk with officials to ask questions, such as:

- How can we get our supplies in?
- How do we handle money?
- What's your labor law contract?
- Is there some sort of registration for permissions?
- What are the standards for water, food, clothing, and accommodations?

While the area affected by the earthquake was relatively large, the national food supply was not disrupted. The problem was the internal movement of food, along with clothing to stay warm. We didn't import any food into Japan because we found enough in local markets. The local emergency services were highly competent and very focused. However, in any major crisis inside a nation, there are always gaps where some segment of the population or some need is not fully addressed. Identifying those is a major challenge in any crisis.

In Sendai, Samaritan's Purse was the first NGO on the ground, alongside the Japanese military. The city government there was very open to us and couldn't have been more gracious, appreciative, and cooperative. As they pointed us in different directions, we were able to start taking action. At the time, they informed us that about one-fourth of Japan's population was over the age of sixty-five. The needs of the many aged and elderly, with their unique health issues, were very different from those of the general population. For so many who had managed to survive, their homes were gone. They had nothing left. The Japanese government was housing people in any available safe public buildings, such as schools and civic centers.

With each passing day, I came to truly appreciate Japanese culture. The people there are very orchestrated, coordinated, and uniform, and their hospitality is world-class. Everything is meticulous and exquisitely manicured. And, as the world has long known, Japanese engineering skills are second to none. Their society is highly structured.

As you've walked with me through the previous chapters, I'm sure by now you can guess what my biggest question was: What was the number-one need Samaritan's Purse could meet? We made the decision to rent a building and create a warehouse operation so we could supply practical necessities, such as clothes, shoes, cookware, and cleaning supplies. Through contacts we had from a crusade that Dr. Billy Graham had done in Osaka and another that Franklin had done, we put out the word asking Christians to come to Sendai and help us. While there were not many churches, there was an executive committee that helped in evangelical events. We went to them and asked for help making connections with the body of Christ in Japan. Their plan was to try to mobilize believers. Soon, hundreds of volunteers began driving to Sendai from all over the country.

The warehouse in Sendai became our base of operations where we had a large map on the wall. When anyone returned from making assessments or deliveries or when word came back of other needs, we marked it on the map. When any partners or volunteers wanted a place to help, we were able to direct them where to go.

Yet we soon realized there were Christians and churches in Japan that we didn't know about. For example, there is a large immigrant population from Brazil, and one church in Tokyo was predominantly made up of Brazilian Christians. They were a very energetic and passionate Pentecostal group, and I really admired their energy and enthusiasm—exactly the kind of people I love to work with. They weren't shy or pious like some groups tend to be in those types of ministry settings. Their contagious joy and hope was a breath of fresh air amid so much tragedy.

Morioka area, Honshu

Dozens of churches of all sizes stepped up to help. In some heavily affected areas, we found congregations with a handful of people and their humble pastors, Christians who were trying to be faithful but didn't know how to deal with the disaster. While I have never wanted to turn churches into relief agencies, if God calls a body to step up, then I want to support them in helping their people.

A Japanese congressman, Reverend Ryuichi Doi, a devout Christian, came to Sendai to tour the devastation with me. At seventy-two years old, he took the train and then made the drive to reach us. (A YouTube video of that visit is available.[10]) Before leaving, Doi invited me to come to the National Diet in Tokyo, a historic building, where the legislature meets—the lower house (House of Representatives) and the upper house (House of Councillors).[11] At the end of World War II, General Douglas MacArthur intentionally protected this building from destruction for two reasons: he recognized its role in Japanese history and culture, and he knew the preservation of parliament would help build bridges in their postwar government.

Upon my visit, we went to the third floor to the cafeteria, where they served great food on white linen tablecloths. After our meal, Doi walked me over to this grand, ornate stairwell, about twenty feet wide, closed off with velvet ropes. He told me this was where the emperor walks into parliament, accompanied by all the pomp and circumstance.

I was so honored to get to know Congressman Doi, a brother in Christ. After his death at the age of seventy-six, at his memorial service on March 26, 2013, former Korean Agriculture and Forestry Minister Kim Young-jin, who founded the Korea-Japan Federation of Christian Parliamentarians, shared, "Doi embraced true historical awareness, God's justice, and God's suffering people. He cried and prayed for them. He was God's faithful servant for our times."[12]

A driving influence in my life has been that Jesus died for *all* people. We must always remember that God's Kingdom is not made up only of people who look like us. We can find brothers and sisters in Christ anywhere on the planet. His Kingdom is not from one country or culture or color but consists of all those who have trusted Jesus by faith. In Ephesians 4:3–6, Paul reminds us, "Make every effort to keep yourselves united in the Spirit, binding yourselves together with peace. For there is one body and one Spirit, just as you have been called to one glorious hope for the future. There is one Lord, one faith, one baptism, one God and Father of all, who is over all, in all, and living through all" (NLT).

Protection and Provision

After about two weeks, the missionaries returned to their home, so we had to locate a different place to live. The next house we were able to secure was a two-story home that actually had heat. By this point, everyone had gotten more comfortable with the potential threats, so the ladies were upstairs and the men downstairs. With twenty-five people on the team, we were always living in very close quarters, and most of us still had to sleep on the floor.

One night around eleven o'clock, I was reading while lying on the floor of one of the bedrooms. Because of the winter weather, I was wearing insulated long underwear. Suddenly, the entire house violently shook like God had punched the earth. Sitting straight up, I could literally feel the ground continuing to move and shake. I jumped up to run outside. From that point on, I felt like my body was moving in slow motion, and my vision was like peering through a tunnel. Outside the room, I saw one of our team holding open the front door, but as he spoke, the words sounded like they were in slow motion as well. I had never experienced a strange sensation like that before, nor have I since.

With all the women filing down the stairs, everyone was trying to get out of the house as quickly as possible. Outside in my insulated underwear in the cold and falling snow, I realized I was barefoot. But, thank God, we were all safe. Several transformers in the area began to explode, adding to the trauma. The event we experienced was reported at a magnitude 7.2. In that moment, our team understood firsthand how absolutely frightened and helpless you feel when the ground below suddenly feels unstable and unpredictable.

Almost every day, there were aftershocks at varying levels. In the warehouse where we were running our supplies operation, besides the windows in the building, there were a number of three-quarter-inch glass panes that had been hung from the ceiling as if to muffle or deflect sound. At least, that was my guess. Frequently, you could see those panes swaying or shaking. As you can imagine, going about your life and work in such an unstable environment creates anxiety. In fact, a lot of people we encountered were still struggling with some degree of shock. After a while, I was able to get accustomed to the feeling. I recall thinking, *Okay, I'm not going to worry about this. If God's going to take me this way, there's nothing I can do about it. I'm here, and I'm not leaving.*

Because the needs of the people were so vast, I knew I had to find a local source for food, clothing, coats, and household supplies in large quantities. But where could I find a place like that? Richard Brown was one of our team members, a retired automotive engineer, who ran our procurement and logistics. He had stayed behind in Tokyo while the others went to Sendai. He inspired us all with his wonderful attitude toward mission and service in Jesus' name. Talking to Richard one day about our need, he suggested, "Why don't we go and talk with Costco?" Lo and behold, there was a Costco Wholesale in Tokyo!

I took the infamous bullet train and went back there. Richard and I drove to Costco where I flashed my card and asked to speak to the manager on duty. Soon, I was visiting with a kind lady, telling her who we were and what we were doing. After I showed her a list of the kinds of items we needed, her response was immediate, "We want to help." I've seen there's a natural instinct in people to want to do something when a crisis occurs, but most just have no idea how or where to start. On that first trip, the total was somewhere around $80,000. (And no, I don't believe there were any $1.50 hot dogs from the food court on that receipt.)

At the register, I pulled out my trusty American Express card. (The same one I had used to charter a cargo plane in Ethiopia.) After I ran the card, a message popped up to contact American Express. (By now, I halfway expected that to happen anyway.) With a train of carts and dollies behind me, I called the 800 number, and, after explaining my dilemma to the representative, I had to verify my identity and go through the usual drill. But then the person asked me, "How are you planning on paying for this?" (Fair question.) I answered, "Well, I'm *not* paying for this. The organization I work for, Samaritan's Purse, will pay it." At once, they put me on hold to call our office and verify the purchase. Soon, the transaction was approved and all was well.

As we wheeled everything out to the trucks, the manager followed me. She told me she was a Buddhist and admired what we were doing. After we loaded up, she handed me a thick computer printout and said, "This is the packing list for our ship out in Tokyo Harbor right now. You look it over and tell me what you want. Then you can access the goods directly from the ship."

While she wasn't offering anything for free or at a discount, she was giving us first choice and simplifying our trips. Her offer was a huge help to get the much-needed supplies straight from their own economy to continue helping those who were displaced and homeless in Japan. Richard became the Costco manager's primary contact for us. He and I were grateful to God for them and their proactive manager.

As we continued our work and expanded into northern Japan, we bought some small economical Japanese pickups called Kei trucks that have a two-seater cab that resembles the front of the classic Volkswagen van. They're very practical at eleven feet long and under seven feet high. Most of them have an open low-wall flatbed behind the cab and a top speed of sixty-five miles per hour. Daihatsu, Subaru, Suzuki, Mitsubishi, and Honda make them, and the quirky vehicles are all over the roads in Japan.[13]

Figuring out that we could get a strong pressure washer and a seventy-five-gallon water tank in the bed of a Kei, we equipped churches with these trucks to use for mudding out houses. (Anytime floodwaters wash into a house or building and then recede, mud and debris are left on the walls. Mudding out is the term for washing off this residue.) These trucks with the water tanks and pressure washers were a practical way to help people start to clean up their homes and businesses. People on our team taught church members how to operate the equipment and then let them take the trucks out to get busy.

Dignity and Deference

In meeting so many people around the country, we came across a missionary group whose founder was a US military World War II veteran. He had married a Japanese woman and had several children. His brother and family had moved there as well to help. While they spread the Gospel, their legal reason for being in the country, their "tent-making," so to speak, was starting multiple businesses. They owned everything from computer information services to film production. After launching throughout Japan, they moved into Mongolia and Nepal to continue their mission and evangelism work. Everywhere they went, they planted a new business, creating jobs and supporting the local economy. We enjoyed partnering with them in many ways, and they generously let us use some of their office and warehouse space.

As a direct result of the disaster, Japan's economy took an obvious hard hit. The Japanese are extraordinarily honest people and very thrifty with money. I was told that it was common prac-tice there to stuff a mattress with cash or keep your money in a safe in your house. With that knowledge, I was able to witness a fascinating aspect of this dynamic. Because homes and businesses had been swept away, near the shoreline I saw large quantities of Japanese yen in various denominations lying around and blowing in the wind. You might also see a safe sitting in a random spot out in the open that had been

Dr. Chiles (far left), Ken, and two US Marines coordinating a US response

carried away by floodwater. But here's the most amazing part: Because personal honor and integrity are so important to the Japanese, no one would touch the cash or a safe. Nobody touched *anything* that wasn't theirs. There was no looting. Eventually, trillions of yen were collected and turned in to police departments. I can't imagine that happening anywhere else in the world.

While we continued to mud out houses, I also wanted to take the next step of repair and restoration. After Samaritan's Purse Vice President Luther Harrison began reaching out through our North American Ministries net-work, we were able to recruit hundreds of volunteers to come to Japan and replicate the same kind of ministry model we have always used in the US following any natural disaster that caused flooding—volunteers through churches clean out homes and repair them inside. In fact, we recruited so many volunteers to come to Japan that we started setting up base camps in affected areas. A unique detail I learned about Japanese home construction was, because of the threat from earthquakes, builders use wooden pegs, so they aren't nailed tight. That intentionally leaves some play so that walls and roofs can "move" with tremors.

In one particular town, we discovered a couple in their eighties stranded on the second floor of their house. The first floor still had several feet of water standing with mold growing everywhere. They were too feeble and frightened to venture out and didn't want to ask for or accept help for cultural reasons. That was actually a common problem we kept running into, Japanese beneficiaries not being receptive to help. Because they live very private lives and don't reach out to others, accepting help was difficult for them. I could see that what we needed was essentially a "demo" or "model home," so to speak, to prove to folks what we could do.

Edward Densham, our International Director of Projects, whom I have previously mentioned, was there with the team, so I decided to challenge him, "Edward, you go to that couple's house, and, no matter what it takes, you work your way in there and figure out how we're going to help those people. We'll get everything out of the first floor of their house and fix it for them." True to Edward's nature, that's exactly what he did.

As we began sifting through their belongings, we discovered another cultural dynamic. They wanted anything and everything touched by floodwater to be thrown out—from clothing to furniture to the washing machine—gone. That's part of that meticulous dynamic of being very clean and extraordinarily hygienic. We cleaned out the bottom floor of the couple's house, and, after seeing our first day's progress, they were in tears. Next, we tore off the wallboard, brought in fans, dried everything out, did mold remediation, and put up new drywall. They were overwhelmed and couldn't believe the help and love they were receiving.

From the restoration of that one home, word spread. After people saw what we could do and that we were legit, a lot of people began coming to us to let us know their needs. I was looking for a catalyst, a tipping point, and we found it. Through Edward's persistence, God opened that door, and, in our time there, we helped around 2,000 families restore their homes.

Next, I decided to take Micah Lawrence to Fukushima where the nuclear reactor had been damaged to assess the needs in that area. Knowing we would have to deal with potential radioactivity on the eastern side of Japan, when we began working in Sendai, I wanted to be cautious to ensure the safety of our team. For that reason, we each wore personal radioactivity detectors called dosimeters. I reached out to Dr. Tom Wood, the epidemiologist who had predicted and helped us in the cholera outbreak in Haiti, in whose assessments and advice I had total confidence. After he agreed to monitor our exposure, every day I gave him our readings to maintain a constant check on our health.

After about a week in Sendai, Dr. Wood said, "Kenney, I figured this out. At the present rate of exposure, you're going to be overdosed in fourteen years. Did you take enough clothes?" I've always loved how he communicated our lack of risk in that way. That put the circumstances into perspective for me. There was certainly radioactivity around, but not anything lethal, at least in our location at that time.

But in going to Fukushima, we had to take our caution to another level. On the way to visit a church community center run by a foreign missionary, our first stop was a church where the pastor had refused to leave. There were about fifty people in the building with him, and they were serving a daily lunch. All the windows looked like they had been coated with acid rain, and everything was covered in dried muddy grit.

My dosimeter was reading in a normal range—that is, until I walked over to a grassy area outside the church. I also had a larger handheld dosimeter with me that allowed us to check vehicles, cargo, and other materials. While I was holding that unit out in front of me, immediately, the peg panned hard to the right and the alarm started beeping and chirping. "Micah, we have to get out of here *now*." That night when we returned to the house, our personal dosimeters registered high exposure for the day. While we were still okay according to Dr. Wood, that situation showed me the seriousness of the radioactivity around Fukushima. If the people in those communities, Christian or not, chose to stay, that was a choice they had the right to make and we would respect.

In any sort of disaster where there have been mass deaths, the way corpses are handled depends on the culture. In Sendai, they gathered the bodies of victims in a sports stadium. Until they could obtain a positive identification, they wouldn't count the person as dead. They wouldn't announce total death rates until they had identified the individuals. While from a reporting standpoint, that was a disadvantage, I thought it was very respectful and showed dignity to the dead and also to their families.

Morioka area, Honshu

Franklin knew a crusade director in Japan with the Billy Graham Evangelistic Association whom we integrated into our DART structure. After Dr. Paul Chiles had gone home, the director became my deputy. While talking to him about the activity in the stadium, he told me they wanted to plan a festival in that venue as soon as possible. Franklin's answer was clear. "Right now, that stadium is full of death. But we'll come back in a year and, through Jesus Christ, bring new life to Japan." As promised, right around the one-year mark in March of 2012, Franklin went to Japan to put on a crusade in the stadium. I was able to attend and spoke briefly to the crowd. I also had the opportunity to share at several relatively large churches during that event, which was a truly emotional time because it was the one-year anniversary. That visit was deeply meaningful to me, and I believe it was to the Japanese Christians as well, as they heard from others who had been there to help during such a difficult time. Saying that our times of great suffering are also when we see Christ at work is always a hard confession to make, but it is true. I was so blessed to encourage the Japanese people that I had come to love in my time there.

In total, I stayed around seven weeks in Japan, and Samaritan's Purse stayed for the next two years. We maintained our volunteer camps and kept bringing people over to help. Because so many fishermen had lost their boats, and therefore their livelihoods, in the tsunami, we also started a program to replace fishing vessels.

In any disaster, water filtration equipment is the one thing we always provide. There was a man from Ghana, John Akudugu, whom I had sent to the north while I was in Tokyo. John got his PhD in hydrology in Japan. Now, a guy who has a Ghanaian accent speaking fluent Japanese definitely gets everyone's attention. They don't have a lot of migrants come there. Because it's an island surrounded by water, people can't get there easily. Adding to that, Japan is very protective of its borders. When I told John that I had water filtration equipment on the plane and planned to try to use it, he was adamant, "Ken, there is no way. They are never going to let us take that equipment off the plane." I took him at his word. Turned out, he was right. The Japanese have such a high standard to meet for clean water that we weren't able to help.

Evidence of the Gospel

I want to come full circle, back to where we began this story when Franklin and I first talked about going to Japan. Since Japan had the second-largest economy in the world at the time, there was no earthly reason they should have allowed us to come there. Yet, in retrospect, I believe there were four reasons that Samaritan's Purse was allowed in.

First, we were able to fill a niche, supplying necessities to people, from food to clothing to cookware to bicycles. Second, we were able to do it by mobilizing the body of Christ with churches and individual Christians getting involved. Third, we were given great favor by the government, with particular help from Congressman Doi, who helped open many doors for us. And last, but never least, was God's favor. We saw a great spiritual harvest come out of our efforts. That tends to be a common by-product as we work hard to be a witness for Christ and minister to people as Good Samaritans. Yet that is the one aspect of what we do that we cannot plan. We simply count on the Lord to take care of that, just as He promised us in Matthew 6:33, "But seek first his kingdom and his righteousness, and all these things will be given to you as well."

After being home awhile, several weeks later, I returned to Japan to check on our programs. We ran the warehouse for another three to four months to continue to supply people with necessities. As we always have, we adjusted our work wherever we discovered gaps and watched for ways we could intertwine the Gospel with our relief efforts.

When you minister to people in other parts of the world, you have to allow for cultural differences. Forcing our Western ways just won't work. For example, in the US, when you ask someone if he or she has a personal relationship with Jesus and the person says no, then you explain the plan of salvation. But for people in other cultures, receiving the Gospel is not a one-time event but a gradual process. They need more context, mostly because they have not had the same level of exposure to the Gospel that we in the West have.

If someone in another country tells me he or she is a Christian and I ask, "When did you accept Jesus?" most often, the person can't point to a singular moment. Many times people in other cultures come to faith by learning about the Bible through a much slower process, and oftentimes an ongoing relationship with a Christian is involved. We should recognize that people come to Christ because He draws them. We can't gauge anyone's salvation in any country simply over Western Christian buzzwords and misperceptions.

Sadly, today there are people sitting in pews every Sunday who don't have a true relationship with Jesus. Because of my work for decades now, I have to say the Bible is clear that simply doing good works doesn't make a person a Christian and won't get anyone into Heaven. Helping people in the name of Jesus should be a response of obedience to His death, burial, and resurrection. His followers simply display the fruit produced by a life fully surrendered to Him.

What good is it, my brothers and sisters, if someone claims to have faith but has no deeds? Can such faith save them? Suppose a brother or a sister is without clothes and daily food. If one of you says to them, "Go in peace; keep warm and well fed," but does nothing about their physical needs, what good is it? In the same way, faith by itself, if it is not accompanied by action, is dead.

But someone will say, "You have faith; I have deeds."

Show me your faith without deeds, and I will show you my faith by my deeds. (James 2:14–18)

To find out more about a relationship with God through Jesus Christ, scan the QR code below.

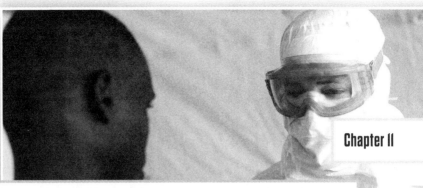

Chapter 11

This May Be His Only Chance

Liberia
2014
Ebola

Saturday, July 26, 2014, was a beautiful day in the Appalachian Mountains of western North Carolina. Carolyn and I were celebrating the wedding of some friends, a Mexican couple who proudly displayed their heritage in the ceremony. The entire bridal party looked amazing in their formal dress. Their vows given by the priest were very moving. As is normal for me, I cried during the wedding. There has always been something deeply moving to me about the union of a man and woman with "'til death do us part" always melting my heart and bringing me to tears.

Following the presentation of the couple, we were all invited to the basement of the small church for their reception. Around one o'clock in the afternoon, as the eighty guests finished lunch, just as the wedding cake was being cut, my wife received a text that read: "Please have Kenney call urgent." Edward Densham had been trying to reach me. My phone battery had died earlier in the day. In my line of work, the word *urgent* goes far beyond a challenging deadline or an impatient client. Words like that most often indicate an actual life-and-death situation.

When I stepped outside to call Edward, he answered and said, "Dr. Brantly's results for his test came back. He tested positive, Kenney. He has Ebola." Hearing those three words, I immediately felt as if some huge invisible fist punched me in the gut, taking the breath right out of me. Instantly, my emotions shifted from the joy of my friends' wedding to the horror of knowing firsthand what this disease did to people. Ebola is a relentless, unforgiving, brutal virus.

What came to mind right away was the first case that had come across our path in Liberia in March of that year. A ten-year-old boy had gone to a funeral. In West Africa, the ritual preparation of the body—washing and dressing—is participated in by family and community members. Sometimes, these ceremonies even include the mourners drinking the bathing or washing water. Because Ebola is extremely contagious, a person who has just died is at a maximum point of shedding the virus. *Any* contact with the body, even through clothes and linens, is dangerous. These sorts of cultural factors are always a significant driver in the spread of disease.

When the boy became ill, he was taken to a small health clinic that we managed in Foya, Liberia. Fortunately, Doctors Without Borders (the organization I first mentioned in the chapter on Bosnia) had visited our clinic on several occasions and shared knowledge and training with our staff on proper protection techniques in a highly contagious environment. We had been helping by teaching people in the villages simple precautions, such as not going around people who are sick, not participating in certain rituals, and having a "safe and dignified burial" (the phrase we used). Doctors Without Borders medical personnel had been coming from Sierra Leone to Foya, and we were very grateful. At first, we avoided setting up and running an Ebola treatment center because of the unique care and treatment the disease required. But, before long, the deadly virus eclipsed our reservations.

After Edward laid out the facts for me on the phone, I knew Carolyn and I would have to leave right away. I had to get back to our operations center in Boone to assemble the team and make some tough decisions. While we are accustomed to working in high-risk situations around the world, at that point the mortality rate for Ebola was approaching 90 percent. My mind began to race, feeling like a pinball machine, randomly bouncing from thought to thought, emotion to emotion, with the reality that the life of one of my team members was at risk.

Dr. Kent Brantly, only thirty-three years old at the time, was in our two-year program as a post-resident physician. He and his wife, Amber, along with their two young children, had come to Liberia in October of 2013. Our goal is to give young doctors a short-term opportunity to see if they're called to become career medical missionaries. Amber and the kids had left Africa only the week before to return to the States for a wedding. This news would be devastating to them. Having been on the ground there, his wife knew all too well the usual outcome of the virus.

When the first infected patients came to Eternal Love Winning Africa (ELWA) at the Serving in Mission (SIM) hospital in Monrovia, we knew we had to make a difficult and dangerous decision. Were we going to get involved in receiving and treating Ebola patients or not? I felt deeply that we were spiritually and morally compelled to support the fight, which meant we were going to set up and scrub in. We could not turn away. We had medical and logistics personnel. There was no one in the region with more capacity than us to take

At the River Gee

this on. So I made the decision and told the team, "Let's do it. We've got to. If Kent is willing, let's get the people together and fight." Regardless of the conviction, it was a heavy moment because we all understood how high the stakes were.

After I gave guidance to my team, I figured a little manual labor would be a good release and give me some time to think and pray. I drove out to our farm and started digging a hole to install a water spigot. About an hour later, when I was literally standing three feet deep in the ground, my cell rang. I dropped the shovel and reached my dirt-caked hand down into my pocket for my phone. Looking at the screen, I saw that Franklin was calling.

His voice and demeanor were different from how he usually spoke (our talks are typically brief and to the point). But he was softer in his approach this time, which made me curious, as he said, "Kenney, I feel that if God is calling our people to fight Ebola, we shouldn't get in the way of that." Hearing

his concern, I realized that somehow he had the idea I might be against it. Without hesitating, I interjected, "Franklin, there is no light between me and you on this subject. I agree." After a momentary pause, he stated, "Okay, great," and hung up.

On June 11, our first cases showed up as an ambulance brought a young woman and her uncle to our hospital. Within a short time, both died. Knowing more suffering from the virus would soon be coming, we decided to convert the chapel into a six-bed isolation ward. When that filled up, we created a larger facility with twenty beds until that also reached capacity. The size and severity of the virus was obvious to us all. The staff, along with Liberian helpers, began working eighteen-hour days to provide the level of care required.

When we first began to treat Ebola patients, as a staff, we discussed the options of what steps we would take if one of our team were to fall ill. At the time, our only recourse was to provide locally available treatment at the hospital. But now, with Dr. Brantly's diagnosis, this was no longer some academic exercise regarding medical care for a person who *might* have a lethal disease. The reality and weight of what we faced was crushing to the entire team.

Pressure, Persistence, and Providence

As Carolyn and I made the forty-mile drive from the wedding back to our offices in Boone, I ran through so many potential scenarios. Before long, the media had somehow gotten word of Kent's diagnosis. TV trucks started showing up in our parking lot and extending their broadcast dishes high into the air. Huge lights were positioned for nighttime news broadcasts. It was clear these folks planned on camping out for a while.

When I walked into the Incident Management Team (IMT) Command Center, many of the staff had already assembled, and we were soon met with more bad news. Another team member, Nancy Writebol, a missionary with SIM, who had been helping us, also tested positive for Ebola. She and her husband, David, had come to Liberia as missionaries. In a tight-knit community, she had become like a grandmother to the Brantlys' children.

Nancy had been involved in the "donning and doffing" process, where medical personnel meticulously go through the dressing and removal of their personal protective equipment (PPE) to go in and out of the "hot zone"—contact with the Ebola patient. The intensity of that environment cannot be overstated. Each step can take thirty to forty minutes to execute. No shortcuts can be taken. No skin can be exposed. Both donning and doffing are equally important to prevent contact with the level 4 pathogenic Ebola virus. The slightest mistake creates a great risk.

After news had spread that Nancy was also infected, throughout the day, and even in the middle of the night, the news media was in the parking lot filming updates, and all I could think was, *What are they talking about? We've not given them any more information.* Watching a news cycle at work firsthand is crazy. When Franklin arrived home from a trip to Alaska and saw the circus outside our offices, right away, he gave us an order, "No talking to the media." He was concerned about what might happen when we tried to bring either of them home for treatment. Fear and hysteria can create a lot of bad outcomes. So out of an abundance of caution, we started shaping our messages, offering only carefully drafted statements.

As I began to work on a solution to bring Kent back home for treatment, I was searching everywhere. One air carrier in South Africa with a level 3 containment plane told me they could get him only as far as Europe. Also, they wanted more than a million dollars, which was out of the question. We also needed a higher level of containment to safely transfer someone with Ebola.

Someone I knew in the State Department connected me to Phoenix Air, an aviation company that had the ability to make biocontainment flights in specially outfitted planes with a protective bubble for an infected patient and the medical equipment and staff for situations like Kent's. But no one with Ebola had ever been out of Africa. I spoke with Dent Thompson, the COO, who immediately told me no, that there was no way they could do it. He said the planes were actually owned by the Department of Defense, and he wasn't able to help me.

Countless people were now praying. Because being in a third world country made Kent and Nancy's circumstances even more difficult, folks were also calling representatives and senators to ask for help to bring them back home for treatment. By now, Kent's condition was deteriorating, and all of us were carrying the heavy burden of worry and fear for his and Nancy's lives.

Two days later, Dent called me back and said, "I don't know who you guys know or what kind of strings you're pulling, but you should call Dr. Will Walters at the Department of State. He helps get ill Americans out of foreign countries and back home."

Once I got the doctor on the phone, everything began to move quickly. We walked through every detail of the extraction, working to answer questions like "Where will the ambulance pick him up?" and "Where is the plane going to land?" As we mapped out each step of the journey, Will's help was invaluable. He was willing to go the extra mile to bring two Americans home, particularly with the substantial controversy surrounding patients with Ebola being allowed into the US.

Soon, I was notified that the flight had made its departure to head toward Liberia. But, about two o'clock in the morning, I got a call, "Mr. Isaacs, the plane has cabin pressure problems out over the Atlantic Ocean, and it has to turn around and come back." I responded, "No! A man's life is at stake! You have to find a way to go get him." I don't mind admitting to you that I got forceful and a little irate. The Phoenix Air dispatcher calmly responded, "I'm really sorry, but you don't want a pressure problem on an airplane flying over the ocean, especially one that is carrying a critically ill patient."

I could tell they weren't going to change their minds. Operational safety required the plane to return for repairs. My pleas and protests weren't going to help, and, of course, the safety of the crew was just as crucial as that of the patient. Hearing that the flight was no longer headed to get Kent was yet another very difficult and heart-wrenching moment for me. Bad news just seemed to keep coming. As I lay in bed staring at the ceiling after that call, my prayers were mixed with tears.

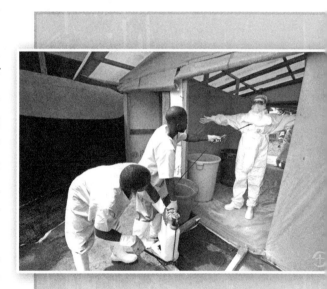

Disinfection at the Ebola clinic exit, ELWA Hospital

After I contacted our staff in Liberia with news that the flight wasn't coming, another member of our DART there, Dr. Lance Plyler, knew his two colleagues might not survive much longer. We had sent Lance there specifically to oversee the medical response of the Ebola crisis after the first patients had come to the hospital.

Allow me to pause here and give you some detailed backstory leading up to that Saturday when I received the news about Kent.

On Wednesday, July 23, after Kent woke up, he realized he didn't feel well. He called Lance to tell him. Later, talking about receiving that call, Lance said, "I remember verbatim what [Kent] said to me.... 'Lance, don't freak out, but I have a fever.'" They decided Kent would quarantine at his home until they could figure out what was going on.[1]

At first, they suspected it might be malaria, which is what I had originally

been told before the call that Saturday. But the test came back negative. Next, they knew they had to check for Ebola. While the first test was negative, the protocol was to do a second one. By Saturday, Kent's fever was up. After Lance got the results, he went to Kent's house where he was in isolation. Through the outside bedroom window, he said, "Kent, bud, we have your test result.... I'm really sorry to tell you it's positive for Ebola."[2]

In an interview before falling ill, Kent stated, "Ebola is a humiliating disease. It's humiliating for patients who have to be isolated: They have no direct contact with another human being; they lose control of their bodily functions. But it is also humiliating ... for the healthcare workers who are trying to take care of these people because there is so little that you can do." Once Kent realized a patient was dying, he often held his or her hands and sang as the person passed. He added, "Death was ever present." At that point, there had been only one patient in their care who had survived the virus. Later, Kent reflected on his diagnosis, "I had a very real sense of peace in that moment that I can only attribute to the grace of God.... My first words were: 'Okay, what's next? What's our plan?' And then my next thought was, 'How am I going to tell Amber?'"[3]

Later that Saturday, when Nancy's test came back positive, Lance delivered the news to the staff. It would be natural at that point for them all to be thinking, *Am I next?* Everyone had carefully followed the safety protocols and had no idea how two of them had become infected, especially Nancy, who had not been in direct contact with patients, only participating in the disinfecting of the clothing. Just before this, a Liberian physician's assistant, nurse, and hygienist had each become infected, and two of them had died. After that, some of the Liberians stopped coming to work. They were understandably afraid of contracting the virus, just as everyone was. Facing an invisible deadly enemy that no one knows how to defend against is terrifying. I had never seen a team so crushed.

After finding out the plane was no longer coming for Kent, I knew we had to devise some sort of a plan. Someone from the National Institutes of Health (NIH) called me to say there was an experimental therapeutic medicine called ZMapp. They asked if we would be interested in considering it. I jumped at the opportunity and was given the name of a field researcher.

When I passed the information to Dr. Plyler, I was surprised to hear that he knew the researcher, someone who was also in Liberia at the time. He then started working out the logistical details to get the medicine. We learned that a group of scientists had developed ZMapp—a mixture of genetically engineered antibodies devised to support the immune system's response to Ebola, derived from mice cells and tobacco plants. But the drug had been tested only on animals, not on humans yet. The medicine could possibly create a catastrophic reaction in a person. The dilemma was very real—the treatment might kill the patient before the virus did.

Miraculously, the researcher told us that a dose was available in neighboring Sierra Leone. It had been sent there for another doctor who had contracted the virus. For a number of reasons, his team decided to not give him the experimental drug. He later died. When the doctors there heard our story, they agreed to give us the ZMapp.

The medicine had to be kept in a container maintained at a temperature of twenty degrees below zero. There were three bags, eight ounces each, that had to be injected one at a time by a drip IV. Soon, the treatment was flown to the border of Liberia, brought by canoe across the river, and then driven to Monrovia, the capital of Liberia, where someone on our team would pick it up.

But there was just one problem. There were *two* sick people, and Lance was told there were only enough dosages for *one*. In fact, if it was going to work at all, the scientists plainly told him that "it would take all three doses to knock out the virus" in one person. "Whatever you do," they said, "don't split the course."[4]

Throwing a Hail Mary

The morning the ZMapp arrived, to everyone's surprise, Kent had woken up feeling better. Hopeful that he could be turning the corner toward recovery, Kent told the staff, "Look, I'm younger, so give the dose to Nancy. I'll be okay."

The container with the medicine was taken to David and Nancy's home where she was quarantined and being cared for. Needing to thaw the drug while also having to be careful to protect the antibodies, they decided to lay the medicine up against Nancy in her bed with a blanket.

But, later that night, on a Thursday, suddenly Kent's condition took a turn for the worse, and he began to crash. By the time the medicine was sufficiently thawed for Nancy, Lance told me, "Kent has a 105-degree fever, he's breathing about thirty times a minute, and he has this incredibly toxic appearance. He's not going make it. He's going to die."

The team on the ground felt deep spiritual heaviness and darkness. Kendall Kaufelt, our country director, went to all the houses in the missionary compound asking people to pray. They had been under a no-touch protocol for about two months at this point, but our team gathered together, pleading for God to save Kent's life. With him on the threshold of death, the blow was devastating to their morale.

In response to Lance's report, I asked him, "Have you given Kent any of the ZMapp yet?" He told me no, that they had only discussed the regimen and the ethics of using an experimental drug. They had also attempted to calculate the drip rate at which to administer it. I can only imagine the daunting task they faced, giving a man a medicine that had never been put into any human. Yet, knowing Kent's life was in imminent danger, I stated, "Lance, you have to get Kent the medicine right now. Go get it, and give it to him. This may be his only chance."

Lance raced over to the Writebols' house to ask her attending physician, Dr. Debbie Eisenhut, who also worked for SIM, to get the medicine from Nancy's bedside. The doctor, fully draped in her PPE with facemask and gloves, put it in a plastic bag, sprayed it down with chlorine solution, and then gave it to Lance in a bucket. Wearing no PPE himself, he simply put on a pair of gloves, took the chlorine-sprayed bucket, and drove back to Kent's house. He handed it to Dr. Linda Mobula, a member of our team, who, through her full PPE suit, administered the drug in Kent's IV drip. She calculated the administration by counting the drops and measuring the time—a method that is a far cry from the sophisticated monitoring systems that make medicine so easy and proficient today in Western hospitals.

Almost immediately, Kent went into severe, violent tremors known as rigors. Then, after about an hour, the shaking began to subside, and his fever started to come down. He was responding to the treatment, which was a miracle, especially given the fact that only an hour before he was on his deathbed. And then, Kent actually got up under his own power to go to the bathroom when he couldn't even walk the day before. His body's reaction to the medication was incredible.

By August 2, the biocontainment plane was repaired and headed to Liberia. When the flight arrived, Kent was able to walk out of his house, fully dressed in PPE, and get into the back of an "ambulance," which was actually a Toyota Land Cruiser, to be driven to the airport. Our team gathered nearby, clapping and cheering at the incredible sight of Kent walking to get into the truck.

The Liberian officials at the airport worked graciously with us to facilitate direct access to the private plane that was coming to get him. Honestly, no one wanted to deal with being around an Ebola patient because, by now, everyone knew the virus was incredibly contagious and deadly.

Because Kent had responded so well to the single dosage, Dr. Bruce Ribner at Emory Hospital in Atlanta, the medical facility that had agreed to treat Kent and Nancy, acknowledged that he had acquired ZMapp and would be ready to administer the other doses. Because of this news, we were able to leave the other two doses in Monrovia to give to Nancy until she got to Emory. While the effects were not as extreme for her as they were for Kent, she too experienced improvement. The plane returned for her extraction on August 5.

By now, several miracles had taken place:

- An unknown experimental drug had actually been created for Ebola.
- There was a dose available in neighboring Sierra Leone.
- Kent experienced immediate, vast improvement after only *one* dose.
- While it had never been used in a person, the medicine worked.
- The airplane's cabin pressurization problem resulted in the aircraft having to turn around, unknowingly yet miraculously providing the perfect timing for Kent to receive his first treatment and Nancy to receive the other two during Kent's evacuation.

Ultimately, the lives of two people were saved, while the entire world watched, literally.

Everyone on our team, along with the Emory University Hospital staff, had agreed to keep all the details around Kent's extraction confidential. But, just like his initial diagnosis, somehow the information leaked to the media. Because his arrival back in the US as an Ebola patient was a first-time, historic event, most news outlets covered the story. NBC and CNN had cameras rolling live when the containment flight landed in Atlanta. We had even switched landing strips to one that was more remote outside of the city. I'll never forget the surprise of seeing the TV cameras focused on the very spot where the flight would land and taxi in.

When the plane landed and pulled in next to the hangar, a TV camera positioned from a long distance away zoomed in for the live shot. The on-air reporters were wondering which one coming out of the airplane was the patient, because they were watching for a gurney. Back in the command center, we were thanking God and cheering through tears of joy to see Kent walking off the plane. While we knew which of the people was Kent, the cameras showed the

entire medical crew, all in full protective gear, looking like astronauts. Unless you knew the staff positioning like we did, you couldn't tell which one was the patient. Of course, then the camera crews followed the ambulance by helicopter with a live shot all the way to Emory as the FBI and local police escorted the emergency vehicle the entire way.

A very similar scene replayed at the side entrance door to Emory Hospital. The EMT driving the ambulance came around and opened the back door, while two men in space suits came out. One took Kent's hand as he stepped out under his own power to walk. The EMT encouraged Kent to see if he could make it out and then walk through the door. The archived news footage will forever document that incredible moment when Kent did just that—stepped down from the back of the ambulance and walked into the hospital, fully under his own power.

Reporters marveled that he was able to walk at all. Just like at the airport, news commentators were asking, "Where's the patient? Which one is the patient?" Everyone had been expecting to see a completely sedate person strapped to a gurney. Knowing Kent was now in the hands of an incredible medical team and the plane would soon be leaving to return to extract Nancy and bring her home, all of us at Samaritan's Purse had tears of joy praising God.

Before Kent's arrival, an NBC reporter interviewed one of the infectious disease doctors, asking, "Do you have any fear yourself?" He answered, "No. The unit where he will be taken is staffed with experts—physician experts and nursing experts—in the infection control practices that are necessary to both contain the virus and maintain the safety of both the patients in the hospital and the general public."[5]

While waiting for Kent to get to Atlanta, I was able to track down the man who owned the company that created ZMapp. We had talked on one other occasion. On that Friday night after Kent's arrival around eleven o'clock, he called me, saying, "Your folks have put out a press release, and it talks about ZMapp. You have to pull that back. You need to stop it. People can't know about this. Lives are in the balance."

I understood his perspective and the problem, but it was out of my hands. I responded, "Well, it's not my press release. I can't pull it back. That's Dr. Brantly's wife's decision. She can say whatever she wants to the media." He was obviously worried about the fact that the drug had never before been tested on humans. I continued, "Sir, I'm going to give you some advice. You need to release a press statement of your own in the morning, saying whatever you need to communicate to cover your bases." Just as I had advised, he had his own release that next morning.

Once Kent was settled into his containment room, Amber was able to see and talk to him through protective glass. Afterward, she released her statement, "It was a relief to welcome Kent home today. I spoke with him, and he is glad to be back in the U.S. I am thankful to God for his safe transport and for giving him the strength to walk into the hospital. Please continue praying for Kent and Nancy, and please continue praying for the people of Liberia and those who continue to serve them there."[6]

The doctors were supplied with enough ZMapp for both Kent and Nancy to complete their treatments. Kent received his other two doses in Atlanta, and Nancy got her final dose once she was admitted to Emory. Kent was also given plasma donated by his one former patient who had survived Ebola. The fact that they were diagnosed quickly and treated to the best of our staff's ability definitely helped in their recovery. In a later interview, when asked about the miraculous nature of their healing, Lance stated, "Prayers and antibodies—in that order."[7]

On Tuesday, August 19, 2014, Nancy was privately and quietly discharged from the hospital. Her husband, David, released a statement to the media, saying that Nancy "was greatly encouraged knowing that there were so many people around the world lifting prayers to God for her return to health. Her departure from the hospital, free of the disease, is a powerful testimony to God's sustaining grace in time of need."[8]

Two days later, on Thursday, August 21, Kent was officially discharged from Emory. At a press conference, his doctors stressed that he and Nancy were fully recovered and that their release posed no public health risk. With his family and medical team around him, Kent shared, "I am thrilled to be alive, to be well, and to be reunited with my family. As a medical missionary I never imagined myself in this position." Dr. Bruce Ribner, the medical director of Emory's Infectious Disease Unit, added, "The Emory Healthcare team is extremely pleased with Dr. Brantly's and Mrs. Writebol's recovery, and was inspired by their spirit and strength, as well as by the steadfast support of their families."[9]

When the brief speeches were over, Kent and Amber hugged the medical staff, with the hospital employees applauding and cheering as the Brantlys made their way to the exit.

There's Always More to the Story

One very important aspect of this event that must be shared is God's timing. Often, we can look at a circumstance through our natural eyes and think that He is *not* answering a prayer, or possibly that He is somehow letting us down. But, if Kent had gone out on the first plane, he would have missed the dose of ZMapp. He would have gotten the sickest when he was in the air. I believe he most likely would have died en route, somewhere over the Atlantic Ocean. I'm convinced of that. The "problem" with the air pressure on the plane that upset us all, that made me feel like we would now surely lose Kent, was actually the very thing that saved his life. God was at work and proactively answering thousands of prayers to take care of Kent and Nancy.

But the Lord wasn't done yet.

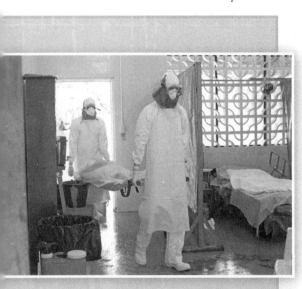

ELWA Ebola clinic

Ironically, with the entire world watching this situation, Samaritan's Purse was suddenly in the infectious disease business at a level we hadn't ever even considered. As with COVID, the US didn't anticipate the serious fallout that could happen with Ebola. I was invited to testify before a House committee on August 7, 2014. Such a testimony requires a written submission and then a verbal presentation, followed by questions from congressional leaders.

The room was packed with cameras as the government witnesses went first. Then the nongovernment witnesses took a seat before the committee. I felt great frustration and was deeply disturbed by the lack of action to help the people of West Africa, specifically the countries of Liberia, Sierra Leone, and

Guinea. While I was sitting behind those who were testifying first, I received an email from my staff in Monrovia asking if we could send another planeload of PPE to the country. In the room, I was hearing one of the government witnesses testify that a specified number of tons of PPE had already been delivered there, but, judging by the reality on the ground, the response by the US government and, in fact, the entire world was vastly insufficient.

When it was my turn to speak, I stated that the international response had been a total failure. The intelligence coming out of Liberia was horrible. At the time, hundreds had died, but thousands of people were going to die. And not just die, but suffer horribly before they passed. I was able to claim these projections based on the great work of epidemiologist Dr. Tom Wood. His accuracy never ceased to amaze me. I had full confidence in his analytical skills to track diseases and project the outcomes.

Dr. Tom Frieden, the director of the Centers for Disease Control and Prevention (CDC) at the time, finally traveled to Liberia weeks later and saw what was going on with his own eyes. I was told by friends and staff at the CDC and in DC that, upon his return, Dr. Frieden was visibly and emotionally shaken by what he had witnessed firsthand. He flew back to Washington on a Saturday night and met with President Obama on Sunday. He convinced the president that the US had to take action. It was clear that the three impacted countries, and even the World Health Organization (WHO), lacked the operational capabilities to coordinate an effective response. By mid-September of 2014, President Obama had dedicated US military resources to help with logistical support in Liberia, along with building Ebola treatment centers.

The strategic questions that had to be raised were:

- What does the world do when a deadly infectious disease crosses borders and becomes an international event?
- Who is in charge?
- What does a coordinated effort look like?

In the US, there is a federal government, but there are also fifty states with anywhere from 3 to 254 counties each that have a health department that gets to make some decisions for their local communities. We had the same problem in West Africa with no answers to these questions when we desperately needed them. No one knew where the buck stopped.

We experienced the same challenges during the COVID pandemic with the often illogical application of lockdowns and the mantra coming from health officials everywhere that they were following the science, all while their actions were conflicting with the efforts of other healthcare officials and political leaders around the globe.

On the same day of my testimony, that evening, WHO finally declared an international event of public health concern on Ebola. By the end of what was such a difficult and stressful string of events, here was yet another amazing story of how God works in the lives of His people, yet also among the nations.

Following this incident, after being certain none of our other Liberia staff was infected, we ended hands-on treatment and went back to community education and preparation to try to stop the spread. In 2017, a documentary about this crisis was released titled *Facing Darkness*, which is available via streaming services. The title is spot-on about how our team felt literal darkness coming over them. We felt a distinct spiritual battle from Liberia all the way to the US.

As for Kent, after his brief brush with "fame," including being on the cover of *Time* magazine, he and I were in New York together to meet with Doctors Without Borders regarding Ebola containment and treatment. We were sitting and visiting in the lobby of the small hotel where we were staying. Two ladies came up to Kent and asked, "Dr. Brantly, can we have a picture taken with you?" Kent humbly and shyly agreed. We then left the hotel and, out on the street, someone else recognized him and asked to take a picture.

Finally, I asked, "Kent, do people often come up to you for pictures and to shake your hand?" In his usual wonderful demeanor displaying humility and servanthood, he responded, "I can't say that a lot of people come up to me, but I can say that I never go out anymore and not get recognized." Obviously, catching Ebola had profound effects on Kent and his family's life that went far beyond the physical effect on his body. He and his family went on to become missionaries in Zambia. Kent says he feels like God allowed his situation so he could raise awareness about Ebola, which was certainly crucial because 11,000 people died from that particular outbreak.

On that beautiful Saturday at our friends' wedding, I will never forget the moment I went outside to take the call about Kent's diagnosis. In that moment, I couldn't help but think of King David's words in Psalm 23:4—"even though I walk through the valley of the shadow of death" (NASB). I have been in so many circumstances where you can literally *feel* those words. This was certainly one of those situations. But, thank God, He always has more to the story, and, for the believer, He never leaves us alone in the valley.

The LORD is my shepherd, I lack nothing.
    He makes me lie down in green pastures,
he leads me beside quiet waters,
    he refreshes my soul.
He guides me along the right paths
    for his name's sake.
Even though I walk
    through the darkest valley,
I will fear no evil,
    for you are with me. (Ps. 23:1–4)

Chapter 12

This Is the Life I've Got, and I'm Going to Live It

Carolyn
2016–2017
War in Iraq

After being threatened, held captive, shot at, and surviving many close calls from bombs and land mines, on my way home from a disaster or war zone, I would often ask myself, *How many of these ordeals will I be allowed to get through and make it safely back to my wife?*

And then the very sobering question, *What will Carolyn do when I get killed?*

Throughout the Bible, there are numerous accounts of God's favor and protection for His faithful people, yet, for many, including most of the disciples, their lives ultimately ended in martyrdom. For those who believe in Jesus, eternity is guaranteed; safety is not. God has a purpose for every day He gives us breath, but there is also a purpose in death as well. The apostle Paul often touched on this subject, as in Philippians 1:20–21, "Christ will be exalted in my body, whether by life or by death. For to me, to live is Christ and to die is gain."

In what country and what crisis would it simply be my time? I also smoked for twenty years, finally quitting on June 13, 1993. If you have ever been addicted to anything, you understand why I know the exact date. After that, at my wife's insistence, I took up running and, starting in 1997, began participating in marathons (which, like skydiving, is a very helpful activity for PTSD).

Finally, I decided to have "the talk" with Carolyn. "Honey, you know that we have a will together. I have a will. So everything is taken care of. The only big decision you're going to have to make, when something happens to me, will be to answer the question, Is there anything worth bringing back home, or do you just want to bury me in whatever country where I die? It doesn't matter to me. You do what you want."

Carolyn was always my greatest encourager and supporter. Each time I came home from dealing with so much death and destruction, while I didn't like to own up to it, I legitimately needed counseling to process what I had been through. I confess I was strangely distant, often in a bad mood, and struggled with an internal anger at the world. I also carried feelings of guilt for leaving behind people I had come to know who could not escape their lives. Through it all, my wife was very skilled at managing me through those hard times.

As I would start to settle back in, Carolyn would intentionally be very quiet. The only questions she would ask were superficial, like, "How was your flight home?" or "What would you like for dinner, honey?" Often, on my first day back, she would wake me up at four o'clock in the morning and say, "Hey, let's go for a walk." I would answer, "Ah, babe, do you realize what time it is? Come on, just let me sleep. I'm tired." She would persist, "Yeah, come on. Let's go for a walk. You'll feel good. It'll help you get back in our time zone."

While definitely being grumpy and protesting, I would finally give in, get up, and go with her. We would walk out into the darkness to the local trail or go for a jog. We didn't talk but would just be in each other's company. No matter how long I had been gone, she put *zero* pressure on me to share anything. Applying no expectations, Carolyn was a master at supporting me through her ministry of presence and service. In fact, her love language was acts of service. She would be incredibly patient with me until, finally, depending on the severity of the circumstances I had been through, after a week or two, maybe as long as a month, I would start talking. She would listen intently and actively engage with me, gently being there to help me process my transition.

While I can say I should have seen a therapist that specializes in PTSD, long before the condition became a household word, God gave me the gift of my own personal counselor. While Carolyn never went through any formal training, as I would share my stories, she was in tune with me. As I began to open up, she would ask questions for clarity to be certain she understood. Even though we had a rocky start when I agreed to go to work for Samaritan's Purse,

God moved in our marriage, and Carolyn quickly became an anchor for me. All those years, she was like a bastion I could cling to for survival and protection. She was very strong in her faith and support of my calling.

On Saturday, June 25, 2016, we were at our little farm about twenty miles outside of Boone where we had built a second home as our getaway place. Carolyn and I were sitting on the back deck when our daughter-in-law, Laa from Thailand, asked in her heavy Thai accent,

Yazidi holy site in Lalish, Kurdistan region, northeast Iraq, 2016

"Granma, is your arm swollen?" I looked over at Carolyn to see that her left arm was very puffy. Surprised, I said, "Honey, stretch out your arm by your other one. Let me see it." Laa was right. Something about the difference felt ominous to me.

I took a picture with my phone and sent it to Dr. Lance Plyler, who was so integral in the treatment of Kent and Nancy during our Ebola crisis. Out of the hundreds of doctors I know, Lance is the best diagnostician I have ever known. Right away, he called, "Kenney, you need to take her to the hospital to let someone check that out." Hearing the urgency in his voice, I asked, "Okay ... so, this is an emergency?" He answered, "Well, it looks like it's probably a blood clot."

Trusting his guidance, we drove to the emergency room in Boone. Upon telling them what Dr. Plyler had said, along with their examination, they gave her a blood thinner. By now, it was late Saturday afternoon, so they told us to come back first thing Monday morning to run more tests.

Carolyn and Ken underneath the Lalish holy site

When we returned to the hospital, the female technician doing Carolyn's scan told us, "Yeah, you've got a blood clot. I can see it right here." To me, when you can *see* something, that means you can fix it. (Well drillers think practically that way. But the human body is certainly more complicated than a water well.) Then she added, "I'm just going to continue up your arm and take a look." As she slowly ran the device all the way to Carolyn's collarbone, she said, "Hmmm, this lymph node is larger." That's when my heart fell. A swollen arm and now an enlarged lymph node; I knew something wasn't right.

They wanted to do a needle biopsy of a lymph gland, so I stepped out into the little waiting area beside the procedure room. Soon, the doctor came out and said, "We finished. She'll be out in a few minutes." I asked, "Doc, tell me.

What do you think we're looking at here?" Solemn, he answered, "Well, with my seventeen years of experience, I have a feeling you're looking at a malignancy."

In about a week, the biopsy results came back. Dr. Paul Dagher, who was on the church board with me, had agreed to call us to discuss the results. His father, Sammy Dagher, was a pastor and very close associate of Franklin's, as well as a spiritual mentor to me and countless others. When Paul called, with the phone on speaker, he confirmed a malignancy, metastatic breast cancer. He then started talking about the three primary female hormones and how the identification of one or two of those with a tumor can allow for a targeted response with chemotherapy. Lastly, he said, "The needle biopsy doesn't indicate any of those, so it's triple negative." "Triple negative" sounded like a good thing. Yet what he was explaining to us was that there were no viable targeted treatment options.

This news was emotionally devastating to us both. We were reeling, trying to come to terms with our sudden new reality. What we soon learned was that the cancer had spread, and tumors were all over her body, even down her spine.

For a second opinion on potential treatments, we went to the Mayo Clinic, where we met with a recommended oncologist who was a Christian. As he was looking over everything, he seemed nervous, stopping a few times to scratch his head and rub his brow. As he began to talk about options, he said, "Of course, we've always got chemo in our back pocket." To me, it sounded like he was saying that while there are better treatments, we've always got chemo to fall back on. But no, what he was actually saying was chemo likely wouldn't help. When he finished writing on his chart, he handed us an information sheet on TNBC—triple-negative breast cancer. In the middle of the page, there was a bold line that read "life expectancy nine to eighteen months." My brain was screaming as I tried to take in those words.

After this news, Greta Van Susteren, a good friend who was involved with our work in Haiti, put us in touch with the CEO of MD Anderson in Houston, where Carolyn entered into a research trial. While there, we discovered an interesting fact—one of the foremost experts on triple-negative breast cancer was in Chapel Hill, North Carolina, a two-and-a-half-hour drive from our home. We ended up going through two trials and then radiation. During those treatments, she lost the use of her left arm from paralysis.

For years, Carolyn loved running on nearby trails while communing with God and nature. She always kept a meticulous log of her progress on every outing. When she could no longer run because the nerves in her right leg were starting to be pinched by a tumor, one day we drove to nearby Blowing Rock Park. After walking about a hundred feet on the trail into the woods, she looked at me and said, "I can't go any farther, honey. I've got to go back to the car now." That was her last time. Even still, in her logbook, she recorded that day as walking one-tenth of a mile.

Through these trials, Carolyn stayed resolute. I would see her trying to do something that was clearly very difficult for her and offer, "Honey, let me do that." With great determination, she would tell me, "This is the life I've got, and I'm going to live it."

By March of 2017, Carolyn's right leg was paralyzed, and she had to use a wheelchair to get around.

Throughout her illness, Franklin was enormously gracious to us. When we walked out of the Mayo Clinic after having received the second opinion that confirmed Carolyn had terminal cancer, emotionally exhausted and shaken, we sat down on a bench. Our world was reeling. At that very instant, Franklin called. I spoke to him and Carolyn spoke to him, and then she handed the phone back to me. Franklin said, "Kenney, you need to spend all the time you can with your wife while you've got her." Heeding his guidance, I began working mostly from home. There were also times my coworkers would come by to go over something with me.

They'll Do What They Say They'll Do

During this season in 2016, I sent a DART to northern Iraq—two medical teams in mobile clinics that went into the many villages across the region. Beginning in 2014, the Islamic State's violent attacks had brought about thousands of deaths, as well as the displacement of hundreds of thousands of people. These teams were essentially outpatient clinics offering limited treatment in the Nineveh Plains. (Yes, the same Nineveh that caused so much upset for Jonah before and after he answered God's call.)

Due to the obvious potential threats to Christian humanitarian teams in the region, our typical security system was led by a point of contact who had researched the area, spoken with local officials, assessed the risks, and then made the teams aware of how to take any and all necessary measures to mitigate danger. I began getting word from the medical team leaders that they desperately needed more staff and capacity. They were encountering an increasing number of patients with chronic diseases and a variety of complications. As their requests were coming in, the threat level on the ground was elevated. With that intelligence, the security team lead wanted to limit where the medical teams could go.

This created two issues: The first was the growing pressure from the medical teams to expand our capability. The second involved the security department's responsibility. The question was, ultimately, who decided what our mission was. I knew we needed to find a

IDP Camp, Kurdistan region, northeast Iraq, 2016

way to work together to avoid any contention, a dynamic that appeared to be developing. Clearly, someone needed to resolve these organizational conflicts.

At home, Carolyn was hearing my phone calls regarding the situation in Iraq. Knowing me so well, she quickly picked up on my concerns. Finally, she said, "Listen, I'm going to have about ten days coming up where I will be in a treatment cycle, and I'll be good here. I have people to call if I need help. Why don't you get on a plane, go to Iraq, and solve these issues?"

I heard her out, but I refused. I didn't want to leave her. Now, in every chapter before this one, I have shared how when the call came regarding a crisis, I left with no hesitancy and Carolyn was supportive. So for me to know the problems in Iraq and say no should tell you a lot about my concern for my wife and my understanding of where my priorities had to be. But Carolyn ignored my protests. She started to gently push, "You go. I'll be right here when you get back. You need to go to Iraq. You need to get this done."

Finally, I relented, "All right. Fine. I'll go.... I don't want to, but I will."

In December of 2016, I flew to Iraq, landing in Erbil, located in the northern Kurdish territory where we had an office. There, I met up with our Vice President of Security, Jamie Gough, who would work with me to find solutions. Over the next several days, we made our way across the plains of Nineveh. (You may recall that back when I was making the decision about Samaritan's Purse all those years ago, the story of Jonah was a major motivator for me to listen to God. Actually being in Nineveh when I did not want to go was not lost on me. A full circle moment, for sure.) Jamie and I began to visit local towns and villages where our mobile medical teams were helping victims

Preparing for large-scale food distribution to IDPs, Iraq, 2016 of ISIS. Right away, I saw that they were indeed very mobile, working off card tables with gear brought in duffel bags.

Next, we met with the local security team leader. While I heard and appreciated his concerns, I also felt that by avoiding places that had any possibility of danger, we were not fulfilling our call to ministry. Discussing the issue, he told me that he wanted to go meet with a certain Iraqi brigadier general. Essentially, he felt like an officer from the Iraqi army would be a helpful card in his pocket, should he need it.

We went with him as he drove to the location to meet the general. While he was inside, Jamie and I waited out in the vehicle. Looking around, I realized we were in a place called Bartella, which appeared to be deserted. That made sense because we could hear the bombing and fighting in Mosul, about ten miles away from where the front-line battle with ISIS was taking place. Seeing a checkpoint nearby, we watched as some people walking down the road were stopped by soldiers at gunpoint. They were commanded to reach down and carefully pull their coats up to show there wasn't a bomb strapped to them. Satisfied, the soldiers lowered their guns and let the people pass through. This was clearly a constant threat for the soldiers and a common occurrence for the locals.

After a while, the security leader walked out, got back in the vehicle with us, and said, "Okay, I met the general. I feel good about everything now." During the two-hour drive back to the city, Jamie said to him, "I think we can work here in the plains of Nineveh and move around to the various villages. I don't think it's a closed door." Then, he asked, "Do you agree?" The security leader echoed the agreement. Case closed.

While in the region, Jamie and I went to meet with our country director in Iraq, Matt Nowery, in Erbil. Matt had worked with us for fifteen years. In our conversation, he said, "Oh, Ken, Lise Grande is here right now. She said she knew you from South Sudan and wants to know if you would like to get a cup of coffee with her and catch up?" Lise was the special representative to the secretary-general at the UN.

I responded, "Sure, I know Lise. She's a nice lady and a very professional diplomat." So that afternoon, Matt and I arranged to meet with her and her assistant. After "talking shop" for a while, Lise, who is always very friendly, asked, "So tell me, what's going on in the world of Samaritan's Purse?" I told her how we had just launched a successful deployment of our emergency field hospital in our own DC-8 airplane following an earthquake in Ecuador. Hearing that news, Lise perked up and asked, "You have hospitals?"

After I confirmed, she explained her interest, "Well, just last night, I gave a lot of money from the UN to WHO to buy three hospitals." I started laughing and said, "Lise, you can't just *buy* a hospital. You have to secure medical personnel, doctors, nurses, biomedical technicians, and engineers. You have to build a whole team. Plus, you need equipment. There's no such thing as a hospital-in-a-box." While I was being very direct, with the kind of money I knew the UN had likely given, I felt an obligation to be honest with her. Lise took out a pen and pad and wrote down a name and phone number. Sliding the paper across the table to me, she said, "This is Altaf Musani, the country director for WHO in Iraq. I think you need to go talk to him."

Honoring Lise's request, I called Altaf's office and made an appointment. The next morning, Matt and I drove to the WHO compound, which was quite large. Around the permanent buildings there were a number of mobile offices housed in twenty-foot-by-eight-foot shipping containers, essentially a large metal box. Altaf was an American who had graduated from Emory and was clearly quite smart. He was seated behind a desk with his hands clasped on top of a legal-size notebook about three inches thick. Right away, I could tell that his body language indicated skepticism about me and our organizational capability. His reservations were warranted, knowing the extreme complexity of medical work involving surgery in war zones.

After introductions, I got right to the point, "Yesterday, Lise, the SRSG, told me you're looking to put up hospitals." His answer was reasonable, as he stated, "Yes, but this isn't something that some NGO can just come and do." I responded, "Okay, well, are you looking for a tier 2 or tier 3 hospital, and how many ORs were you expecting?" As soon as he heard my questions using that terminology, he could tell I knew what I was talking about. From there, I called Ian Norton, a doctor I had met in the Philippines in 2013, who was the head of medical teams with WHO and was aware of the development of our hospital program and the progress we had made. Ian kindly explained, "Samaritan's Purse will do what they say they're going to do. They have the capability, and they're very professional."

Satisfied with the call, Altaf opened up the thick notebook to a map, then said, "WHO needs to put three hospitals down." As he pointed to a specific spot, my glance went straight to the area where we had been the day before—

Bartella. This was the same kind of situation that had happened in Haiti, where we met the pastor of the church and then got involved in the World Food Programme's food distribution. Once again, I saw a place where I had just been "by chance." What I didn't know at that moment was that Bartella was actually a Christian community.

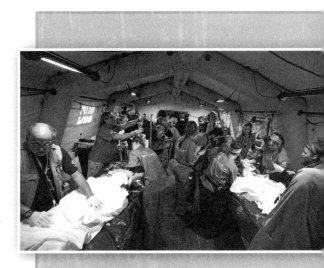

I looked up from the map and said, "I am not committing yet, but I will tell you I'm at least 85 percent sure we'll

Medical staff treating patients in emergency room, outside of Mosul, 2017

do it." I felt God speaking to me through another providential convergence regarding a spot on a map and a need that He wanted met.

Altaf and I developed a great working relationship. Later, he sent me a note asking about the potential of starting another project in Yemen and said, "Together, we can change the world."

Why Are These People Being So Kind?

Back at the hotel, I called Franklin. "Hey, I met with Lise Grande, a lady I know from South Sudan. She asked me to speak with the WHO field office here in Iraq. Bottom line, they're asking us to put together a proposal to place a hospital here."

Franklin Graham giving the address at the dedication of the Emergency Field Hospital, Bartella, January 2017

Over the years, in situations such as this, my conversations with Franklin have often been very brief. As usual, in this conversation, he asked me questions: "Can we get the access we need?" "Can we handle the logistics?" "Can we do it now?" "You think we can pull it off?" To each question, I answered, "Yes, we can do it." Franklin's final question was "Kenney, do you *want* to do it?" I responded, "Yes, I do." His closing words were "Then let's do it!" A massive decision in a brief, simple conversation. But that's what years of trust can produce.

I called the Incident Management Team (IMT) Command Center back home and spoke with Dr. Elliott Tenpenny, our Director of International Health, and said, "Listen, we're talking about a tier 3 hospital that has to be here. It's needed *now*. The location will be about ten miles outside Mosul. We can expect trauma wounds from gunshots, mines, booby traps, and explosions. War zone emergencies. I need you all to get a concept paper together right away."

After assigning our IMT the responsibility, I flew back home. Even though I knew that asking them to develop a plan quickly created a lot of pressure, from there, everything began to come together. I have always felt that if government funding is available for something that God has called us to do, then we should display excellence to qualify. God's people should reflect His qualities in all we do.

After the hospital proposal was written and submitted, WHO processed the paperwork extremely fast. They knew the circumstances in Iraq involved life-and-death situations where wounded people needed treatment. Typically, with a proposal this complicated and expensive, most of the details are worked out before the ink is ever on paper. The normal process can go on for weeks or even months, but in this case, we signed agreements within ten days.

To get started, WHO committed up front to roughly half of the $20 million it would ultimately cost to complete the project. We soon realized that our single DC-8 airplane could not fly enough equipment over to set up a tier 3 hospital. We also knew that we didn't have the necessary permissions to take our plane into Erbil. While we needed another flight, it wouldn't be allowed to come into Erbil either. The Iraqi military had shut down the airspace. In fact, a French flight had landed there rather than Baghdad, and the government impounded the plane. Iraq wanted flights to land in Baghdad so they could formally clear all imported goods coming into the country, which obviously presented bureaucratic delays and issues. In our case, it was not in anyone's best interest to waste time.

Here was yet another obstacle to overcome: Christmas was just around the corner, and 747s essentially become Santa's sled to move things around the world. At "the most wonderful time of the year," 747s are like flying reindeer—*very* hard to find. They're all booked up far in advance. So with our whole team working on this problem, finally, we located a carrier called Silk Way in Azerbaijan that had a 747-400 available. To our surprise, not only did they inform us that we could charter the plane, but they also said they had clearance to fly into Erbil two days every week. Their cargo planes had standing permission to land there—the proverbial two birds with one stone. Once again, God made a way where we thought there was no way.

We had the 747 land in Greensboro, North Carolina, where we loaded it up. The flight would be coming into Iraq on Christmas Eve with its landing permission good only until midnight. But the flight was late arriving to us, and, on top of that, one of the pieces of equipment that lifted the freight up into the airplane was broken. And, as if these problems weren't enough, the plane had to fly to Baku, the capital of Azerbaijan, refuel, and then fly around Iran into Iraq. After the flight had been in the air long enough to know it had to be getting close to Erbil, we called Silk Way's operations desk to ask, "Sir, we're just checking on our expected landing time. Our people there are telling us the airspace will close in forty-five minutes." A man with a heavy Russian accent assured us the plane would be there on time before the deadline expired.

People fleeing Mosul area during time of conflict, 2017

At 11:45 p.m. local time in Erbil, our cargo plane touched down.

We had flown a large DART over there on commercial flights. With such a massive amount of cargo that had to be unloaded, the operation involved a lot of people, forklifts, and vehicles to move the supplies and equipment two hours west to the hospital site. Our security team was working with contractors to build double blast walls, grading the area and hauling in mountains of gravel. We also had to put a strict security contingent in place because of the constant concern of suicide bombers coming to try to stop us.

We created three rings of protection. First, we coordinated with the Iraqi military to guard the external perimeter from about ten kilometers out. For the middle ground protection, we hired a private contractor. Around the actual hospital wall, we had another private contractor provide men carrying side-arms. Inside the hospital, we had to come up with a protocol for how to get patients through, making sure they didn't have weapons or explosives on them. As has so often been the case, our team did a masterful job. Within two weeks, the hospital was up, equipped, staffed, and ready to open.

Back home, just as Carolyn had told me, she was able to be self-sufficient during that ten-day window while I went to Iraq. In early January of 2017, Franklin oversaw the dedication of the hospital in Mosul. He called me from there and said, "Kenney, I wish you could be here." I detected he was emotional as he spoke. I said, "Well, I wish I could be there too, but I'm where I'm supposed to be right now. Thank you for letting me be home, Franklin."

After he had toured the hospital and led the dedication, Franklin called me again, so excited. "Kenney, this is the best thing we've ever done! You wouldn't believe it. The people on the team are all amazing." I could not have agreed with him more. But what a satisfying and affirming word to hear from the president of our organization. As he has always been so faithful to do, Franklin proclaimed the Gospel there at the hospital in Iraq.

From January to September 2017, Samaritan's Purse ran the hospital in that location treating 4,000 patients with 1,700 lifesaving surgeries. The Iraqis we worked with were enormously warm, gracious, hospitable, welcoming, and appreciative. They knew that no one else was willing to go there and commit to such a project.

Once again, we come back to Jesus' parable of the Good Samaritan. While we so

Outside of Mosul, 2017

often focus on how the Samaritan met the needs of the wounded man, we cannot dismiss the other side of what Jesus was teaching: the priest and the Levite wouldn't go near the victim in the ditch to help. Social, cultural, and political divisions took precedent over ministry. In our hospital, besides the Iraqi people, Christians treated ISIS fighters, men that so many people would avoid for all the same reasons the wounded man was avoided in Jesus' parable. To this day, I don't know how those fighters got into the hospital, but when they did, we treated them just like everybody else.

To support this point, I have to share an amazing story I heard from a translator there. We had a section in the hospital designated for military-aged men, particularly those who came in having the appearance of combat-hardened fighters. For obvious security reasons, we had to watch them, taking no chances, because the environment was so hostile. He heard this one man, who had a long beard and the typical clothing of an ISIS fighter, ask, "What is going on here? Why are these people being so kind to us? These are the people that we're trying to kill." This was evidence that those who were being treated were starting to ask questions they had never asked before, namely, "What could possibly motivate these people to help us?!"

Displaced Iraqis, northeast Iraq, 2017

When ISIS was overrun and pushed out of Mosul, the hospital's structures and equipment were divided up and sent into various communities. Eventually, the Iraqi government gave us permission to bring our DC-8 in and land directly in Erbil every week with medical supplies. During the operation of the hospital, we had to maintain our supply lines for medical equipment, as well as for medicines, narcotics, and anesthetics. The prime minister of the government of Iraq gave us special permission to manage our own pharmaceutical supply and signed off on all the necessary permissions. Our witness there was strong and, as always, came about from focusing on relationships, taking the time to build trust, and remaining committed to being persistent, consistent, tenacious, and pervasive in difficult environments.

Looking back, several things are very poignant to me. The domino effect is so clear. God worked through Carolyn to motivate me to go to Iraq. Had I not met with our security team leader, I wouldn't have gone to Bartella. Had I not worked in South Sudan, I would not have known Lise Grande. If Lise had not met with Matt, she would not have requested a meeting with me. Had I not met with Matt, I wouldn't have met with Lise Grande. Had I not met with Lise, I wouldn't have met with the man from WHO and wouldn't have seen Bartella on his map. Had I not known Ian, I may not have gotten the attention of the WHO country director. Considering all these individual factors, we would never have had the invitation to build a hospital. None of that would have happened. Plus, I have to go back to the fact that I did not want to go. Had God not worked through Carolyn, there may not have been a hospital in Mosul when one was desperately needed to save many lives.

Lastly, everyone who worked at that hospital walked through fire together. And people who walk through fire together become uniquely bonded. They dealt with all sorts of emotional trauma and pain as they met together every morning for devotions inside concrete walls for protection from shelling. Those same people put Bible verses and prayer notes for Carolyn on those walls. Today, I have pictures of that display of their love and commitment. God worked through my wife to get to me, but then when the dedication was made and the actual operation began, it wasn't His will for me to be there. The glory was God's and God's alone. It was not what any one person did but what He did.

Your Will Be Done

Month by month in 2017, Carolyn got worse. During that time, literally hundreds of people came by our house to spend time with her. When she reached the point where it was becoming physically difficult for me to take care of her alone, I had to have help. At that time, I received some wise advice, "In the final days, you don't need to be her caregiver; you need to be her husband." I heeded that wisdom, and, from that point on, I was only her husband. I wanted to be there with her for every moment, to be close to her, to love her, as I always did.

In the final weeks, her body was in an emaciated state. She was gaunt, and her hair became wiry like steel wool. Her cheeks were sunken, and her skin appeared burned from the chemo and radiation. In the final days, we all started to feel a special presence in the room. Something heavenly. I began to wonder if there was an angel sent to watch over her or escort her home.

After midnight on October 3, she became very weak, and her pulse grew faint. As I sat by her bedside, there were a couple of hospice nurses with me, monitoring her vitals. Suddenly, Carolyn's right arm rose up into the air, and her eyes looked up toward the right-hand corner of the bedroom. I thought she was having some sort of seizure, so I gently took her hand, brought her arm back down, and began to rub her shoulder. When I let go, she put her arm right back up in the air as she continued gazing upward. That's when I realized she was worshipping.

In that moment, the nurses, our sons—Coy and Jamey, who were now in the room—and I all felt the strong, manifested presence of the Holy Spirit, as if Jesus was there to receive her. Certainly, the intensity of the supernatural feeling that there was a powerful presence in the room was substantially accentuated. Listening with a stethoscope, at 12:55 a.m., as we all softly sang "It Is Well with My Soul," I heard my wife's final heartbeat. She took her last breath on this earth and stepped into Heaven with her Lord, who had surely come into the room moments before, getting her attention, causing her to lift her gaze and raise her hand, to do what He promised her in John 14:2–3, "My Father's house has many rooms; if that were not so, would I have told you that I am going there to prepare a place for you? And if I go and prepare a place for you, I will come back and take you to be with me that you also may be where I am."

At Carolyn's memorial service, hundreds of people came to honor her life and her God.

A few weeks later, Franklin called and said, "Hey, Kenney, why don't you come down to Florida? There's so much going on after Hurricane Maria that we can't keep up with it all." I was honest with him, "No, I don't want to do that." He persisted, "Come on. Come on down and join us." Franklin has always been great about knowing when to help someone get back up after they've received a blow in their life. I agreed and, from there, returned to what I was called to do.

Fast-forward several months to February 19, 2018. I was in Juba, South Sudan. That night, I had the most vivid, realistic, incredibly intense dream I have ever had. I saw Carolyn. Her hair was white as snow, very thick and full, down to her shoulders. She was wearing a whitish-silver woven blouse and skirt. While I knew her face, I couldn't clearly see because she was so extraordinarily bright and radiant that the light hurt my eyes, and I had to squint. But as I tried to look at her, I realized the light wasn't emanating from her. Rather, she was a reflection from another Source.

Construction of hospital's blast walls, Bartella

Around her eyes and face, there was something there that I can only describe as a tiny solar system, like little planets and stars in a formation. As I watched

her, for just a moment, she glanced at me, but then her head went back up to look above and past me again—not that different from what I had witnessed her doing in her final moments before she passed as she looked up at the corner of the room. Then, and in my dream, her eyes were fixed on something or Someone beyond me.

In the dream, I walked toward her, asking, "Aren't you glad to see me?" As I got to her, Carolyn raised her left arm into the air. That was significant because her left arm had been paralyzed in her final months. As I put my arms around her, I felt her physically. I felt her body pressed against mine, as I had countless times in our marriage. She gave me a fraternal pat on my shoulders, yet she never took her eyes off whatever she was looking toward. That's where the dream ended. It was so profound and so real to me that I awoke, got up, and wrote down the details I just shared with you.

As I processed everything I had just witnessed, I believe that God allowed me to see my wife in Heaven. And then I realized something far more important: what Carolyn was looking toward was also exactly what she was reflecting—the glory of God. Now, here is what I also came to understand that I believe He wanted me to know: my earthly relationship with her was of minimal importance compared to the glory of Christ. We often wonder about who *won't* be in Heaven, but the real point is who *is* there: Jesus. Because of the light of Christ, we *won't* be sad; we can't be sad. There will be no tears. God's glory will supersede everything, as evidenced in passages such as John's words in Revelation 21:

And I heard a loud voice from the throne saying, "Look! God's dwelling place is now among the people, and he will dwell with them. They will be his people, and God himself will be with them and be their God. 'He will wipe every tear from their eyes. There will be no more death' or mourning or crying or pain, for the old order of things has passed away."

He who was seated on the throne said, "I am making everything new!" (vv. 3–5)

In the months when my wife lay dying, our prayer changed from "Lord, would You give us ten more years?" to "Lord, Your will be done because we trust You." At forty-six and a half years of marriage, in front of several hundred people, we publicly renewed our vows in church with Carolyn in her wheelchair. We had always thought we would take that step at our fifty-year anniversary, but we saw we weren't going to make it. That was not a lack of faith, just the realization of what we sensed as we prayed for His will.

We arrived at the conclusion that God doesn't owe us anything. However many years we had, in light of eternity, would be but a vapor, gone in the blink of an eye. Even if God were to heal Carolyn and give us twenty more years, we were going to eventually end up right back here anyway. One of us was going to die first. Through that journey, we realized the importance of trusting Him in life and in death. Carolyn trusted Him. I trusted Him and still do. And the dream that God gave me reinforced that trust deeper than ever as an affirmation of our aspirations and beliefs as a couple about Heaven and eternity with Him.

Starting the day with team prayer, near Mosul, 2017

Today, I know exactly where my wife is. I know she is with Jesus, the One she couldn't turn her eyes away from. All the questions of earth simply fade in the light of His face.

There was a special spiritual connection between Carolyn and the Lord in her request, encouraging me to go to Iraq. I believe that sacrifice she made in our final days will be one of her many treasures in Heaven. She glorified God by insisting I go.

Lastly, that little solar system, for lack of a better description, that I saw on her face—I believe with all my heart that had to do with her rewards, the jewels in her crown given to her by Jesus.

As for me, my life has already been poured out as an offering to God. The time of my death is near. I have fought the good fight, I have finished the race, and I have remained faithful. And now the prize awaits me—the crown of righteousness, which the Lord, the righteous Judge, will give me on the day of his return. And the prize is not just for me but for all who eagerly look forward to his appearing. (2 Tim. 4:6–8 NLT)

View of EFH, outside of Mosul, 2017

Called to Follow, Called to Go

Back in my days as a well driller, I stood at a machine that was at work at the bottom of a hole, often five hundred feet away, straight down. I couldn't see it. I didn't know what was actually going on down there. I heard a loud smashing sound as my hands were on the controls and the drill rod. Through repeating that process over and over again, in those first twenty-two years of my life, I was able to develop the ability to perceive and respond to that which I could not see.

My life and work as a well driller has always made Hebrews 11:1 an unusual and real-time metaphor for me: "Now faith is confidence in what we hope for and assurance about what we do not see." As I lowered the bit to start breaking through the ground, I had to be confident that, while I could not see it, water was where I hoped it would be. As my hands guided the controls, I had to have the assurance of the reality far below me. Every day of the past thirty-five years working for Samaritan's Purse, I have taken a similar action, except it may be a phone call to a country director in Africa, a text to a pastor in Ukraine, a letter to the president of South Sudan, or a face-to-face sit-down in Washington with the National Security Council. In each setting, I am working to get lifesaving, life-giving resources to victims and survivors around the world while applying the faith, the confidence, and the assurance that God is leading my heart and guiding my hands.

In my story you have just read, I simply testified to what I have seen and experienced, which is exactly the same purpose of the Gospels, to offer written accounts of Jesus' work in the lives of people. I'm grateful that, early on, I began to understand that work is not about me, but Him. Throughout my life, I have been well aware that I am not the one driving the bus. But I have been blessed to get a good seat as God saw fit to educate me through His own means, not by the ways of this world, but in His very eclectic, unique, and creative manner.

Everything I learned was in the field, through hard work and trial-and-error problem-solving. My commitment has been to live by the biblical principles of honesty, integrity, and compassion where my primary job is to find a workable and practical solution. In the beginning of my career, I was bothered when someone would comment, "We noticed you don't have a degree." But it wasn't long before I realized that my God-given opportunities were actually my education.

In reality, my life's work, just like the organization where I work, has borne out Luke 10:25–37, the story of the Good Samaritan. One day, an expert of the law came to Jesus and started a conversation, not about being a good neighbor, not about good works, but about a spiritual, eternal question:

> "Teacher," he asked, "what must I do to inherit eternal life?"
>
> "What is written in the Law?" [Jesus] replied. "How do you read it?" (vv. 25–26)

I find it interesting that the Lord's response was not to give an answer but to offer the expert two of His own questions, essentially, "How do you understand it? How do you interpret it?" The man answered with text that was familiar to them both:

> "Love the Lord your God with all your heart and with all your soul and with all your strength and with all your mind"; and, "Love your neighbor as yourself." (v. 27)

Those themes come from two different places in the Old Testament with "love God" being from Deuteronomy 6:5 and "love your neighbor" from Leviticus 19:18.

> "You have answered correctly," Jesus replied. "Do this and you will live." (v. 28)

Now, to truly "do this"—to love the Lord with all your heart and your mind and soul and to love your neighbor as yourself—would require a life of perfection, which Jesus lived. But we know the state of the human race: "For all have sinned and fall short of the glory of God" (Rom. 3:23), the very reason we need Jesus.

So with a sense of arrogance, the expert wanted to test the Lord.

> But he wanted to justify himself, so he asked Jesus, "And who is my neighbor?" (Luke 10:29)

Now, comes the parable:

> In reply Jesus said: "A man was going down from Jerusalem to Jericho, when he was attacked by robbers. They stripped him of his clothes, beat him and went away, leaving him half dead. A priest happened to be going down the same road, and when he saw the man, he passed by on the other side. So too, a Levite, when he came to the place and saw him, passed by on the other side." (vv. 30–32)

Every time I read this, I tell myself, *I never want to be like those two men. I don't want to be someone who is too afraid or too pious or too hurried or too comfortable to stop and help.* But a fascinating and surprising twist came next, especially in that day, as Jesus made the hero of His parable a social outcast, someone despised by the Jewish religious leaders.

> But a Samaritan, as he traveled, came where the man was; and when he saw him, he took pity on him. He went to him and bandaged his wounds, pouring on oil and wine. Then he put the man on his own donkey, brought him to an inn and took care of him. The next day he took out two denarii and gave them to the innkeeper. "Look after him," he said, "and when I return, I will reimburse you for any extra expense you may have." (vv. 33–35)

Now, notice that the Samaritan didn't ask, "So, who did you vote for?" or "Which side do you fight for?" or "Who do you pray to?" or "Who do you sleep with?" In fact, he didn't ask anything. There were no prerequisites, qualifications, or requirements. He simply took action. By bandaging the man's wounds and taking him to the inn for care, the Samaritan made a choice that saved the man's life.

Called to Word and Deed

Allow me to break this down in the professional terms of humanitarian NGO work:

By bandaging the man's wounds, the Samaritan gave emergency medicine.

By putting the man on a donkey, he provided emergency logistics.

By taking the man to an inn, he provided emergency shelter.

By giving the man the required physical needs, he provided emergency water and food, along with some sort of covering (a blanket or robe), known as NFIs—nonfood items.

In just two verses, Jesus gave the six primary sectors known today in the world of emergency relief:

1. Emergency Medicine
2. Emergency Logistics
3. Emergency Shelter
4. Emergency Food
5. Emergency Water
6. Emergency NFIs

Lastly, the Good Samaritan focused on the man's short-term needs by leaving money and instructions for him to be taken care of. He didn't have a discussion with the innkeeper about where the man might get a job, where he could live, how he was going to provide for himself and his family, or how his kids were going to be educated. The point of Jesus' parable was all about emergency response: "What did you do for the victim during the emergent situation?"

Jesus followed up His story with another question:

> "Which of these three do you think was a neighbor to the
> man who fell into the hands of robbers?" (v. 36)

Essentially, Jesus asked, of the three—the priest, the Levite, and the Samaritan—which acted like a neighbor?

> The expert in the law replied, "The one who had mercy on
> him." (v. 37)

Then the conversation ended:

> Jesus told him, "Go and do likewise." (v. 37)

Not a suggestion, but a command.

We need to understand the connection Jesus makes here between knowing what is required and taking action—the go and do. In the Western evangelical world today, the balance between word—what we say—and deed—what we do—is not as it should be, particularly in light of Jesus' parable. My belief is that when we receive Jesus as Lord and Savior and enter into a relationship with Him, He calls us to both word *and* deed. The scales are balanced as His Holy Spirit fills and empowers us, then His fruit of the Spirit grows and flows from us. We are called to both the filling *and* the fruit.

Called to Stand Firm

Another hallmark passage for me in my life and career comes from Matthew 24.

> As Jesus was sitting on the Mount of Olives, the disciples came to him privately. "Tell us," they said, "... what will be the sign of your coming and of the end of the age?"
>
> Jesus answered ... "You will hear of wars and rumors of wars, but see to it that you are not alarmed. Such things must happen, but the end is still to come. Nation will rise against nation, and kingdom against kingdom. There will be famines and earthquakes in various places. All these are the beginning of birth pains." (vv. 3–4, 6–8)

War has been a common catalyst for Samaritan's Purse's response to help the victim and survivor, the refugee and the displaced. I have told you stories about wars, nations against nations, famines, and earthquakes. Today, there are most certainly wars and rumors of wars. These "birth pains," as Jesus called them, have also been Samaritan's Purse's calling. That *is* our mission for this time in history.

Jesus continued:

Then you will be handed over to be persecuted and put to death, and you will be hated by all nations because of me. At that time many will turn away from the faith and will betray and hate each other, and many false prophets will appear and deceive many people. Because of the increase of wickedness, the love of most will grow cold, but the one who stands firm to the end will be saved. And this gospel of the kingdom will be preached in the whole world as a testimony to all nations, and then the end will come. (vv. 9–14)

I am certainly no prophet, and I am not a preacher. But I can testify that the cadence, the rhythm, the speed of the fulfillment of prophecy certainly appears to be picking up in my lifetime. Simply take a look at the pace of technology and changes of recent years. Around the world, deviousness, brutality, and savagery, the "increase of wickedness" is clear. With the way information is given or withheld, the way that power is centralized in governments, and even the concentration of power and authority that exceeds governments, how much longer can the world continue on this trajectory?

In the meantime, Jesus told us what to do: stand firm for the Gospel of His Kingdom.

Called to Follow

Those who believe Jesus' promises also believe He will come back. With that as our future reality, my encouragement to you is to get involved in the lives of others. That starts by not walking past the wounded on the side of the road, whether a neighbor in your community or on the other side of the world.

There is an ongoing dialogue in the NGO community that says, "Okay, so you helped someone. You gave someone fresh water and a blanket. That's great. But what about next month?" In every need met that I have witnessed, whatever has been done to help right now has had merit in and of itself. No, we will never be able to fix all the ills of poverty and political challenges in this world. While we cannot begin to resolve all that is wrong, we also cannot casually walk by someone and ignore when he or she is hurt, bleeding, and in need.

I have also seen that when people get help, they don't forget. They ask, "Why did you do that?" That witness for Christ is my encouragement to never let your heart grow cold, as He warned would happen to many. I believe it is time for those who follow Him to step forward and get involved. I literally see thousands upon thousands take that challenge every year. You can join them. Step up to help your brothers and sisters. Don't take tomorrow for granted. Put in the work to see the harvest. Invest. Take the time. Decide to live in the Kingdom of God on this earth where, when an enemy is bleeding, he or she is no longer a combatant but a patient.

I have seen horrific things that I cannot unsee but wish I could. Yet I have also seen God work in ways that I could never have imagined. I have seen Him open doors no one believed could be open. Followers of Jesus will be a part of that work in His Kingdom to help the suffering in this world, those who are our neighbors.

Called to Go

At Samaritan's Purse, when I have to make decisions after a catastrophe has occurred somewhere in the world, I believe Jesus' words are not an optional suggestion but a direct command. That brings me back to His final words to the expert in the law, "Go and do likewise" (Luke 10:37). In the first book of the New Testament, the Gospel of Matthew, we find the word *go* constantly given—to the forgiven, to the healed, to the wealthy and the poor alike, and, finally, to His followers.

> Go and be reconciled.
> Go with them, not one but two miles.
> Go, show yourself to the priest.

Go, let it be done just as you believed.

Go, take your mat and walk.

Go and proclaim this message.

Go, sell your possessions, and give to the poor.

Go to the street corners.

Go and make disciples of all nations.

But to anyone who claims He is Lord, His command is clear: Go.

The only question that remains is, Will you?

Will you help in Jesus' name?

Will you run to the fire?

Notes

Chapter 2: Go, Even Though There Is No Road—Ethiopia

1. Haley Hudson, "Khat Addiction and Abuse," Addiction Center, updated March 2, 2025, www.addictioncenter.com/drugs/khat-addiction-abuse.

Chapter 3: Now's the Time—Afghanistan

1. "Sikorsky S-70A: UH-60A Black Hawk," Igor I Sikorsky Historical Archives, accessed February 4, 2025, https://sikorskyarchives.com/home/sikorsky-product-history/helicopter-innovation-era/sikorsky-s-70a-uh-60a-black-hawk.

2. "Special Forces: Serve among the Most Elite in the Force," U.S. Army, accessed February 4, 2025, www.goarmy.com/careers-and-jobs/specialty-careers/special-ops/special-forces.

3. "Duhok City," Duhok Private Technical Institute, accessed February 4, 2025, https://dhk-pti.com/website/DuhokCity.php.

4. Rudyard Kipling, "Arithmetic on the Frontier," Kipling Society, accessed February 4, 2025, www.kiplingsociety.co.uk/poem/poems_arith.htm.

5. "Soviet Invasion of Afghanistan: 1979," *Britannica*, updated February 15, 2025, www.britannica.com/event/Soviet-invasion-of-Afghanistan.

6. Julie Elkner, "*Dedovshchina* and the Committee of Soldiers' Mothers under Gorbachev," *The Journal of Power Institutions in Post-Soviet Societies*, no. 1 (2004), https://journals.openedition.org/pipss/243.

7. "Mujahideen: Afghani Rebels," *Britannica*, updated November 8, 2024, www.britannica.com/topic/mujahideen-Afghani-rebels.

8. Nazar Ul Islam and Benazir Shah, "Pakistan's 'Gun Valley': A Town of 80,000 People & 2,000 Weapon Shops," ThePrint, January 22, 2019, https://theprint.in/feature/pakistans-gun-valley-a-town-of-80000-people-2000-weapon-shops/181754.

9. Aaron Y. Zelin, "When Tunisians Fired the Start Gun for 9/11," Washington Institute for Near East Policy, September 9, 2021, www.washingtoninstitute.org/policy-analysis/when -tunisians-fired-start-gun-911.

10. A film depicting this story titled *12 Strong* was released in 2018, based on the book *Horse Soldiers: The Extraordinary Story of a Band of U.S. Soldiers Who Rode to Victory in Afghanistan* by Doug Stanton.

11. "The United States President's Emergency Plan for AIDS Relief," U.S. Department of State, accessed February 4, 2025, www.state.gov/pepfar.

Chapter 4: Anyone Who Welcomes a Little Child—Bosnia

1. "Josip Broz Tito Summary," *Britannica*, accessed February 4, 2025, www.britannica.com /summary/Josip-Broz-Tito.

2. "The Breakup of Yugoslavia," Remembering Srebrenica, accessed February 4, 2025, https://srebrenica.org.uk/what-happened/history/breakup-yugoslavia.

3. John R. Lampe, "Bosnian War: European History (1992–1995)," *Britannica*, updated March 18, 2025, www.britannica.com/event/Bosnian-War.

4. "Bosnia and Herzegovina: Displacement Associated with Conflict and Violence," Internal Displacement Monitoring Centre, accessed February 4, 2025, https://api.internal -displacement.org/sites/default/files/2020-04/GRID%202020%20-%20Conflict %20Figure%20Analysis%20-%20BOSNIA%20AND%20HERZEGOVINA.pdf.

5. "Bosnian Genocide," History, updated October 30, 2019, www.history.com/topics/1990s /bosnian-genocide.

Chapter 5: Tell Them Who You Are and Why You're Here—Rwanda

1. "Rwanda Genocide: 100 Days of Slaughter," BBC, April 4, 2019, www.bbc.com/news /world-africa-26875506.

2. *Time*, May 16, 1994, https://time.com/vault/issue/1994-05-16/page/1.

3. "Remembering Rwanda: A Genocide Remembered," Samaritan's Purse, June 7, 2013, www.samaritanspurse.org/our-ministry/remembering-rwanda.

4. "Remembering Rwanda."

Chapter 6: Will I Die Tonight or Tomorrow?—Zaire

1. "Paul Kagame: President of Rwanda," *Britannica*, updated March 18, 2025, www.britannica.com/biography/Paul-Kagame.

2. Kris Janowski, "Eight-Year Rwandan Refugee Saga in Tanzania Comes to an End," UNHCR, January 3, 2003, www.unhcr.org/us/news/eight-year-rwandan-refugee -saga-tanzania-comes-end.

3. "Mission," International Organization for Migration, UN Migration, accessed February 4, 2025, www.iom.int/mission.

Chapter 7: To Go into the No-Go—South Sudan

1. "A Guide to the United States' History of Recognition, Diplomatic, and Consular Relations, by Country, since 1776: South Sudan," Office of the Historian, US Department of State, accessed February 4, 2025, https://history.state.gov/countries/south-sudan.

2. Peter Tingwa, "Dr. Kenneth and Ms. Eileen Fraser, the Lui Hospital and the Beginning of Modern Health System in the Greater Mundri Counties," *South Sudan Medical Journal*, 2023, www.southsudanmedicaljournal.com/assets/files/Journals/vol_16_iss_1_feb_23 /Lui%20Hospital%20History_Final.pdf.

3. Cédric Cotter, "The Religious Convictions of Henri Dunant, Founder of the ICRC," *Religion and Humanitarian Principles*, International Committee of the Red Cross, November 8, 2021, https://blogs.icrc.org/religion-humanitarianprinciples/the-religious-convictions -of-henri-dunant-founder-of-the-icrc.

My Seventeen-Month Detour through Washington, DC

1. "Indian Ocean Tsunami of 2004," *Britannica*, updated March 19, 2025, www.britannica.com/event/Indian-Ocean-tsunami-of-2004.

Chapter 8: Yes, Mr. President—China/Myanmar

1. John P. Rafferty and Kenneth Pletcher, "Sichuan Earthquake of 2008," *Britannica*, updated May 9, 2024, www.britannica.com/event/Sichuan-earthquake-of-2008.

2. "Number of Dead and Missing in Myanmar Cyclone Raised to 138,000," ReliefWeb, United Nations Office for the Coordination of Humanitarian Affairs (OCHA), June 24, 2008, https://reliefweb.int/report/myanmar/number-dead-and-missing-myanmar-cyclone -raised-138000.

3. "A Chinese Man Walk [*sic*] Past a Clock Tower Which Stopped the Time When Monday's Powerful Earthquake Hit Hanwang Town in Sichuan Province, China, Wednesday, May 14, 2008," Alamy, accessed February 5, 2025, www.alamy.com/a-chinese-man-walk-past-a-clock -tower-which-stopped-the-time-when-mondays-powerful-earthquake-hit-hanwang-town-in -sichuan-province-china-wednesday-may-14-2008-ap-photoandy-wong-image539778845.html.

Chapter 9: Ask the Right Questions—Haiti

1. Richard Pallardy, "2010 Haiti Earthquake," *Britannica*, updated February 19, 2025, www.britannica.com/event/2010-Haiti-earthquake.

2. "Haitian Revolution: Haitian History," *Britannica*, updated February 21, 2025, www.britannica.com/topic/Haitian-Revolution.

3. "Haiti Cholera Outbreak: October 22, 2010–March 15, 2011," CDC Office of Readiness and Response, accessed April 8, 2025, www.cdc.gov/orr/responses/haiti-cholera-outbreak .html.

4. Pallardy, "2010 Haiti Earthquake."

Chapter 10 Like God Had Punched the Earth—Japan

1. Kenneth Pletcher and John P. Rafferty, "Japan Earthquake and Tsunami of 2011," *Britannica*, updated March 19, 2025, www.britannica.com/event/Japan-earthquake-and -tsunami-of-2011.

2. Pletcher and Rafferty, "Japan Earthquake and Tsunami."

3. Laura Castañón, "Fukushima and the Ocean: A Decade of Disaster Response," *Oceanus*, April 1, 2021, www.whoi.edu/oceanus/feature/fukushima-disaster-response.

4. "Comparing Fukushima and Chernobyl," Nuclear Energy Institute (NEI), October 2019, https://www.nei.org/resources/fact-sheets/comparing-fukushima-and-chernobyl.

5. "Snow Adds to Japan's Misery," CBS News, March 17, 2011, www.cbsnews.com/pictures /snow-adds-to-japans-misery.

6. "What Is the Richter Scale," SMS Tsunami Warning, accessed February 4, 2025, www.sms-tsunami-warning.com/pages/richter-scale.

7. "Japan Video Shows Moment Tsunami Hit Fukushima Nuclear Plant," Channel 4 News, YouTube, accessed April 8, 2025, https://youtu.be/f9AcMn6ygq8?si=vs5Yvpl2d_dZ3eYe.

8. Peter Durfee, "A Tsunami Landmark to Come Down," Nippon.com, September 10, 2013, www.nippon.com/en/nipponblog/z00014.

9. John P. Rafferty and Kenneth Pletcher, "Aftermath of the Disaster in Japan Earthquake and Tsunami," *Britannica*, updated March 19, 2025, www.britannica.com/event/Japan -earthquake-and-tsunami-of-2011/Aftermath-of-the-disaster.

10. "Samaritan's Purse—Japanese Congressman Doi Visits Tsunami Damage," Samaritan's Purse, YouTube, accessed April 8, 2025, https://youtu.be/QLILuVFIKyQ?si=6x22NJhGAa Ad2CZb.

11. "Diet: Japanese Government," *Britannica*, updated March 7, 2025, www.britannica.com /topic/Diet-Japanese-government.

12. Narae Kim and Yeara Ahn-Park, "Korea-Japan Memorial Service for Ryuichi Doi: 'Man of God with a Religious Conscience,'" *Kukmin Daily*, March 30, 2016, www.kukmindaily.co .kr/article/view.asp?arcid=0010490670.

13. Mike Gagliardi, "Move Over, Ford and Chevy: Kei Trucks Are Pulling Up as Customers Opt for Smaller, Cheaper Vehicles," NBC News, June 12, 2024, www.nbcnews.com/business /autos/kei-trucks-are-gaining-popularity-us-small-size-low-prices-rcna156653.

Chapter 11: This May Be His Only Chance—Liberia

1. Alexandra Zavis, "Great Read: Ebola Doctor's Dilemma: Two Patients, and Drugs Enough for One," *Los Angeles Times*, December 24, 2014, www.latimes.com/world/la-fg-c1-ebola -rescue-20141224-story.html.

2. Zavis, "Great Read."

3. Zavis, "Great Read."

4. Zavis, "Great Read."

5. "Ebola Patient Dr. Kent Brantly Walks into Emory Hospital," NBC News, August 2, 2014, www.nbcnews.com/video/ebola-patient-dr-kent-brantly-walks-into-emory-hospital -314595907884.

6. Tara Fowler and Nicole Weisensee Egan, "Two U.S. Patients with Ebola Being Brought to Georgia for Treatment," *People*, August 1, 2014, https://people.com/human-interest/u-s -patients-with-ebola-being-brought-to-georgia.

7. Zavis, "Great Read."

8. "'Miraculous Day': American Ebola Patients Discharged from Atlanta Hospital," CBS News, August 21, 2014, www.cbsnews.com/news/ebola-patients-kent-brantly-and-nancy -writebol-discharged-from-hospital.

9. "'Miraculous Day.'"

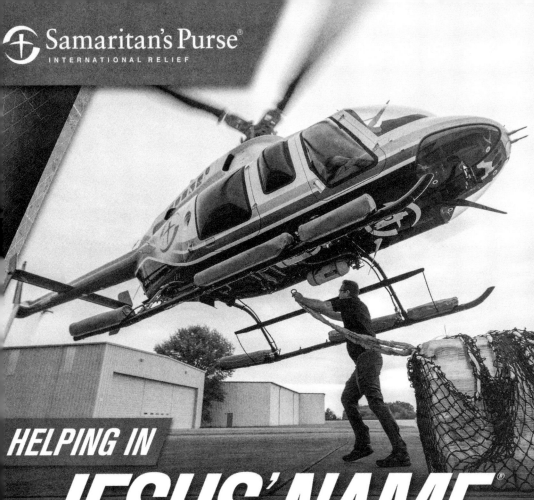

![Samaritan's Purse INTERNATIONAL RELIEF]

HELPING IN
JESUS' NAME®

THE WORLD NEEDS MORE GOOD SAMARITANS

Help us run to the fire to share the eternal hope of the Gospel of Jesus Christ.

"Go and do likewise." —Luke 10:37

Hurricane Helene Response

Samaritan's Purse®, Franklin Graham, President
P.O. Box 3000, Boone, NC 28607 | 1-800-528-1980
© 2025 Samaritan's Purse. All rights reserved.

samaritanspurse.org